Teaching Outside the Box

Teaching Outside the Box

HOW TO GRAB YOUR STUDENTS
BY THEIR BRAINS

Third Edition

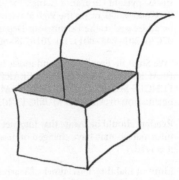

LouAnne Johnson

JB JOSSEY-BASS™
A Wiley Brand

Published by Jossey-Bass
A Wiley Brand
One Montgomery Street, San Francisco, CA 94104—www.wiley.com

Library of Congress Cataloging-in-Publication Data

Johnson, LouAnne.
  Teaching outside the box : how to grab your students by their brains / LouAnne Johnson.—Third edition.
    pages cm
  Includes index.
  ISBN 978-1-119-08927-8 (pbk.)—ISBN 978-1-119-08921-6 (ePDF)—ISBN 978-1-119-08922-3 (epub)
  1. Teaching.   I. Title.
  LB1025.3.J6395 2015
  371.102—dc23

2015026173

Cover Design: Wiley
Cover Image: ©CSA Images/Getty Images

Printed in the United States of America
THIRD EDITION
PB Printing V10002956_080218

CONTENTS

ACKNOWLEDGMENTS

Thank you to the teachers who taught me to believe in myself and follow my heart: Mary Ellen Boyling, Evelyn Hodak, Eleanora Sandblade, Caroline DeSalvo, Jerry Novelli, Jim Miller, Mary Ann Greggan, Diane Herrera Shepard, and Jane Allen.

A shout out to my posse—the unforgettable, lovable, "unteachable" students who taught me how to teach.

Muchas gracias y abrazos fuerzas a los estudiantes en mi primer clase de Limited English, especialmente Isabel Jimenez y Francisco Diaz. Their English may have been limited, but their desire to learn was unlimited. They taught me what a joy teaching can be, how to teach nonnative English speakers—and how to speak Spanish "like a Mexican."

Special thanks to all the teachers who tested the techniques from this book in their own classrooms and reported their results along with suggestions for improvement. And special thanks to Pam Prosise, Lori Montejano, and Cindy Detler for sharing their own creative teaching strategies and providing much-appreciated moral support.

THE AUTHOR

LouAnne Johnson is the author of nine nonfiction books about education, the young adult novel *Muchacho* (Knopf, 2009), and two illustrated books for young readers. At present, she teaches English language arts full time at a public high school in rural New Mexico.

A native of northwestern Pennsylvania, Johnson served nine years on active military duty, achieving the rank of Journalist First Class in the Navy and 2nd Lieutenant in the Marine Corps. She holds a BS in psychology, an MAT in English, and an EdD in educational leadership.

Prior to earning her teaching license, Johnson worked as a newspaper reporter, ballroom dance instructor, and executive secretary. In 1989, she began teaching as an intern at a Northern California high school. Two years later, she was appointed head of the school's program for at-risk teens. During the government evaluation of ten similar pilot programs, Johnson's group rated first in academic achievement, increased self-esteem, and student retention. Her memoir about those early teaching years, *My Posse Don't Do Homework* (St. Martin's Press, 1986), was adapted for the 1995 hit movie *Dangerous Minds* (directed by John N. Smith), starring Michele Pfeiffer, and has been published in eight languages, including Italian, German, and Japanese.

After teaching high school for six years, Johnson returned to graduate school. Subsequently, she served as lead ESL instructor at Lexington Community College in North Carolina, adjunct instructor of developmental reading and writing for Western New Mexico University, adjunct English instructor at New Mexico State

University, and associate professor of teacher training at Santa Fe Community College. In 2014, she returned to her first passion—teaching teenagers.

In addition to teaching, Johnson has also designed and presented workshops in classroom management and motivation for teachers across the country. A staunch advocate of school reform, limited testing, and student-centered teaching, Johnson is a popular keynote speaker. She has presented keynote addresses to over one hundred organizations, including the National School Boards Association, the National Council on Curriculum Development, the Association of Texas Professional Educators, the National Council of Teachers of English, Stanford University, Texas A&M University, National Hispanic University, the Puerto Rico Department of Education, and the European Council of International Schools. She has appeared on several television shows, including *Oprah, CBS Eye to Eye, NBC Weekend Today, Maury Povich,* and *CNN Talkback Live.*

INTRODUCTION

When I faced my first class of students twenty-six years ago, I could not have stated my teaching philosophy in one simple sentence. I was too busy trying to organize paperwork, plan lessons, referee arguments, convince students to cooperate, find a disciplinary approach that worked, maintain my sanity, and extinguish the thousand tiny fires that erupt in every classroom every day. A disenchanted student helped me focus my thinking. When I was assigned to teach a class of sophomores whose regular teacher suddenly decided to retire, I entered the classroom with high hopes and boundless energy and found myself facing a group of students with zero hope and subzero motivation.

"It don't matter what we do," the girl complained. "Before she left, our teacher done flunked us all. Wrote a red F in the grade book beside everybody's name." At the mention of the grade book filled with Fs, I watched the students collectively slump their shoulders, droop their heads, and issue a giant group sigh.

I could feel their hopelessness, so I hurried to assure them that I didn't have their previous teacher's grade book and that I intended to start everybody in my new grade book with an A—in red ink. It may sound melodramatic, but I swear I could hear the hope fluttering in those students' hearts. Every face turned toward me, even those who insisted that they didn't care one fig about school.

From the back of the room, I heard a boy whisper, "She's lyin'."

"Shut up!" another boy shushed him. "What if she ain't lyin'? I ain't never had a A before."

In that moment, my philosophy of teaching was born, and it has served me well. That philosophy is based on one simple belief:

When students believe success is possible, they will try.

Once I learned how to put that idea into action and succeeded in convincing every student in the room that he or she was an intelligent person capable of learning, teaching became so much simpler and infinitely more enjoyable. My students stopped fighting me and started learning. Before long, they were hooked on learning, and I was hooked on teaching.

During the following years, using student behavior and achievement, along with ongoing research and self-reflection, as my guides, I developed new philosophies about discipline, grades and exams, motivation, classroom management, positive discipline, and how to use simple psychology and brain science to engage students' attention. I developed a toolkit of successful strategies and practices. Thousands of teachers from around the world have generously shared their own theories, strategies, and experiences with me. I'd like to share our combined wisdom. What I would really like to do is sit down for a few hours and talk with you about teaching—why we chose to be teachers, why we still teach considering all the frustrations of the job, our best and worst practices, and how we can help each other be more effective, more confident, and more satisfied with our work.

This book is my side of our imaginary conversation—my attempt to share everything I have learned about effective teaching in one practical package for future teachers, beginning teachers, and experienced teachers who have lost some of their shine and are seeking moral support and inspiration. Instead of writing a formal standard textbook, I chose to write a more conversational, anecdotal text that would serve equally well as a guidebook for individual teachers or as a text for teacher training or staff development courses. My hope is that this book will be a helpful tool in your quest to become the teacher you have always dreamed of being.

Dear Teacher:
An Open Letter

Dear Teacher:

Thank you.

Thank you for being a teacher, for choosing to use your time and talents to teach when you had so many other career options, most of which offer better pay, more comfortable working conditions, and much more respect from the general public than the teaching profession does.

Thank you for taking yet another exam to prove your competence, although you have already completed five or more years of college and hundreds of dollars' worth of standardized tests.

Thank you for getting up at 5 or 6 a.m. every day to work in a graceless room bathed in artificial light or a windowless closet or a dilapidated trailer that has been desperately labeled as a learning center—and for continuing to teach higher-level thinking skills and advanced academics, in spite of having test after test after test added to your curriculum requirements, without any additional instruction time.

Thank you for coping so often with ancient, malfunctioning, or nonexistent air conditioning and heating, and for eating your lunch out of a paper bag in a sparsely furnished lounge where a working coffeemaker is a treat and a functioning microwave oven is a luxury.

Thank you for spending your so-called time off grading papers; making lesson plans; and attending professional development conferences, committee meetings, restructuring meetings, parent–teacher conferences, school board meetings, and continuing education classes.

Thank you for working countless hours of unpaid overtime because it is the only way to do your job well and because you cannot do less—and for not reminding people constantly that if you were paid for your overtime you could retire tomorrow and never have to work again.

Thank you.

For spending your own money on pens and pencils, erasers and chalk, paper, tissues, bandages, birthday gifts, treats, clothing, shoes, eyeglasses—and a hundred other things that your students need but don't have.

For accepting the achy back, creaky knees, tired legs, and sore feet that go with the teaching territory.

For consistently giving respect to children who don't know what to do with it and don't realize what a valuable gift you are offering.

For caring about children whose own families don't care—or who never learned how to demonstrate their love.

For spending sleepless nights worrying about a struggling student, wondering what else you might do to help overcome the obstacles that life has placed in his or her path.

For raiding your own children's closets to find a pair of shoes or a jacket for a child who has none.

For putting your own family on hold while you help a struggling student.

For believing in the life-changing power of education.

For maintaining your belief that all students can learn if only we can learn how to teach them.

Thank you.

Thank you for giving hopeless children enough hope to continue struggling against the poverty, prejudice, abuse, alcoholism, hunger, and apathy that are a daily part of so many tender young lives.

For risking your job to give a child a much-needed hug.

For biting your tongue and counting to a million when a parent insists that your incompetence is responsible for the misbehavior of his or her undisciplined, spoiled, obnoxious child.

For taking on one of the most difficult, challenging, frustrating, emotionally exhausting, mentally draining, satisfying, wonderful, important, and precious jobs in the world.

Thank you for being a teacher.

You truly are the unsung American hero.

You have my respect and my gratitude,

LouAnne Johnson

Are You Teacher Material?

"**H**ow can I tell if I'm really teacher material?" a teacher candidate asked me by e-mail. "Can I learn to be a good teacher? Or is it something you have to be born with?" She went on to explain that she had recently abandoned a well-paid position in advertising to pursue her dream of becoming a teacher.

"I know I will make a lot less money as a teacher," she wrote, "and I have accepted that reality, but now I'm wondering what will happen if I get my degree and get a job, and then I hate teaching. What if I find out that I just can't do it? I have a feeling that teaching is going to be very different from being a student teacher or observing experienced teachers. I guess what I'm asking is: Do you have any advice that might help me make the right decision about becoming a teacher?"

To teach or not to teach? is a question that stumps many people. Far too many of us know bright, energetic people who spent five or more years earning a bachelor's degree and teaching credential only to quit after one or two years in the classroom. New teachers give up for a long laundry list of reasons, but the most common complaints include disrespectful and disruptive students, apathetic administrators, overwhelming stacks of paperwork, lunchroom politics, parental pressure and pestering, and mental or emotional exhaustion.

Those complaints are valid. I have to say that I have worked with some excellent administrators, and their support enabled me to be a better teacher. But even with good support, teaching is very demanding and difficult work. Children today suffer from a host of emotional, mental, and physical challenges that affect their behavior and ability to learn. And unfortunately many of their role models encourage them to treat themselves and others with disrespect. Dealing with children requires abundant reserves of patience and tact. An indestructible sense of humor also helps. Government regulations have created a testing and accountability monster that consumes mountains of money, paperwork, time, and energy—and teachers have the task of feeding the monster. The monster is fickle, too, so if last-minute changes upset you, teaching will tax you to the limits of your flexibility. If you don't bend, you will definitely break. Of course, you already know that the pay is atrocious, primarily because people outside of education view teaching as babysitting with books. Thus, if wealth and prestige are important to you, teaching will be a disappointment. And teaching can be physically painful: hours of standing on your feet, bending over to read small print on small desks, and lugging boxes of books and papers to and fro can send you home with tired feet, an aching back, and a heavy heart.

And then there are the students. It might seem facetious to say that you should like children if you plan to teach school, but apparently many people overlook this obvious fact. Every staff lunchroom has at least a few (and most have a large handful of) complainers and groaners who spend their breaks and lunch hours plotting against the enemy, sharing their strategies for revenge, nursing their wounds, and displaying their battle scars. These are not necessarily bad people, but they are people who grew up and immediately forgot their own childhoods. Like people who fall in love with the idea of owning a dog, dreaming of the unconditional love a dog will offer and forgetting that puppies pee on the carpet, vomit on the bath mat, chew your slippers, and poop on the lawn, some would-be teachers envision themselves standing in front of a quiet, orderly classroom, facing a sea of silent, adoring, obedient, angelic little faces. When those angelic faces turn out to belong to noisy, messy, ill-mannered, selfish, and obstinate little stinkers, those teachers go into shock. Some fail to recover. They become bitter, humorless, and overly strict, and they spend the rest of their years in the classroom making themselves and their students miserable by trying to make reality fit their impossible fantasies.

All right, that's the downside of teaching. If you're still reading, still thinking you might like to be a teacher, then you are persistent and optimistic—two very helpful attributes for would-be teachers. And you are right to be hopeful because the upside of teaching is so much bigger and so much more important than the downside.

Teaching is the most wonderful profession in the world. As a teacher, you make a direct, tangible contribution to the future of our country and the world by helping young people acquire knowledge and skills. You know that you are spending your life in an honorable pursuit and that your life has a purpose. Teaching provides endless challenges and opportunities for growth. Every day, teaching tests your interpersonal communications skills, your academic knowledge, or your leadership ability. On a good day, you'll be tested in all three areas, and you'll pass all three tests. You have the opportunity as a teacher to share your passion for learning with young people. If you are a good teacher, you will also inspire, motivate, and challenge those youngsters to develop their individual strengths and talents, and you will feel the incomparable joy when one of them (usually far more than one) realizes how much you have given and makes his or her way back to your classroom to give you a hug and a teary thank-you. And you will cry your own tears. And when you go home, you will share that student's thank-you with your family and friends, and they will all cry a few tears. When you go to bed that night, the last thing you will think before you go to sleep is, I did a fine thing. I helped a child become a successful adult. And that night, you will dream the sweetest dreams.

SUPER, EXCELLENT, OR GOOD?

Teachers come in three basic flavors—super, excellent, and good. (Of course, there are mediocre teachers and, sadly, terrible teachers. But teaching poorly is not acceptable or excusable, so such practices are not included in this discussion.) Which flavor of teacher you decide to become depends on your personal strengths, intimate relationships, professional goals, and individual priorities.

Before you begin teaching, seriously consider how much time and emotional energy you can afford to spend on your work outside the home. Take a long look at your life, your relationships, your financial and emotional obligations, your personal and career goals. If you find it hard to view your own life objectively, discussing your situation with a friend or close relative may improve your perspective. If your sister points out that you like expensive clothes and your husband reminds you that you become impatient and overly critical under stress, for example, you will need to decide whether you are willing to trim your wardrobe and do the hard work required to develop more patience.

Decide what is important to you and which aspects of your life should take priority. Will your children, parents, spouse, or partner feel neglected if you spend some of your free time creating lesson plans or counseling students? How much emotional energy will you need to conserve during the day to have enough left over for your family at night? Will you feel comfortable counseling students about their personal problems, or would you rather leave such things up to their own parents or guardians?

There is no right or wrong answer to these questions, but if you know the answers before you begin teaching, you will be a happier, more successful instructor. Not everybody can or should be a super teacher. It is perfectly acceptable to be an excellent or good teacher.

Super teaching requires the highest amounts of physical, emotional, and mental energy. Super teachers usually arrive at school early and stay late. They also attend seminars and continuing education classes, volunteer for student activities, and make themselves available to students who need extra help, both in and out of the classroom. Because super teachers enjoy a solid rapport with their students, they don't have to focus so much time or energy on discipline in their classrooms. Instead, there is a give-and-take, an ebb and flow, the teaching equivalent of the runner's high that so many athletes find addictive. Unfortunately, unless they are extraordinary people with impressive reserves of natural energy or unless they make an effort to rejuvenate themselves regularly, super teachers may find themselves in danger of burning out.

Super teaching demands huge amounts of physical and mental effort, and depending on your budget it may absorb some money as well. If you are single, childless, and unattached, you may choose to devote the bulk of your energies to teaching for some period of time. However, if you are a single mother with three young children and have a close friend or intimate partner, you may not be willing or able to devote the amount of emotional energy that being a super teacher requires. Having children doesn't disqualify you from becoming a super teacher; it simply means that you will need to make sure that your family understands and supports your teaching. If your children are well-adjusted, self-motivated, and respectful of you and your partner, if your partner supports your career goals, and if you have a high level of energy, then you may be able to handle the stresses involved in super teaching. But don't beat yourself up if you can't be extraordinary. Being an excellent or good teacher is a true achievement.

Excellent teachers enjoy their work, but they limit the amount of time and energy they devote to teaching. They care about their students and do their best to help them—but not at the expense of their own families. Excellent teachers do work overtime because teaching well requires a certain amount of unpaid overtime (grading papers, making lesson plans, and supervising field trips), but excellent teachers put a limit on the amount of overtime they are willing to work.

Excellent teaching requires less energy expenditure than super teaching, but excellent teaching may still wear you out if you aren't careful; you still need to make time to nurture yourself and your family. And you may have to explain more than once to your friends and family that your job is a high priority and that you need to spend some time in the evenings and on weekends developing your lessons and skills. Again, don't be too hard on yourself if you find that you can't juggle so many teaching balls as you thought you could, especially during your first few years. Mastering just the basics of sound teaching is a major accomplishment, and students still thrive in the classrooms of good old everyday teachers.

Good teachers do their jobs well but know their own limits. They make a very clear distinction between professional and personal time. They treat their students with respect and do their best to make sure that all students learn the material required for the next level of education, but they don't feel obligated to save every student. Good teachers arrive at school early enough to be prepared, but they don't hold open house before school or during lunch hour. And they don't spend hours in their classroom after school for informal chats or counseling sessions. They lock the doors to their classrooms at night and focus on their own lives, their own educations, their hobbies, their friends, and their families. By creating a distinct division between their personal and professional lives, good teachers conserve their emotional and mental energy. As a result, they often enjoy long and successful teaching careers; they are the ones who sadly wave good-bye to the excellent and super teachers, who overestimated their personal resources and burst into flames after a few years of teaching at Mach speed.

Sometimes teachers confess that they feel a bit guilty for not having the energy or natural ability to be a super teacher. I tell them—and I am absolutely sincere—that there is no shame in being an everyday good teacher. Not everybody can be a rock star, and not everybody needs to be. The world needs all kinds of people—those who are satisfied by doing good work, raising decent children, caring for their neighbors, and contributing to their communities as well as those who are compelled to create and invent or to seek fame and fortune. Not every teacher wants or needs to be a Jaime Escalante or an Esme Codell. And millions of students in this country are learning from—and loving—their everyday ordinary teachers. I may be biased, but I believe that an everyday ordinary good teacher is still a hero. (And I'm sure those millions of students in this country would agree.)

Regardless of whether you choose to be a super, excellent, or good teacher, you will still be contributing to society, performing honorable and necessary work, and helping to shape the future of our country. Aside from yourself, your students, and a few supervisors, nobody will know how much energy you devote to your job. But we don't become teachers out of a need for public recognition or reward. We don't teach out of a desire for prestige; we teach because we believe it's important. Teaching superbly is like running a marathon by yourself in the dark. Few people even notice what you're doing, and those who notice don't pay much attention—but their oblivion doesn't slow you down. You still enjoy the thrill and satisfaction of finishing the race, and you are definitely a winner.

EARN SOME EXTRA CREDIT

Let us assume that you have a strong desire to help young people, a passion for your subject, a solid education, and a license from an accredited teacher-training institution. Are passion, motivation, education, and training enough? My answer is a very loud *no*. Those attributes can create an excellent foundation, but teaching requires much more than knowledge and the desire to teach. Teaching requires a solid grasp of motivational techniques, leadership and conflict resolution skills, human psychology (child, adolescent, and adult), computer literacy, the ability to whittle an impossibly huge pile of paperwork into a succinct and teachable curriculum, and the ability to think on your feet. (A pair of extremely comfortable shoes for those feet will help.)

Some teacher-training programs include excellent components in some of those areas, but based on the e-mails and letters I have received and the conversations I have had with teachers throughout the country far too many teacher-training programs are heavy on theory and light on practical skills and techniques that teachers must have in order to teach effectively. Designing work-sheets, lessons plans, and exams requires important skills. Creating intriguing bulletin boards, art projects, and group activities can make the difference between a stuffy classroom filled with bored underachievers and an exciting classroom buzzing with the electricity that motivated little learners can generate. But even the most enthusiastic, creative, accomplished, and intelligent new teacher will struggle if he or she doesn't have a firm grasp on the basic concepts of human psychology and behavior: what motivates people to act the way they act, how to convince people to change their behavior voluntarily, how to challenge and inspire people to attempt difficult tasks, how to develop a solid rapport with people from diverse economic and cultural backgrounds, and how to quickly and effectively convince people to follow your lead.

Look for teacher-training programs that focus on successful leadership techniques instead of ineffective punitive disciplinary approaches. If possible, opt for a program in which teacher candidates do their student teaching during the first part of their education program instead of the last. Some people realize after just a few days in the classroom that they weren't meant to be teachers; it's a shame when those would-be teachers have to face the choice of continuing in a teacher program in which they don't belong or changing to a new major and spending thousands of dollars preparing for a different career. And heaven help both the students and the teachers when those teachers who know that they have chosen the wrong field decide to teach until they can afford to go back to school or find another job. Everybody loses in that situation.

If you have the choice, opt for a full year of student teaching (I would recommend two years), preferably at a number of different schools where you will have the opportunity to work with students at different age levels and from different backgrounds. (An Internet search for schools of education will allow you to review and compare different programs across the country.) You may find that, although you thought you would enjoy teaching kindergarten, high school is where you belong. Or you may find that the squirrelly sophomores who everybody complains about are the ones you enjoy the most.

Make sure that your student teaching experience actually provides teaching experience. If you are assigned to a single master teacher for your entire student teaching time frame and that teacher does not allow you to interact with students beyond distributing papers (or, worse yet, expects you to sit in the back of the room and observe for weeks on end), then ask your college advisor to change your assignment. Don't complain about the master teacher; just say you believe you need a more hands-on approach to make sure that teaching really suits you. Your advisor may try to discourage you from insisting on a change, but be firm. You are the customer. You are paying for your education, and you deserve to be taught how to teach. Your instructors may label you difficult, but I promise you that a little flak from your professors is nothing compared with the flak you will take from students if they sense that you are ill prepared to teach.

If your teacher education program allows you the opportunity to take elective courses, then psychology, leadership, conflict resolution, and time management are good choices. The more you can learn about what makes people tick (and how to wind and unwind them), the easier it will be for you to establish a controlled learning environment in your classroom. Community colleges often offer a variety of continuing education courses as well as courses designed to improve the quality of life for local residents. If you don't have access to classroom instruction, countless courses are available online—although some are little more than advertising bait to sell books and other products. Some of the products may be worthwhile, but unless the Web sites offer you a generous sample of their materials and a money-back guarantee for instruction you would be wise to check with librarians, teachers, or other people who might be able to point you in the direction of quality instruction.

Fortunately, thanks to the Internet, you can learn quite a bit about a number of subjects on your home or public library computer. The Web site www.teachers.net, for example, allows you to read the logs of conversations between teachers on topics ranging from classroom discipline to motivational lesson plans. If you enter "classroom discipline" or "motivational techniques" into a search engine, you will find a host of provocative articles, Web sites, and pointers for future reading.

THOSE WHO CAN'T TEACH CAN STILL DO

Don't despair if you find that, in spite of your desire to nurture and guide young people, teaching children isn't your bag of books. Or perhaps you lack the resources to complete the increasingly complex licensure and teacher testing programs. Nonteaching jobs in education still enable you to provide instruction, guidance, and counseling: teacher aides, security officers, bus drivers, coaches, counselors, curriculum designers, independent consultants, test proctors, and career planners all make important contributions. You might consider working as an adjunct, adult education, or English as a Second Language instructor at a community college, library, or detention facility. Teaching adults requires many of the same skills as teaching youngsters, but adult students are much more likely to be motivated, well behaved, and receptive to instruction. In addition, there are opportunities to teach in day care centers, after-school programs, church-sponsored community service programs, mentor programs, literacy programs, tutoring programs, and school-to-work programs that match students with adults who help them prepare to enter the workplace.

If you have a burning desire to teach a subject you love, you may have to do some searching of your soul, your situation, and your options, but there are students who want to learn as passionately as you want to teach.

WHAT IS TEACHING ALL ABOUT?

If you think carefully and analytically about your own favorite teachers, from elementary school through college, you will recognize some common traits and behaviors. Although they undoubtedly used different techniques and approaches to teaching, successful teachers communicate clearly their expectations for students, their attitudes about learning, and their basic belief about the teacher–student relationship. Many teachers say, "Please come talk to me if you have any concerns," but we don't always accept that offer because we know that it isn't always sincere. How do we know? Because students learn very early on to pay more attention to what teachers do than to what they say. One young girl, a fifth grader who wrote to me about her own teacher, provided a perfect example.

> My teacher always says, "Don't be afraid to ask questions," but then if you ask a question she makes a face and says, "Do you really need to ask me that?" so I stopped asking questions.

It's very important, especially at the beginning of a school year, and especially for new teachers, for your attitude and behavior to be consistent with your words and instructions. One way to guarantee consistency is to be able to articulate your teaching philosophy simply and succinctly. If you can't state your philosophy or if you are unsure that your philosophy is correct, then I suggest that you browse a few textbooks on teaching methods and ask other teachers to state their own philosophies. Often it's easier to start by articulating what we don't believe than articulating what we do believe. For example, I once met a teacher who told me, "I provide students with all the information they need. If they aren't interested in learning, f—k them." Naturally, I was shocked, but the teacher shrugged and said, "I'm burned out, but I can't afford to retire for a few more years, so I'm just hanging on by my fingernails." I tried to avoid spending time with that teacher because his negative attitude was so distressing to me, but his comments helped me define my own ideas about the teacher–student relationship.

Here are some common philosophies. Perhaps one of them represents your own approach, or represents an approach you definitely don't want to take:

Teachers should never appear to know less than students. A teacher who makes mistakes, or admits making mistakes, loses the respect of students and is unprofessional.

Students should respect the teacher simply because he or she is the teacher. Teachers should never tolerate disrespect from students for any reason.

Mutual respect is the cornerstone of a successful teacher–student relationship, and it is the teacher's responsibility to set the tone and model respectful behavior.

Students must be held accountable for their behavior. I want students to understand that their behavior has consequences so they will learn to make better choices.

A teacher's job is to teach academic information and skills only. Parents are responsible for character education, values, and ethics.

A teacher is a role model, guide, and mentor in addition to being an expert instructor in academics, arts, or sports.

Effective teachers set the stage for learning—then step aside and let students learn through discovery and experiment. A teacher is really a guide.

I will explain how I arrived at my own teaching philosophy in the next chapter, but basically my philosophy is based on one simple belief:

When students believe success is possible, they will try. If they don't believe they can succeed, it doesn't matter how easy the material or how smart the students—they will fail. Therefore, my primary job is to convince my students that success is possible and then to help them succeed in my class.

Don't panic if you can't articulate your teaching philosophy this very minute. Let the idea percolate in your brain. Just as a computer can continue background printing or operations, your brain will tackle the topic and wrestle with it until, eventually, your philosophy will emerge. You may decide later on to do a little tweaking or a major overhaul. If you realize you believe only certain students can learn, imagine yourself standing in front of your class, face-to-face, and explaining to your pupils why you don't believe some of them are capable of learning. Hopefully, that visualization will help you imagine what it feels like to be on the other side of the desk from a teacher who has low expectations for your success.

There's nothing wrong with changing your mind and adopting a different philosophy or approach based on experience, observation, or serious reflection—but if you enter your classroom with a clear idea of why you are there and what you expect from yourself and your students, you stand a much better chance of being a successful teacher.

WHAT DO YOU THINK?

1. How do you feel about the idea of categorizing teachers as good, super, or excellent? Can you suggest an alternative method of categorizing teachers?

2. How important do you believe psychology and leadership skills are to new teachers? Is it possible to develop such skills on the job and still be an effective teacher?

3. Which of the teaching philosophies from the list in this chapter do you agree with? Which do you disagree with and why?

4. Briefly state your own teaching philosophy.

Do Your Homework

Why do so many teacher candidates ace their education courses, read all the latest journals, carefully observe good teachers, shine like stars during their student teaching, and then crash and burn during their first year in the classroom?

Because education, desire, intelligence, passion, and talent do not automatically enable you to communicate complex ideas to other people.

Because in teacher training programs, the instructors are on your side and have a vested interest in your success, whereas your students (and, sadly, even some fellow teachers) couldn't care less if you fail. In fact, some of them find it entertaining to watch you flounder.

Because unlike your college classmates, who admired your pretty lesson plans and praised the cleverness of your lectures and worksheets, your students may not be at all interested in learning.

Because effective teaching is more a matter of psychology than pedagogy. As one young man wisely explained to me, "You can make me sit here and hold this stupid book all day, but you can't make me read."

Fortunately, psychology is interesting to read and think about, relatively simple to understand, and eminently applicable to teaching. Perhaps you have detailed instructions about what you are expected to teach, with curriculum guidelines that list specific reading selections and activities that your class must complete during a given time. Or perhaps you have the freedom and responsibility of creating your own curriculum. In either case, if you grab your students by their brains quickly, during the first days of class, they won't have the time or inclination to resist your instruction.

CHOOSE YOUR PERSONA

Your classroom is a miniature theater: it holds a small, captive audience and an even smaller cast—you. You are the star of the show, and when you first stand on that stage your small audience can seem overwhelmingly large. The brighter your spotlight, the faster you'll capture your audience. Later on, you may choose to share the stage with your students, but until your students have learned their roles you will need to take center stage. I don't mean that you should posture grandly and strut about your room; however, you do have a show to run and specific goals to accomplish. Your responsibility is to lead your cast toward those goals; their role is to follow, although it is perfectly acceptable for them to politely suggest changes in the script.

Because your students will take their cues from you, it's very important that you decide before you step onstage how you will portray your character. What kind of image do you want to project to your students? How do you want them to see you? As the scientific expert, the hip dude who knows algebra inside out, the cool nerd, the toughest but best chemistry teacher on earth, the drill sergeant grammarian, the stand-up comic who happens to know all about history, the serious student of literature or science, the hard-boiled journalist, the tough but tender coach?

Let me be very clear: I am not suggesting that you adopt a fake personality. You must be yourself. Pretending to be somebody you are not is a terrible idea and one that is bound to fail because students are very adept at quickly assessing their teachers' characters. They will decide during the first few moments they see you what kind of person you are. They will look at your clothes, your hair, your skin color (not so much to judge you but to assess how you may judge them). They will note your subtlest body language, your gestures, your posture, the length of your stride, the tone of your voice, your expression as you observe other students, and especially the look in your eyes when you look at them. They will decide whether you seem crabby or nice or tough or easy or scared or confident or boring. All of this will happen within the first few seconds of your first class meeting—long before you begin to teach. And once your students decide who you are, you'll have a hard time convincing them to change their perceptions. You can change their minds, but it demands so much time and energy that if you goof and get started on the wrong foot (as I have done more than once), you may be inclined to simply cope with the status quo and hope things will improve over time. Coping and hoping, however, are poor substitutes for self-confidence and leadership.

Whatever persona you choose, it should be one that is natural for you, one that you can maintain for the entire school year. I am advising you not to put on a mask or try to change your personality but to consider how to make best use, as a teacher, of your unique characteristics, traits, and talents. You don't have to be an extrovert to be an effective teacher. Some extremely shy or introverted people blossom as teachers and enjoy a persona in the classroom that highlights their otherwise hidden talents and skills. But it is not a good idea to try to force a completely different personality in the classroom simply because you lack confidence in yourself. Instead of donning a false persona, it would serve you better to spend some time working on discovering your strengths, which will lead to increased confidence and self-esteem. And always remember: children tend to be more accepting of different personalities than adults may be. Students don't care so much about your good looks or your sparkling wit as they do about whether you treat them with dignity and respect.

It took me a while to perfect my drill sergeant/stand-up comic/counselor persona, and I made many changes along the way. My first year I tried too hard to be cool, and it caused discipline problems. I joked around a lot because I wanted the kids to like me, to think of me as an older friend. What I didn't realize at that time was that they didn't need more friends. They had plenty of friends—friends who offered them dope and cigarettes and plagiarized research papers, friends who thought heavy metal was great music and that Ripple was fine wine. What my students needed was for me to be a teacher, an adult who would accept my responsibility as their guide and a leader who sometimes had to be the bad guy so I could help them. During my second teaching year, I took the advice of a veteran teacher who said, "Don't smile until after Christmas." I decided to be the drill sergeant who could stare a student to death. I couldn't do it. I'm a smiling kind of woman, so my message was inconsistent and my students responded by misbehaving half the time.

Finally, I sat down and figured out what my biggest strengths and weaknesses were as a person. Then I combined my three strongest personal assets and came up with a combination that worked for me as a teacher. Once I could define my persona, I could communicate it to students effectively. Now I know who I am as a teacher. I am a strict but flexible professional educator who has high standards and expectations for my students, and I am a caring and compassionate human being. I am inclined to use humor instead of threats, I am intolerant of rude or disrespectful behavior, I am passionate about my subject, and I am willing to meet students halfway. I make a few important rules that cannot be broken under any circumstances, I take the time to know each student personally, and I use humor whenever possible to make my point without making students lose face.

DRESS THE PART

In the search for my most effective persona, I discovered an interesting student response to my clothing: they perceive some outfits as more serious than others, and they behave accordingly. If the lesson for the day requires creativity, spontaneity, and lots of student input, I wear more informal clothing—corduroy pants and a sweater, perhaps. On days when I want to limit the amount of spontaneity, such as during an important exam or a lesson that will serve as an important building block for future lessons, I wear a suit.

Using clothes to project an image is basic psychology, and we see it all around us. The makers of TV commercials, especially commercials for pharmaceuticals or health products, often dress their announcers in white lab coats that give the impression of medical authority so that viewers will be more inclined to believe them when they tell us that we'll have fewer gastrointestinal disturbances or sinus headaches. Difficult students often use clothing—leather jackets and ripped jeans, for instance, or turquoise hair—to advertise their contempt for authority and send a clear challenge to adults, a warning to keep our distance. Corporate executives are often very adept at power dressing. Young teachers or people who tend to be shy and introverted may take some tips from the fashion experts who advise young executives how to give the impression of authority: wear black pants and a white shirt, for example.

When you select your teaching wardrobe, keep in mind the persona you wish to convey. Make sure that your clothes don't send a conflicting message. If your goal is to create a very authoritative persona, for example, you may not be so successful if you dress very informally, especially if you wear the same clothes your students wear. They may tend to treat you as a peer instead of a teacher, in spite of your verbal instructions.

While we're on the subject of clothing, I'd like to suggest that you pay special attention to your feet. Many new teachers, myself included, are sorely surprised to find out how much their feet can hurt after just one day of teaching. Even if you are in good physical condition and are used to spending long periods of time on your feet, teaching will still take its toll on your soles. I strongly recommend investing in a pair of well-made, comfortable shoes such as those made specifically for people who spend a lot of time on their feet by companies like Born, Birkenstock, Clarks, Dansko, Keen, Mephisto, Merrell, Naot, Naturalizer, Reiker, and Walkies.

TRAIN YOUR LITTLE DARLINGS

How do you want students to feel and act in your classroom? Do you want them to sit quietly and raise their hands before responding to your questions, or do you want them to speak freely even if it means interrupting each other or you? Do you want them to feel free to come into your classroom early and chat with you or with other students, or do you want them to keep their socializing outside the classroom and focus solely on academic activities inside your room? Do you want students to engage in enthusiastic discussions in which they freely voice their personal opinions (which may lead to interesting arguments), or do you prefer to control any discussion to avoid conflict and keep the conversation on topic?

Consider your students' age, the difficulty of your subject matter, and the number of students in each group you teach. How do you envision them behaving during a given class period? Perhaps you picture them sitting at their desks, politely raising their hands for you to call on them. Or perhaps your vision involves a more energetic, less controlled environment, where students wave their hands wildly or feel inspired to shout out their ideas. After you have developed a good rapport with your students, you will be able to change the pace and procedures to fit different kinds of lessons, but you are likely to develop a better rapport and experience fewer discipline problems if you stick to one method for at least the first few weeks of classes.

Here's just one example. If you want students to raise their hands before speaking, you need to state your expectations and act accordingly. If you have stated a preference for hand raising and then acknowledge students who speak out of turn during your lessons, you will have just demonstrated that you don't mean what you say. If you persist in acknowledging your shout-out talkers, you may soon find that you have a lot of talkers and a lot of other students who have lost respect for your authority. On the other hand, if you don't mind the movement and noise that accompany student spontaneity and you allow students to speak out during lessons, you may find it very difficult to get those students to sit quietly and raise their hands during a given activity if you decide later on that you need a more orderly classroom to teach a specific skill. Until you are sure that your students will follow your direction, it's best to stick to the one method that you would prefer them to use most of the time. I think of it as setting my students' default behavior. Unless I give specific instructions, how do I want them to behave?

If you aren't certain what kind of classroom environment you want to create, think about your own school days. Which classes did you enjoy most? Which did you dread attending? What kind of environment did those teachers create? How did they communicate their attitudes to you? Chances are good that you will teach the way your favorite teachers taught you—or the way your worst teachers taught you. Far too often, teachers whose own teachers humiliated them will turn around and use those same techniques on their students without even realizing what they are doing. In my opinion, humiliating children is cowardly and emotionally abusive. You can be strict without being cruel, and students will accept a strict but fair teacher as easily as they will accept a laid-back, tolerant teacher. But if you start the year using one approach and then try to change midterm, you may confuse some students, and they may not cooperate when you try to retrain them. Children can be especially resistant to change because they are more likely to feel insecure about many aspects of their personal lives.

Of course, you may choose to change your approach to one that you believe will improve your teaching, but be wary of changing your teaching style as a reaction to student behavior. If you begin the year as a soft-spoken, even-tempered teacher and then become a shouter or develop a short fuse that ignites at the smallest disruption, students will realize that they can control your behavior. Some students will then do their best to push your buttons because watching a teacher fume can be highly entertaining.

Training students is very similar to training puppies. If you let a puppy sleep on the bed every night for a week, she won't understand why you are punishing her by making her sleep on the floor the next week. She will wait until you are asleep and hop up onto the bed. And if you wake up and boot her off, her tender feelings will be hurt, and you will feel like a big bully. Likewise, if you train your little canine companion to sleep on the floor, and then one night you decide you'd like a foot warmer, she may be hesitant to jump up onto the bed. She may agree to warm your feet for a while before jumping back down to her proper place on the floor. Or she may enjoy the change of pace so much that she refuses to sleep on the floor the following night. Either way, you have one confused puppy on your hands.

CONTROL YOUR CLASSROOM, NOT YOUR STUDENTS

Later, I will discuss discipline plans in detail, but right now I'd like to share with you one of the most important lessons I have ever learned. When I began teaching, after nine years on active military duty and seven in the corporate sector, I thought I had a good grasp of the basics of discipline. When my master teacher left me in charge of his sophomore honors English class, I was determined not to take any flak from my students. Unfortunately, my students didn't care one whit about my determination. The harder I tried to control them, the harder they resisted. They all threw their books on the floor at the same time when my back was turned, so I made a seating chart that separated friends from each other. They coughed loudly if anybody tried to answer a question that I had asked, so I gave them harder assignments. They crossed their arms and refused to look at me when I talked to them, so I sent the ringleaders to the office, where they sat for a while before returning to my classroom with a note asking me to be more specific about what infractions they had committed, because refusing to look at the teacher wasn't a punishable offense under the student code of conduct. So I sent them to lunch detention or after-school detention or in-school suspension. And when they returned, they acted exactly as they had before they left my room—except now they were determined to exact revenge.

One day I lost my temper and started screaming. I threw books and papers on the floor and pitched a proper childish tantrum. Those college-bound students looked at me, but they were more amused than impressed. The following day, I asked Al Black, a veteran teacher, to sit in on that class and observe the hostilities. After the students had left the room, Al sighed and shook his head.

"You don't like those students," he said.

"They didn't like me first," I protested.

"That doesn't matter," Al said. "You're the teacher. You create the classroom environment. And right now, you're creating conflict because you're acting like a bully."

After a sleepless night, I realized Al was right. It was up to me to fix the problem. I had been so focused on changing the students' behavior when I should have been looking at my own. I wasn't sure what to do, though, and Al refused to make it easy for me. "Figure it out" was the only advice he would offer. Since I couldn't figure it out on my own, I decided to ask the students for help. The worst that could happen is that they would refuse—which wouldn't change anything and I'd have to think of something else.

The next afternoon, when the students arrived for class, I thanked them for arriving on time. They gave each other quick "what's up?" glances but didn't respond. Then I said, "We started out all wrong, and now nobody likes this class, including me. I don't dislike you. I just don't like what has been happening in this room. So I'd like to start over. I'll be nice to you if you'll be nice to me." After a few stunned seconds, one of the students—and one of the ringleaders—smiled and gave me a thumbs-up. "Deal!" he said. Several others followed suit. And just like that, it was a different classroom. The human dynamic changed completely. Even the air felt different, lighter somehow.

Finally, I realized what those bright, capable underachieving students had been trying to teach me: I cannot control my students' behavior, but I *can* control myself and my classroom. As soon as I understood that simple concept, I stopped responding to their behavior and started making them respond to mine. After that day, when a student disrupted the lesson or refused to cooperate, instead of becoming upset or issuing warnings or threats I immediately held a quick private conversation (sometimes five seconds was enough!) wherein I offered that student the opportunity to change his or her behavior without losing face. While the disrupter considered my offer, I returned to teaching the cooperative students and made sure to thank them for their behavior. Once I stopped letting students dictate my behavior, I had far fewer discipline problems in every class, even when I taught at-risk and remedial students.

I don't mean to suggest that we ignore misbehavior—although it's not a bad idea to ignore small disruptions that may fizzle out on their own. I do mean that if we focus on giving our attention to those students who are cooperating with us and on verbally praising them for their excellent behavior instead of on letting students derail the teaching train, we are more likely to arrive at our destination, and everybody is far more likely to enjoy the trip.

PLAN FOR BATHROOM BREAKS

Some people (including, sadly, some school administrators) believe that bathroom breaks are unimportant. They have better things to think about. I maintain that students can't think about learning if they are preoccupied with avoiding a humiliating accident. As a child, I once peed my pants on a bus because the teacher said I didn't need to use the bathroom when I asked to go. So I speak from personal experience, and I hope you will understand why I am so passionate about this issue.

Using the bathroom is a biological need, not a privilege. Instead of limiting bathroom breaks and ignoring individual student needs, we will enjoy better student morale and subsequent academic achievement if we create plans for making bathroom breaks as fast and efficient as possible.

In a perfect world, teachers would be free to design reasonable and efficient procedures for student bathroom visits. But most of us have to contend with school policies that are often inhumane because their focus is on preventing vandalism or truancy instead of addressing the very real biological needs of students. I have taught at schools where zero bathroom visits were permitted and at other schools where the standard practice was to allow students a limited number of visits per month or semester. And many teachers require students to make up the time they missed from class by coming in during lunch or staying after school. One teacher laughingly described the pee dance that he requires students to perform (grabbing their crotches and hopping from foot to foot) to show that they sincerely need to go to the restroom. (Oh, how I wish his boss would make him do the same dance!)

As always, I ask teachers to put themselves in the place of their students. What if your supervisor informed you on the first day of work that you would not be permitted to go to the restroom for any reason except during your lunch hour? Or that you had to work late or give up your lunch break to make up for using the restroom during work hours? That sounds ridiculous—because it is.

It's inhumane and cruel, in my opinion, to deny people the right to use the bathroom because they are children. Some students have weak bladders. Others have medical conditions or take prescription medications that cause them to need more frequent bathroom breaks. When faced with restrictive restroom policies, they face both emotional and physical pressures. They are shamed by their need to go to the bathroom. And many students will stop drinking liquids to avoid having to go, which makes them dehydrated, which is physically and mentally unhealthy. Our brain needs water and glucose to function well.

Another factor that many teachers overlook is safety. Sometimes students are reluctant to use the bathrooms during breaks or passing periods because of bullies, smoking, drugs, or sexual activities that take place in the restrooms, so they wait to ask to use the restroom until the next class has begun.

So what's the solution? As a group, teachers need to collaborate to design humane school policies. Individually, teachers can do much to counter cruel school policies that can't be changed. For example, when I taught at the high school where students were never permitted to use the restroom, I took my freshman classes as a group to the bathroom immediately after taking attendance. We were very quick and very quiet. Usually we took our books with us so that we could be on a reading field trip if questioned—but we never were because we didn't make noise or disrupt anybody else's learning. My students, grateful for being treated with dignity and respect, repaid me by working harder in my class, and their grades skyrocketed as a result.

Many elementary teachers have found, to their surprise, that young students can be extremely responsible about signing themselves out. Because they are treated like big kids, they try hard to live up to the compliment.

If you are free to create your own policy, make it a small deal rather than a big one. Create a bathroom pass using an item that is clearly visible and not easily broken: a small stuffed animal, a wooden toy, a thick plastic ruler. Attach a keychain or string so that the pass can be hung near the doorway. Make a sign-out sheet for students to use, and then make it very clear that the bathroom pass should be used only for visiting the restroom. Most students will not abuse the system. Serious consequences need to be assigned if students do go somewhere else when they are carrying the bathroom pass. (High school students like to coordinate their visits to meet friends or business associates in the hallways.) I don't deny those students the opportunity to use the restroom in the future, but they are required to have an escort until they prove themselves trustworthy again. If the restroom is nearby, I escort them personally and wait in the hallway. If necessary, I assign a large and responsible student (or call a counselor) to act as my deputy escort. The offenders quickly shape up.

Your bathroom plan should suit your students. The point is to create a workable, flexible system that you can tweak as needed. But your primary goal should be to allow students to use the bathroom when they need to use the bathroom without punishing or shaming them—and with the least disruption to other students. We have far better ways to teach students self-control than by making young people miserable or physically ill. By the way, I have a theory that teachers who humiliate students often are the same teachers who have serious discipline problems in their classroom. I can't prove it. I'm just suggesting.

YOUR OPTIONAL AGENDA

What are you really teaching in your classroom? During my first year in the classroom, I confessed to Al that I was afraid I wasn't teaching my students enough. I explained that I believed students should reach a minimum standard to achieve a passing grade but that I wasn't sure where to set the minimum standard for my different English classes.

"Minimum standard of what?" Al asked me. "Commas, spelling, vocabulary? Should a kid know four ways to use a comma and the correct spelling of four hundred words? Should he know what *defenestrating* means? What if he doesn't know that particular word, but he knows a thousand other ones? What is the standard? I'm not talking about the district's objectives. I'm talking about your own standards. What is it you expect those kids to know when they leave your class?"

"I don't know," I admitted, "but I worry about whether I'm really teaching them anything."

"All teachers wonder whether they're really teaching anything," he told me. "I used to wonder it myself, hundreds of years ago when I was your age. But then I learned something important. You aren't teaching English. 'What are you teaching?' you may ask. You're teaching kids how to analyze information, relate it to other information they know, put it together, take it apart, and give it back to you in the form that you request it. It doesn't matter what the class is; we all teach the same things. We just use different terms. You use commas and adjectives; biology teachers use chromosomes and chlorophyll; math teachers use imaginary numbers and triangles. And you're also teaching an optional agenda: you're teaching your kids to believe in themselves. So don't worry about whether you're teaching them grammar. You're teaching those kids. Trust me, you're teaching them."

After I had a chance to think about Al's comments, I realized that what he called the optional agenda is the most important factor in teaching—more important than school district objectives—because it answers the all-important question, What do you want your students to know when they leave your class?

Naturally, as an English teacher, I want my students to have improved reading and writing skills, expanded vocabularies, increased comprehension of abstract ideas, better thinking skills, and an appreciation for literature. So I design specific lessons for vocabulary building and literary analysis and composing logical arguments—hundreds of different lessons over the years, tailored for different levels of ability. After my discussion with Al, when I spread out my various lesson plans and looked for common areas among them my optional agenda became very clear. Time and again I had framed my lessons within larger lessons. One composition assignment, for example, urged students to write about a time they had faced and overcome a problem. A supplementary short story unit that I put together from a variety of sources included fictional accounts of people dealing with challenges such as divorce, the death of a loved one, peer pressure, and prejudice. The poetry I selected for special attention involved pursuing your dreams, standing up for your principles, admitting your errors.

My answer to Al's question is the same today as it was then: I want my students to have better academic skills, but I also want them to have a strong sense of their own ethical standards, an unquenchable thirst for knowledge, a desire to succeed according to their own definitions of success, good problem-solving skills, and the strength of character to treat all people with basic human dignity and respect.

What is your optional agenda?

Your values and ethics will shape your agenda. Even if you don't intentionally try to include your beliefs and attitudes in your lessons, they will be there, hidden within the context of the reading assignments you select, in the methods you use to determine who passes and who fails, in the tone of your voice when you address certain students, and in a thousand other subtle clues. Every day you will be teaching your students what you believe is important. You will be conveying your own ethics, attitudes, beliefs, and moral values to your students. If you can articulate your optional agenda, you can use that knowledge to enhance your teaching. Knowing your optional agenda will also help you avoid unintentionally teaching your students things you don't want to teach them—which brings us to the next area of consideration.

FACE YOUR OWN PREJUDICES

Although most of us try very hard to rid ourselves of prejudices, I have yet to meet a person who is completely free of them. Our cultural and religious backgrounds, our families and friends, our experiences, even our biology combine to make us prejudge people who are blond or brunette, tall or short, fat or thin, ugly or beautiful, extroverted or introverted, brilliant or dim, nerdy or popular, Catholic or Jewish or Protestant or Muslim, black or brown or white or yellow or red.

It is important that we, as teachers, try harder than most people to eliminate our prejudices and minimize the effects of the ones we just can't seem to defeat because so many of our students will remember the things we say and do for the rest of their lives. We most likely spend more waking hours with our students, especially the youngest and most tender children, than their own parents do. Unless they have reason not to, most children love and respect their teachers. Many, many students learn to love and respect themselves—or despise and disrespect themselves—based on the way their teachers treat them. Think about your own childhood: if any teacher ever called you lazy, stupid, hopeless, ugly, clumsy, or worthless, I'm sure you remember the moment quite clearly. I am also certain you remember if a teacher ever called you intelligent, special, sharp, brilliant, charming, talented, or wonderful.

Skin color and ethnic origin are still primary sources of prejudice in our nation. As Americans, we have made remarkable progress toward eradicating prejudices, but we still have a long way to go. During the past decade, I visited more than half of the states in our nation; in every state I met teachers who were dismayed and appalled at the racial and ethnic prejudices they witness on a recurring basis in their schools and communities. In fact, the only people I have met who truly believe racial prejudice is not a problem in our schools are White. They aren't stupid or lacking in compassion; they simply don't see what doesn't exist in their world. Brown people maintain that prejudice is still a big problem, and I believe they are in a position to assess the situation most accurately.

Some years ago, my sophomore class included a young man who happened to have extremely dark skin. He also had an extremely gentle and loving personality, an enthusiastic attitude toward school, and an extraordinary talent for football. The teachers on our team all liked Dante, and we agreed that his was the shiniest of stars in our class. One afternoon near the end of that school year, Dante stayed after school to talk to me.

"I just want to thank you because you weren't afraid to make me do my homework. All the other teachers are afraid of me because I'm a big black man. They act like they think if they make me mad, I'll hurt them." As he spoke, Dante's eyes filled with tears. Watching him, I felt my own tears rising.

"So what do you do when those teachers act like that?" I asked.

"I act like I'm going to hurt them." Dante tried to laugh, but his chuckle turned into a cough that stopped just short of a sob.

For a split second, I nearly laughed myself, because it sounded funny. But I quickly realized that Dante's remark was not funny at all. Those teachers were prompting Dante to act as though he intended to hurt them. Whether intentionally or not, they were manipulating him into fulfilling their stereotype of black men as angry and violent. To fear a child simply because of his or her skin color is the same as saying, "I know that you are inherently violent simply because of who you are. It is only a matter of time before your true nature is revealed."

We all know how indignant we feel when someone accuses us of lying even though we are telling the truth and how outraged we feel when someone accuses us of doing something we haven't done. Adults are sometimes capable of rationalizing, justifying, or ignoring false accusations and insinuations. But children and adolescents are not experienced enough in human nature to justify or ignore adult behavior, and they don't know how to avoid being manipulated by adults. Most certainly, they are unequipped to cope with the overwhelming feelings of frustration, disbelief, indignation, and anger that arise when adults insinuate that they are violent (or stupid or worthless) because of their skin color or ethnic background. I believe that repeatedly exposing children to such subtle but serious prejudice is psychologically abusive and surely will have long-term effects on their self-esteem, their attitudes toward school, and their outlook on humanity. We all know that students tend to meet their teachers' expectations—high or low. So unless we have good reason to believe that a particular student is prone to violent behavior, we must expect the best from all of our students. And we must eradicate our irrational fears because we can't successfully teach children when we are afraid of them.

After my talk with Dante, I suggested that he read an essay by Brent Staples called "Night Walker," in which Staples describes how he has learned to control the rage he feels when people obviously fear him simply for his skin color alone. To defuse potential confrontations, Staples whistles well-known classical tunes to let people know he isn't a mugger—his "equivalent of the cowbell that hikers wear when they are in bear country." (This essay was originally published in *Ms. Magazine* as "Just Walk on By" and was reprinted elsewhere under different titles. It can be found in a number of essay anthologies and online using a quick Google search.) Although reading an essay doesn't solve the problem, it does provide an articulate, intelligent response that may help minority students cope with a difficult world.

FACING MY OWN PREJUDICES

I have yet to meet a person who is free from prejudice, and I include myself in that sweeping statement. After talking to Dante, I sat down and forced myself to face my own prejudices. I had read the journal articles and the psychology textbooks. I knew that studies have shown that most White (and many Black) Americans' anxiety levels are higher when they see Black or Hispanic men approaching them in public. And I had to admit that my own anxiety level would be higher if a Black or Hispanic man approached me than if a White man did. Yet I had never in my life been attacked by a Black or Hispanic male. I had, however, on more than one occasion experienced an unpleasant social encounter with a White male. Therefore, it made no sense for me to fear Black or Hispanic men more than White men.

Because I had been raised in an all-White town in the North where I had no contact with anybody of any color other than White, I had no experiences to shape my attitudes. Other than a handful of men like Muhammad Ali and Jackie Robinson, I don't remember another positive Black male role model from my childhood through my thirties, at which point I stopped watching TV completely. During nine years of active military service before I became a teacher, I had only one slightly antagonistic experience with a Black or Hispanic man but dozens of severely antagonistic episodes involving male White soldiers and sailors who didn't welcome women in their ranks. I could conclude only that I had formed my prejudice from hearing news reports of young Black and Hispanic males waging wars on big-city streets and from watching movies and TV programs that consistently portrayed minority males as pimps, drug dealers, shiftless alcoholics, crack addicts, gangbangers, wife beaters, cop killers, and convicts.

My solution to purging my prejudice was to meet and talk to as many successful and educated Black and Hispanic men as I could. I sought them as mentors for my students. I befriended them in the school lunchroom and during community activities—not simply as research subjects but as human beings. After several weeks I knew I had made some significant progress in minimizing my racial prejudices when I met a Black man I didn't like at all. Disliking that man was pivotal in my rehabilitation. Prior to that meeting, I would have felt compelled to like him or to act as though I did to avoid appearing prejudiced.

After nearly twenty years of ongoing self-treatment, I feel free to like or dislike anybody I meet, of any skin color or ethnic background, based on the way that person treats me—and especially the way that person treats children and dogs. I don't pretend there is no violence in the world. I try to keep my distance from anybody of any color who appears to be drunk, high, sociopathic, or potentially dangerous. But I don't expect any particular person to be violent simply because of his or her ethnic origin. And I have learned to cope with students who have concerns or prejudices toward me because of my ethnic heritage, such as the young man who strutted into my sophomore English class one day and announced as he passed by, without making eye contact, that he didn't like White people.

"I can't help it if I glow in the dark," I told him. "I was born that way, and I can't do anything about it. If you're going to dislike me for something, please dislike me for something that I am directly responsible for, something I can control, such as my attitude, my politics, or my behavior. Why don't you cut me some slack until you get to know me? And I will do the same for you. I will decide whether or not I like you based on the way you act, not on your skin color."

My prejudiced pal just shrugged and pretended to ignore me, but he must have listened—although he rarely spoke to me and clearly did not feel any affection toward me. At the end of his second year as my student, he wrote in his journal that the most important thing he had learned in school that year was that "not all White people are bad." I considered that a high compliment from him. But even more important, I knew that he could no longer be 100 percent prejudiced because he had met at least one exception to his rule. He inspired me to try to introduce other students to their own exceptions.

As teachers, we can't eradicate students' prejudices, but we can—by our own example and by communicating our expectations clearly—lay the groundwork to make tolerance and compassion the rule in our classrooms.

RESPECT YOURSELF

New teachers often ask, "How do I make students respect me when they walk into the room determined to disrespect me before they even meet me?"

Clearly, you cannot make anybody respect you. You can demand respect all you want, but you can't force it. Children already understand this concept, so they aren't simply being stubborn when they resist teachers' demands for respect. They are insulted, just as you would be if a stranger marched up to you and demanded instant respect. Thus, the harder you try to force students to respect you, the more insulted they will be and the more they will disrespect you.

Sometimes we find ourselves with an entire room full of disrespectful students. And some teachers draw the battle lines. They become stricter, establishing rigid rules and inflexible procedures. They allow students to draw them into the teacher-versus-student battle that so many young people enjoy because it is entertaining and easier than doing lessons and, most important, because they already know how to act disrespectful. I know from experience how frustrating it is to try to continue modeling respectful behavior when students greet your efforts with disdain, defiance, disrespect, or complete disregard. And I know how tempting it is to let the children manipulate you into responding as they expect you to. But if you can resist, if you can continue to respect them as human beings, separating the child from the childish behavior, eventually most of them will realize that you are sincere, that you do respect them as people—and it is extremely difficult to go on hating somebody who truly respects and cares for you.

Here's how I approach the issue. I explain to my students on the first day of class that the one thing I value more than any other behavior is self-respect. I explain that I believe lack of respect for others stems from a lack of self-respect so I will be working to help them develop self-respect, self-discipline, self-esteem, and self-confidence. Then I do my utmost to live up to my own high expectations. When a student disrespects me, I call the student out in the hallway to talk to me, but I still speak respectfully to that student. (On the infrequent occasions when the student has managed to push enough buttons to make me so angry that I can't speak respectfully, I either leave the student standing outside the room until I can gain control or ask a fellow teacher or counselor to take my class for a few minutes while I take a walk to calm down.)

Some students may not know how to respond to genuine respect because they have never encountered it before. You may have to continue being respectful for a very long time (an entire year or longer) until students realize that you aren't pretending. They may be suspicious. One boy told me that when he acted belligerent and I continued to address him respectfully, he assumed it was a trick.

"I figured something was up, you know," he told me later. "I'm like, she's slick, but what's she got up her sleeve? Ain't nobody gonna be that nice unless they want something. I finally figured out you was trying to show me how to act right. Do the right thing, man."

You don't have to like a student to treat him or her with respect. I'm sure you work with adults you don't particularly like, but you don't actively disrespect them, especially in front of your peers. Also, I think it's important to accept that not all students may like you. That is fine. Students don't have to like you, just as they don't have to like each other. They can still learn the information you teach. And they can learn to conduct themselves with self-respect so that they can survive school and go on to become successful people who enjoy positive relationships with other people in their personal and professional lives.

After observing both successful and struggling teachers, I have a theory about why some adults have trouble eliciting respect from students, even when those adults honestly believe they respect their students. When a teacher approaches students from a standpoint of wanting to reform, shape up, or save them, it comes across as condescending. Students sense that the teacher feels superior to them, and they resent the teacher's attitude, even though the teacher truly wants to help them. Imagine if another adult approached you and said, "You are such a mess. You make stupid choices, you waste your time and talents, and your values and ethics are inferior to mine. But I can show you how to be more like me so that you can be a better person. I promise I can help you, if you will only listen to me."

How would you feel if somebody said those things to you, even if the person were more accomplished and successful than you are? I don't think you would be receptive because you would be thinking, "What right does this person have to speak to me this way?" Your emotions would block your intellect, and no real communication would occur. Instead, your attention would be focused on trying to assert your own strength, to control your anger, to express your anger, or to return the insult.

If we want students to respect us, we must respect them as human beings deserving of basic human dignity. We must accept that they may have different values and lifestyles and that they may have made choices that we never would have made. But they are young, uneducated, and inexperienced (even if they are streetwise). We can't expect them to make logical, mature, and intelligent decisions unless adults have taught them how to think and have provided them with role models who exhibit mature and intelligent behavior. In fact, considering the rampant law breaking among our national political and corporate leaders, it's disingenuous to stand in front of students and declare that crime doesn't pay.

THE GANG THANG

Here's our chance to provide that missing role model for our students. Instead of criticizing and belittling them for joining gangs, taking recreational drugs, having rampant unsafe sex, and cheating their way through school, we will be much more likely to earn their respect if we ask students why they have made the choices they have made—and listen to their answers as nonjudgmentally as we can. If they ask for our advice, we can and should respond. Otherwise, I think it's best if we keep asking questions until students learn to question their own choices and behaviors. We can't save our students from themselves, but if we can teach them to think, to solve problems, to analyze their choices, and to articulate their ethics and values, eventually they will save themselves.

"Are you asking me to say it's okay to be a gang member?" one teacher asked me. Of course I am not suggesting that teachers advocate gang membership. But I am asking that we refrain from judging students who happen to be gang members. If a student is a second- or third-generation gang member, as many of my own students have been, the moment I say something derogatory about gangs I have insulted the family and lost any chance of ever gaining that student's trust. And it's very difficult to teach people who mistrust you. If we don't know all the circumstances of another person's life, we can't possibly know whether we would have made different choices if we were in the same situation, facing the same pressures. We can't possibly know the intimate details of our students' lives when we first meet them. So, I have learned to say, "I believe people have reasons for the things they do, even when they make different choices than I think I would. The important thing is to think about the choices we have made and if we decide they were not good choices, we must make some changes for the future." And I have to say that some of my smartest and best students have come from backgrounds where gang activity, violence, drug use, and frequent jail visits were the norm among the adults in the community as well as among students.

Another factor for teachers to consider is that street gangs are not like the Boy Scouts or Girl Scouts. Members can't just decide they don't want to attend meetings any more. One young man in my remedial reading class, an active gang member—I'll call him Ramon—was clearly intelligent and a quick learner, in spite of poor reading skills due to his past truancy. He attended class regularly for several months and then disappeared without a word. A few weeks later, I happened to encounter Ramon at a local department store. I expected him to avoid me, but he walked right over and said hello. I said that I missed seeing him in school.

"My girlfriend is having a baby," Ramon said, "and I was thinking about do I want my kids to grow up and do the same things I did. So I decided to get out of the gang. But they beat me down and told me if I come back to school, I'm dead. So I had to quit."

While I was still trying to think of something appropriate to say, Ramon turned so I could see his face more clearly. One side of his head was covered with bruises that still looked painful, although they were fading. Quickly, he pulled down his lower lip to reveal several missing teeth and wounds inside his mouth.

"I'm so sorry," I said.

"Hey, I'm cool," he said.

"That's wonderful. Good luck. I know you'll do well because you're an intelligent young man." I held out my hand, and Ramon took it without hesitation. After a quick shake, he nodded and walked off down the aisle. I never saw him again. I never forgot him, though, and I hope he remembers me as somebody who looked past his appearance and his mistakes to see the fine young man inside who was struggling to find his way.

As you consider how you are going to demonstrate your respect for your students as human beings, please take a moment to recall your own childhood teachers. I would bet my gigantic teacher's salary that you're not thinking of algebraic formulas or prepositional phrases. More likely you remember a compliment that sent your spirits soaring or a humiliation that still makes your cheeks burn. I remember one of my own elementary teachers using masking tape to attach my glasses to my face because I kept taking them off when other kids teased me about wearing them. The teacher said she meant to teach me to keep my glasses on my face and stop acting silly, but what she taught me was how embarrassing and infuriating it is to be helpless under the control of an authority figure who misuses her power. After that day I left my glasses at home and refused to wear them to school ever again. I squinted in school every year until my high school graduation. I still remember the masking-tape–wielding teacher, but I also remember my fifth-grade teacher, Mrs. Hodak, who encouraged me to write and appointed me to the glorious position of class newspaper editor. When I acted silly, Mrs. Hodak would look at me over the top of her glasses and wait for me to come to my senses and settle down. Then she would hug me. Mrs. Hodak taught me to think about my behavior. She taught me to challenge myself and follow my dreams. She taught me the true meaning of respect, and I will love her until the day I die.

GRADES: PERCENTAGE? CURVE? COIN TOSS?

How will you use grades in your classroom: to provide incentives, to record progress, to evaluate your teaching, to disrupt daydreamers, to punish plagiarizers and procrastinators—or all five? I opt to use only the first three because when teachers use bad grades or deduct points as punishment, they contribute to the cycle of misbehavior and failure that undermines our school system. I believe grades should measure how well students have learned the material and skills, and their grades indicate how well I have presented the lessons and motivated my students. A grade book filled with Ds and Fs is a warning flag that I am not doing my job well.

Every teacher must create a grading policy that reflects his or her own standards and ethics, but the most effective teachers maintain high standards, a flexible attitude, and a constant focus on fairness. Effective teachers keep students informed of their progress at frequent intervals to avoid surprises and complaints. Your school may use a pass/fail option, straight percentages, or a letter-grade system. Your department may add its own criteria, 95 percent required for an A, for example. But it will be up to you to assign the grades. Even a more subjective subject such as math leaves room for subjectivity in grading. Will you give credit only for correct answers on homework, or will you allow credit for student papers that have incorrect answers but indicate considerable effort or basic understanding of important concepts? If a student has perfect attendance, completes her homework faithfully, cooperates during class, but suffers from test anxiety that makes her fail every major exam, what grade will you assign her? Will you go strictly by percentage, even though it doesn't accurately represent her ability? Will you assign less weight to her exam scores? Perhaps you'll arrange an alternative testing program for her, allowing her to take her exams after school, perhaps orally, or with a trusted counselor in attendance.

What about your underachiever? If a student is clearly capable of earning an A without studying, but he decides to read comic books in the back of your classroom whenever he can and rarely bothers to complete a homework assignment, will you give him an A when he aces the midterm and final exams? Will your grade reflect his academic ability and natural intelligence, or will you consider his poor work ethic and laziness?

Will you grade every assignment, or will you give full credit on some assignments for students who make a sincere effort to learn a new skill even if they make a lot of mistakes? Will you allow students who work diligently on every task to earn extra credit that may raise their grade a notch to reflect their hard work, enthusiasm, and persistence? Will you start all students at ground zero and then make it as difficult as you can for them to work their way up to an A? Will you just start assigning work and figure out how to grade students after you see what they can do? Will you start all students with an A and work hard to help them keep it?

Because they believe we need to raise the bar, some teachers blast their classes with impossible workloads from the second the school year begins. And some teachers boast, "Nobody earns an A in my class because I'm too darn tough." My questions to such teachers are: What would motivate a student to try hard if he or she knows in advance that an A is impossible to achieve in your class? If the material in your class is learnable and appropriate for the students' ability level, then why shouldn't a motivated, hard-working student be able to learn what you have to teach?

The real question every teacher must answer is not so much what grade your students deserve as it is what you want them to learn. Of course, you must grade major exams according to your district policy. But although grading every assignment strictly by percentage teaches students that they must achieve whatever standards are set for them in a particular situation, it also may teach them that academic ability is more important than social skills, respect for other people, enthusiasm, a willingness to tackle challenges, and the ability to learn from mistakes.

CATCH THE CHEATERS—OR NOT?

Here's what I have learned about cheating, in general, and plagiarizing on major assignments in particular. Yes, some students cheat because they are lazy by nature. But I believe those students are a small minority. I believe most students cheat because they are afraid—that they can't do the work themselves, that their parents will be upset if they don't earn good grades, that the teacher likes students who earn good grades better than those with mediocre or poor performance, that if they don't earn straight As they won't get into college or won't get a good job or some other important, life-changing scenario. And I believe that students who cheat on major assignments such as research papers are either overwhelmed by the scope of the assignment or simply going through the motions without understanding the point of the whole thing. Sometimes it's both and a bit of laziness thrown into the mix.

So what do we do about those cheaters? We can try to catch them. We can use the Web sites and computer applications designed to scan databases and give us the original sources of the plagiarized works. We can create strict policies for punishing cheaters. We might even expel them. We can police our classrooms, wearing sneakers, so we can tiptoe around and try to make sure that everybody is doing his or her own work. But all of these approaches make more work for teachers who already have more than enough to do. And they detract precious time from teaching the students who truly are trying. I know because I wasted too much of my own time trying to solve this problem—until I realized that I was the problem. Students were cheating because they could. So I decided to redesign my major assignments and redirect my approach.

First, I spend more time trying to help students understand that if they truly do their best to learn what's in their required curriculum, whether they love it or not, they will earn passing grades. But if they don't care about their learning, they won't learn. It's that simple. If you stand in front of a class and say, "Please raise your hand if you would like to pass this class," you will see most of the hands go up. Some will shoot up high. Others will stop at about shoulder height. And some will hover just above the waist. Pay attention. The higher the hand, the higher the confidence and motivation. (The smart alecks who leave their hands down and grin at you are usually asking you to love them for themselves—or they want your attention. Ignore them for the moment.) Take note of the students who aren't sure about passing your class. They are worried. They may be poor readers, smart but slow thinkers, kids with hearing or vision issues, emotional distractions at home, or a sense that they are missing some basic academic skills they should have acquired. Work with them individually, through private conferences, to figure out what they need to believe they can pass your class. Sometimes all it takes is for the teacher to believe—and we must believe that all students can learn. If we don't, they won't. It's that simple. Confidence is contagious.

Second, I try to design assignments that eliminate the potential for cheating. If students are reading a novel, for example, I might ask them to complete a Venn diagram about characterization. But before I ask them to compare two characters from the book (half of them will copy from their neighbors when I'm not looking), I ask them to compare themselves to one of the characters. This personalizes the assignment, makes it more relevant, and helps them understand the basic concept. It also reduces the chances of and motivation for cheating. It's interesting to note that sometimes students worry that they got it wrong when they complete a complex assignment successfully. They think school is supposed to be impossibly difficult, so they are surprised and sometimes suspicious when they actually try and find out that learning isn't so hard after all when it means something to them.

How about those big assignments? At my own high school, two recent assignments leap to mind. During the summer, the Advanced Placement (AP) language arts teachers gave major assignments, hoping to give their students a taste of what might be expected of them at college. Unfortunately, the huge majority of students did what overwhelmed college students do—they went on the Internet and searched for the answers. They found them. I know because as a new teacher on staff I inherited two of the classes. In preparation for teaching, I also searched the Internet for information on the two books—*Huckleberry Finn* and *How to Read Literature Like a Professor*. I found a plethora of material to filch from professors, students, chat rooms, and commercial vendors who pander to bewildered AP students. The chapter summaries of both books are available on multiple sites, in paragraph format or bullet points—whichever the teacher requested. Looking for an allusion, a simile, a theme or recurring motif? *Click. Click. Help yourself.* How about examples of other books and stories that illustrate the point? *Click. Cut and paste.*

But students must learn to do research. They must be able to create a thesis about literature—or science or history or art. Common Core Standards say so. But so does common sense. Students need to learn to generate their own questions about the subjects they study in school, about the world around them, about life in general. They need to learn to tap into their own interests, passions and talents. Rather than going through the motions of writing a research paper just to show that they can format a bibliography and articulate their thoughts using grammatically correct writing, I want my students to be so interested in a topic that they can't help asking questions and seeking more information.

Sometimes I forget to take my own advice. Recently, for example, I gave my AP seniors a cognitive quiz to help them determine whether they relied more on the left or right hemispheres of their brains. We watched a *TED Talks* video called

"The Divided Brain," narrated by a prominent neuroscientist. We read six articles, some academic and some anecdotal. We read about experiments with mice that lost their memories when they drank water with food dye in it. We read about brain surgery and the effects of aerobic fitness on academic achievement and the fact that being bilingual reduces a person's risk of getting Alzheimer's disease. My goals were to encourage my students to engage in some metacognition—to think about themselves as learners. I wanted them to analyze and discuss and write about informational texts. I wanted them to compare various sources and evaluate their accuracy and credibility. I hoped to challenge and improve their higher-level critical thinking skills. They loved the quiz and the video, but with each article fewer students actually read the homework and engaged actively in the discussions and writing exercises. They disconnected from the project. Because they all plan to go to college they did the assignments, but their writing and discussions became perfunctory—boring for them to complete and for me to grade. And I knew I'd be reading a lot of material lifted directly from the Internet.

My plan had been for the culminating assignment to be an essay about some aspect of brain science as it relates to learning, based on the various materials we had studied. But I didn't want to read sixty essays by sixty students who were perfectly capable of producing grammatically correct, properly constructed, extremely boring writing. So I scrapped the essay—temporarily. Instead, I created an assignment sheet for "The Brain Project." Each student was tasked with creating and designing a project (report, brochure, video, slide show, questionnaire, experiment, teaching demonstration, illustrated children's book, artistic interpretation) centering on some aspect of brain science and learning that resonated for them. I provided a list of criteria I would use for grading along with a printed contract for them to fill out. The contract required them to state the topic of their project, describe their basic plan, and agree that they would complete the project by the required due date.

I expected my students to welcome the change in plans, but they were stunned. They sat wide-eyed, staring at me as though I had just asked them to remove their clothing and dance on their desktops.

"Think it over," I said. "Talk to each other. Take the rest of the period. Whip out those cell phones and do a little research. You can complete your contracts tomorrow."

Tomorrow came and went. For fifty minutes, one after another, students pulled me aside and confided that they had no idea what to do. They wanted to do well.

They wanted good grades. But they were lost. Couldn't I please tell them exactly what to do so they could do it well? Many of them looked as though they were going to burst into tears. I nearly gave up. But the thought of those sixty boring essays made me persist.

After another day of bewilderment, I flopped into a student seat and faced my first period class. "I guess this is too much for you," I said. "Let me tell you about something that happened to me when I first went to college. My psychology professor announced that our mid-term grade would be based on just one assignment. We were to write our own theories of personality. I had no idea what that meant. I asked him. He said, 'Tell me your theory of personality.' I told him I had no idea what he was talking about. He said, 'Tell me why people have the personalities they have.' I said I didn't know. He said, 'Think about it. That's your assignment.' When I asked him how long the paper was supposed to be, he replied, 'As long as it is.' And that was the end of his instruction."

"What did you do?" one girl asked me.

"I panicked for a while, and then I came up with a theory. I passed the class. Later, I realized my particular theory wasn't important. The professor just wanted me to think for myself and become interested in psychology. I'm trying to do that for you. But I think maybe it's too much for you right now. So I will take all the articles we read and design some kind of test for you that is more familiar."

Nobody spoke for several seconds. Then the same girl said, "Don't stress, Miss Johnson. We can do this. We just needed to think about it for a while." She looked around the room to make sure her classmates agreed. They did. By the end of that class period, students were bouncing ideas off each other, offering encouragement, helping each other design experiments, and teaching each other how to use PowerPoint. One boy grinned at me on his way out the door and said, "My brain is humming."

My first-period students passed the word to my second-period class, who arrived full of ideas and questions. In both classes, a few students needed more help to narrow their topics and articulate their goals, but eventually everybody had a project he or she was actually interested in completing. Those who wanted to stand in the spotlight had the chance to present to the class. Others chose nonverbal approaches. But everybody had something to write about afterward, and none of the essays were boring.

Project-Based Learning can be daunting, even for experienced teachers. You have to let go of control. You have to make students responsible for their own educations. You have to figure out how to grade the end result, factoring in the different academic abilities and the levels of complexity of their self-designed projects. It's worth the effort, though, and in the end projects require much less time and energy to assess because you can design a rubric with various elements that can be checked off as they are completed.

One final note about grading: If you teach subjects that involve abstract principles or concepts, such as ethics, economics, or algebra (especially algebra), be aware that some students may have problems because of their individual rates of development. There is a point in every child's development when the brain makes the switch from concrete to abstract thinking. This switch has nothing to do with intelligence. Conscientious, industrious students who are used to succeeding in school often become frustrated when they cannot grasp new concepts, and you may think they aren't trying because they usually earn high grades. For example, when we study symbolism in literature, many bright students understand the definition of symbolism and the examples I give them to illustrate the technique, but they cannot create their own examples for an exam. Instead of deducting points from those students' papers, I give them credit if they can define the concept and remember some of my examples. My hope is that later on, when they are able to understand, they will recall those examples and use them as a model for creating their own.

COVERING CURRICULUM IS NOT TEACHING

If you are a master organizer with a creative flair and the ability to teach advanced, regular, and remedial students, undeterred by myriad distractions and interruptions, then you probably have no trouble covering all of the curriculum required for your subject or course. If you don't spend a minute worrying about how you're going to fit everything you want to teach into one school year, then you're an uncommonly talented teacher who should skip this section. The rest of us worry because it's common for teachers, especially new teachers, to fear that they can't teach everything they need to teach. There is too much material, too much paper shuffling, too many energy-consuming administrative tasks, and not enough time. Instead of sharing this fear and discussing ways to become more effective teachers, most of us worry privately and fear that our colleagues will think we're ineffective or unqualified if we admit that we sometimes feel inadequate to the task of teaching all the required skills and information for our courses.

The question every teacher must face is this: Given a conflict, where does my priority lie—in covering the curriculum material and preparing for tests or in meeting my students' needs? It's easy to err in either direction. Some teachers take the district guidelines to heart and race their way through the required textbooks and activities, leaving students who can't learn fast enough trailing behind the pack. Unfortunately, sometimes an entire class ends up falling behind, and the teacher is the only one who really understands the material when it's time for final exams. Other teachers bend to the pressure from above and spend all their class time teaching a specific test. Their students may learn how to take that specific test, and the school district may look good on paper. However, I believe those students could be better served if they learned how to think and read and write well, which would prepare them to succeed in college or at work in addition to preparing them to pass exams. Still other teachers turn giddy from the pressure to perform or pay the price (not being offered a contract or granted tenure, for example), so they toss aside the textbooks and spend their entire class periods chatting with students about current events or designing fun projects that take weeks to complete, leaving their students unprepared for the following year's requirements.

It is possible, though not easy, to find a middle ground. My district supervisor gave me a big boost in the right direction when she explained her viewpoint at a meeting of our teaching team. Working together, we four teachers had the task of teaching fifty at-risk teens, students who had severe attendance problems, substandard reading ability, and apathetic attitudes toward education.

"Covering curriculum is not teaching," our supervisor explained. "Nobody expects you to address the problems these kids have, bring them up to grade level, and cover your entire textbooks in one year. I advise you to select the key elements in your texts and teach those elements well. Don't worry about covering everything; just teach the most important concepts and skills, and teach your students how to learn so they can pick up the slack." We took her advice and were amazed at how well it worked. Instead of dividing our textbooks into segments and arbitrarily deciding how long each new skill should take to master, we made a list of what we wanted to teach and started with the most important and basic skills. For example, our math teacher had to back up and reteach the number line and negative and positive numbers. We were a little nervous at first, but when our students realized that we would slow down as they needed to spend time on areas of special interest they repaid us by working harder at the mundane tasks in between. Our students performed as well as the "regular" students in English, history, and computer courses, and our math students zoomed right past the regular geometry classes, earning higher grades and completing more of the same textbook!

Those students reminded us of a lesson we sometimes forget: children are capable of learning much more than we require during a given school year. If we slow down or back up to fill in the gaps in their knowledge base and if they are confident that we have their best interests at heart, they will accelerate their learning and accomplish goals far beyond any we set for them.

SCHOOL IS AN EMOTIONAL EXPERIENCE

One of the most important things I have ever learned about learning is that our brains and our emotions are intricately interwoven. Every time our brain stores new information, our emotions store the feelings we experience while we are learning that information. More importantly, when we retrieve information, we retrieve the emotions, too. This explains why so many people develop phobias about reading, writing, and mathematics. We can't blame the teacher. Not always, anyway. Regardless of a teacher's ability and compassion, some students will struggle with any new information or skill. And children are the center of their own universe. If a teacher displays concern when children struggle, they may become anxious. Children want to please their teachers. They may think, "The teacher is mad at me." The negative emotions become intertwined with the learning and stored away. The next time the teacher says, "Let's read," or "Let's do our arithmetic," these students retrieve the negative emotions and the cycle begins.

Even when students eventually overcome the obstacles and learn the challenging information and skills, the stored emotions remain. This phenomenon became shockingly clear to me when I was teaching a graduate education course at Santa Fe Community College. One day, I asked my future teachers to pair off and share their memories of their first experiences of learning how to read. Within a few minutes, several students were sniffling, including a few of the men. One woman left the room in tears so she could take a walk and regain her composure. During our class discussion of the exercise, student after student recalled the emotional turmoil they experienced— twenty or thirty years earlier!—as young readers. They proved the theory beyond any doubt.

"Oh, wonderful," you may be thinking. "Now, in addition to worrying about my own teaching, I have to deal with the fallout from all the teachers my students have already had." Yes, you do. But keep in mind that plenty of those past teachers created positive emotional learning cycles. Many students start school, enjoy positive experiences, and get hooked on learning for life. You will have some of those students in your classes, and they are a joy to teach.

You will also have some students who got caught in the negative emotional learning cycle. The first step to breaking any cycle is to be aware it exists. Don't take student behavior personally if you introduce a topic of study and students respond with wild emotions. Unless you have done something to offend or upset a student, the behavior is not about you. It's about whatever emotions were stored away in a past classroom and retrieved in yours. It takes time to replace negative learning experiences with positive ones, but it can be done. Learn to practice mindfulness in the classroom—being aware of the tone of your voice, your posture, and your facial expressions and being alert to your students' emotional states. If your teacher training program did not include a social and emotional learning (SEL) component, your school district may include it in ongoing staff development workshops. But even without formal training, teachers can learn the basic fundamentals of creating classrooms where self-awareness, social awareness, and relationship skills are reinforced routinely during lessons and activities. If you do an online search for SEL, you will find abundant resources and online courses. And you may find that as your own emotional storage drawers begin to open you will be flooded with memories of your own feelings about learning as a child. Don't shy away from those overwhelming emotions. Use them to help you empathize and connect with your own students.

THERE IS NO SUCH THING AS A CASUAL REMARK TO A CHILD

Sometimes I think we forget how impressionable children are (even adolescents). We forget how excruciating the smallest pain can be, how exhilarating the tiniest victory, and how lasting the effect of a comment from an adult they admire. One day before class started, a group of football players were boasting about their latest gridiron glories. I noticed another boy, Sean, blush and fidget as he watched the athletes trade playful insults in front of a group of admiring girls and boys. A skinny youngster, all elbows and knees, Sean often dropped things or tripped over his shoelaces. When one of the ball players, Paul, complimented himself on a 65-yard touchdown, Sean sighed and looked out the window. I walked around the room until I stood near his desk.

"I'm very proud of you, Paul," I told the touchdown scorer. "But I hope you go on to achieve great things after school too. I'd hate for you to be one of those people who peak at age sixteen, whose lives are all downhill after high school."

"I'm cool," Paul responded with a grin. "You know the scouts are already looking at me."

I was looking at Sean, who was looking at Paul.

"You're going to be one of those men who peak much later in life," I said softly to Sean.

"Yeah, I was thinking that," Sean said. His cheeks flushed bright red, but he sat up straighter and stopped staring wistfully at Paul and his entourage. Pleased that I had boosted Sean's self-esteem, I took the scenic route as I strolled back to my desk.

In the far corner of the room, as I passed by the desk of an extremely shy girl named Marcy, I stopped and smiled at her. "You too," I said. "I think you're going to be a late bloomer, but you're going to be a big, beautiful flower."

Marcy folded into herself and hid her face as she did whenever anybody looked at her. Not wanting to embarrass her further, I quickly made some chitchat with other students and returned to the front of the room.

I forgot all about the incident until a few months later, at open house. Toward the end of the event, Sean's mother walked into my room and introduced herself. As I reached out to shake hands with her, she took my right hand with both her hands. She squeezed my hand and held on.

"I wanted to thank you for what you said to Sean," she said. "He said you told him you knew he was going to peak late in life and he shouldn't worry about not being the best athlete or the most popular right now. You should have seen him smile when he told me. And he has been a different person ever since. You changed his life. I can't thank you enough."

I was so stunned at her remarks that I just stood there, grinning stupidly at her until she left the room. I had completely forgotten about that day, but Sean had remembered. I floated through the rest of the evening on a little cloud of happiness. One incident like that can keep a teacher motivated for months. But just as I was ready to turn out the lights and lock the door, Marcy's mother peeked around the door frame.

"Am I too late to say hello?" she asked. Some children work hard to be different from their parents, but Marcy was definitely her mother's daughter. I welcomed her into my room and motioned for her to sit down in one of the student desks for a chat.

"Oh, I don't want to take up your time," she said. She held her purse tightly with both hands, and I had the impression that she was resisting the temptation to hold it up in front of her face to hide behind it.

"I just wanted to thank you," she said. "Marcy told me you said she was a late bloomer but that she is going to be a beautiful flower someday. She cried when she told me. We both did. She used to be worried about what would happen to her when she grew up, but she doesn't worry anymore."

I didn't say anything because I knew I would cry if I opened my mouth. I just nodded and smiled at Marcy's mother as she ducked her head and slipped out the door.

After Sean's mother had talked to me, I admit I was feeling a little proud of myself. But after Marcy's mother left, I felt a little frightened. Two students believed that a 5-second forgotten conversation had changed their lives. If that was true, then what about all the other conversations I couldn't remember? Had I said anything that negatively affected children so strongly as those positive comments had? I tried to remember whether I had said anything harsh the last time I had run out of patience or had been frustrated by too much talking or pencil sharpening or giggling or note writing during class. I couldn't think of any negative comments I may have made, but then I had forgotten the late-bloomer comments too.

Before I turned off the lights and locked the door to my classroom that night, I wrote a note on an index card and taped it to the top of my desk as a reminder. My note read:

> Be careful. Everything you say, every single day, may be recorded in your students' hearts forever.

WHAT DO YOU THINK?

1. What is your teaching persona? How does it compare with your personal persona?

2. What is your optional agenda? What optional agendas did your own teachers have?

3. How can teachers effectively establish rapport with students who come from different cultural or ethnic backgrounds?

4. How can teachers design assessment tools that are accurate and fair indicators of individual student progress?

5. How do you prioritize when pressure to prepare for tests conflicts with the activities and lessons you believe are necessary to include in your curriculum?

6. Share some comments that you remember from your childhood teachers. Why do you still remember those comments?

The Big Three: Preparation, Preparation, Preparation

Award-winning realtors often list their top three criteria for success as "location, location, location." And effective teachers often list the top three criteria for their success as "preparation, preparation, preparation." If you don't get your ducks all in a row well ahead of time, you may find yourself dealing with stray quackers all year long, because once the school year begins even experienced, effective teachers find themselves running at top speed on the teaching treadmill. In addition to saving time and energy later on, spending a couple of weeks getting organized before school starts will allow you to focus on the most challenging and interesting aspect of your job—your students.

You will need some equipment and supplies to get yourself organized. Because most schools operate on limited or shrinking budgets, supplies may be scarce. As soon as you sign your contract to teach, ask a friend or relative to host a teacher-to-be shower. Provide a suggestion list for gifts: file folders, storage crates and bins, portable bookshelves, colored markers and art supplies, poster board, construction paper, scissors, tape, staplers, pencils, pens, paper clips, three-ring binders, subscriptions to educational publications for young people, children's books, young adult books, dictionaries, notebook paper, pastel printer paper, and so on. If your friends and relatives are employed and generous, you might add bigger items such as a room-sized air purifier, a portable stereo, and a video or digital camera. Don't be shy. You aren't asking for gifts for yourself; you are asking for donations to help you educate the future leaders of our country. People will be happy to contribute and even happier if you periodically provide them with an e-mail or printed newsletter highlighting your students' achievements.

Another possible resource is Web sites where teachers can list their requests for funds to buy supplies, equipment, books, and other materials to aid their students. DonorsChoose.org is a national database where teachers describe their classroom projects and donors can search by area or need.

Once you have supplies, where do you start? I suggest making three lists of things you need to prepare: your classroom, your paperwork, and yourself. You'll find my own checklists at the end of this chapter if you'd like to use them as a starting point.

PREPARE YOUR ROOM

I often refer to attending school as children's work, and I frequently draw analogies between the many common behaviors and conditions that lead to success in school and at work. In any profession, your environment affects your comfort and efficiency, and your interactions with other people affect the speed and accuracy of your work. As an adult, you have multiple options if you are uncomfortable or unhappy in your job. Students are stuck with whatever classroom environments their teachers create; your classroom environment can mean the difference between a room filled with cooperative, enthusiastic, motivated children and a group of apathetic nonparticipants and disgruntled whiners. Creating a dynamic classroom environment involves four basic elements: sensory details, seating arrangements, supplies and storage, and student information.

Sensory Details

Children are much more attuned to—and distracted by—the world's sensory elements than most adults are. Students may respond dramatically to the way your room looks, feels, sounds, and even smells. You can do a great deal (even with limited equipment and funds) to address those four aspects of your classroom with an eye toward creating an environment that is functional, comfortable, welcoming, and inspiring.

Sound and smell are the easiest aspects to address. If your school is noisy because of traffic, loud air conditioning or heating systems, thin walls, or rampaging students, you can create an oasis of calm in your classroom by playing soft music before and between class periods. Scientists have repeatedly proven that music can either encourage or discourage thinking and positive feelings. Light classical music, jazz, or music designed to enhance meditation can all be used to take advantage of children's natural affinity for melody and percussion.

One teacher I know spent weeks ignoring objections from her high school juniors when she played light classical music during work time for assignments and exams. Finally, she turned off the music. Before long her students began complaining that all the background noise was too distracting—they asked her to bring back the music.

Music can also be a great tool for increasing student participation and motivation. I have had groups in which even confirmed nonreaders agreed to read difficult fiction in exchange for spending a few minutes at the end of the class period listening to their horrible, screeching, "really great" music.

Next, let's talk about smell, an integral part of any school experience. If you close your eyes and let your nose drift, I would bet you can recall at least one distinctive smell from your own school days. My strongest olfactory memory is of new books. I have always loved their smell. But not all school smells are pleasant. In fact, when you take twenty or thirty warm bodies, plenty of well-worn sneakers, several quarts of perfumed personal hygiene products, dust from dry-erase markers, residue from the custodial staff's industrial-strength cleaners, and reams of old papers, you can end up with some nasty-smelling classrooms.

Fortunately, smell is a relatively easy aspect of your room to control, but buying a decent air cleaner is probably going to cost a few dollars out of your own pocket unless you can find a local business to sponsor you or unless your department budget provides a petty-cash allowance. Even if you have to fork over the dough from your paltry paycheck, your investment will pay off. Not only will your classroom smell better, but also you'll find that you have fewer students sniffling during allergy season. And if you buy an air purifier with an ultraviolet light, it will kill many of the germs that congregate in classrooms during cold and flu season.

Do a little research before you buy an air purifier. There are a lot of urban myths surrounding negative ion generation and ultraviolet radiation. Negative ions are not harmful unless they are created in overabundance, and most new air cleaners have built-in controls. When an air cleaner generates the proper amount of negative ions, it creates a fresh, outdoorsy smell. A distinctive tangy odor means you need to make an adjustment. Ultraviolet lights in air filters are not placed where they can injure people's eyes, and they very effectively zap airborne germs and pollutants.

Now we're ready to tackle the feel of your room. Take a walk around the block and then enter your classroom. Notice whether it's too warm or too cold, whether the lights are so bright that they create glare on the desks. Are the walls a nice warm color, or have they been painted an ugly industrial gray or tan to hide the dirt? (I know, I know, you aren't supposed to paint your room. But there are ways to get it done if you are creative.) If you do decide to paint sans permission—I'm not advocating, just suggesting a possibility—buy paint that does not give off gasses. They are called low-VOC paints; read about them at the BioShield Paint Web site (www.bioshieldpaint.com). If you go the law-abiding route and request permission, consult your building custodians for advice.

Does your room feel inviting? Is this a place you'd like to sit for a few hours every day? Visit other classrooms. Compare the way they feel with the way your room feels. If your room is stuffy and overheated or too cold and drafty, ask the maintenance supervisor for advice. Some schools are inflexible about the dates that schools must use heating or air conditioning, regardless of the local weather conditions, and some buildings have a central ventilation system with no individual room settings. However, if you explain that you are trying to make your room as comfortable as possible for your students, your maintenance professionals will probably find a way to help you. It has been my experience that they appreciate being recognized for their knowledge and training and are eager to help you if you approach them with a respectful and patient attitude. At one school, the custodians placed a transparent blue film over the fluorescent lights to reduce the glare and create a more natural color of light. At another school, when I asked about full-spectrum fluorescent lights, the head custodian said, "You tell me what you need, and I'll find it." When I painted my room one weekend—honestly, I didn't know I wasn't supposed to—the custodians shook their heads but pretended not to notice.

Does your classroom look inviting and interesting? If you teach special needs students who are distracted by visual input, you may want to opt for a less busy decor, but if you do decide to decorate try tacking up photos of students from your old high school yearbooks, copies of your childhood report cards, a collection of calendars, restaurant menus, theater playbills, colorful mobiles, or plants (real or fake). Think of theme restaurants you like: the decor has nothing to do with the food, but we still like to sit in surroundings that are beautiful or amusing. Put a fake palm tree and some floor pillows in a corner of your classroom with a nonfluorescent lamp nearby, and kids will clamor to sit there and read. (Don't ask permission to do this. Just do it, and if you get in trouble apologize profusely. If student behavior or grades have improved because of your decor, administrators are much more likely to okay them.)

Does your room have some eye candy for students who daydream occasionally? (Brain science suggests that daydreamers may actually be processing new information.) When students aren't paying attention to your lessons, they will still absorb the information they see on the walls. Motivational quotations are especially effective. There are a number of sites that help teachers create their own posters. (BigHugeLabs.com and poster.4teachers.org are just two of many such resources.)

Here are a few of my favorite quotes to get you started:

> *The hallmark of a second-rater is resentment of another's achievement.*
>
> —Ayn Rand

> *Nobody can make you feel inferior without your consent.*
>
> —Eleanor Roosevelt

> *If you can imagine it, you can achieve it; if you can dream it, you can become it.*
>
> —William Ward

> *Great spirits have always encountered violent opposition from mediocre minds.*
>
> —Albert Einstein

The hardest thing about success is finding somebody who is truly happy for you.

—Bette Midler

There are two tragedies in life: one is to lose your heart's desire, the other to gain it.

—G. B. Shaw

If your only tool is a hammer, you tend to see every problem as a nail.

—Abraham Maslow

One often learns more from ten days of agony than from ten years of contentment.

—Merle Shain

Light came to me when I realized I did not have to consider any racial group as a whole. God made them duck by duck, and that was the only way I could see them.

—Zora Neale Hurston

Rudeness is a weak person's attempt at strength.

—J. M. Casey

Hold fast to dreams, for if dreams die, life is a broken-winged bird that cannot fly.

—Langston Hughes

Keep away from people who try to belittle your ambitions. Small people always do that, but the really great make you feel that you, too, are great.

—Mark Twain

We are each given the same twenty-four hours each day. How we choose to spend our time makes the difference between success and failure.

—K. Brodeur

Just because you're right doesn't mean I'm wrong.

—My mom, Alyce Shirley

The Psychology of Seating

Student seating arrangements have a tremendous impact on their motivation, behavior, and interactions with each other and with the teacher. For very young children who spend most of their time sitting on the pillows or floor mats, the important thing is for them to see and hear the teacher and classroom aides. Once children are old enough to spend their class time seated in chairs, seating becomes a more important issue. The shape and size of your classroom will limit your options, but two considerations should take priority regardless of what arrangement you choose: vision and access. While seated, students must be able to clearly see the board, projector screens, and monitors. Also, you must have quick, easy access to every student in your room. You will have far fewer discipline problems if you arrange student seating with a clear pathway to each student and a maximum of two people between you and a given student.

Creating access can be a challenge in a small room, especially in narrow mobile classrooms. In a smaller room, you may have to create three or more separate areas to have desks only three deep. Try sketching a few different ideas on paper. If you have a small room, you might consider eliminating your own desk if it's big and bulky and you have sufficient storage. A small mobile computer desk and worktable might allow a more effective use of space.

Psychology plays an important role in seating: a round table indicates that all participants hold equal status, whereas a rectangular table usually has a chair at the head for the leader. Large tables with chairs that face across are conducive to communication and discussion. Chairs lined in long, straight rows facing a stage (think of church pews or seats in a theater) create a clear distinction between the speakers and the audience.

Your seating plan communicates information to your students. Long, straight rows indicate that yours will be a traditional classroom, governed by standard rules and regulations. A large circle or concentric semicircles send a different message, usually indicating group discussions or other student interactions. Small groups of desks or tables alert students to be prepared to participate in small-group activities or teamwork exercises.

I use different arrangements for different activities, but I have learned the hard way to avoid arrangements in which students face each other squarely from a distance. At one school where gang activity was a serious problem, both boys and girls would stare down students who sat directly opposite them. Turning desks so that they faced each other at even a slight angle eliminated this problem; it's easy to judge whether you've got it right. Sit in one of the student desks in the front row. If your gaze is directed squarely at another student's desk, then shift your desk so that the direct line of your gaze includes several desks or a wall.

The only time I use straight rows of desks facing the same direction is when we have an important test. Students understand that when they see test formation, they should sharpen their pencils, stow their possessions, and be prepared to work quietly. I don't like long, straight rows as a rule. Students tend to misbehave or daydream when they are seated in rows of six or seven, because no matter where I stand several students are far away from me. Worse yet, students cannot hear or see each other well. Students in the front and back of the room can't hear each other's comments, questions, or answers during class time. Everybody has trouble hearing when students read aloud during class because students are either reading into a void in the front of the room or into the backs of other students' heads—not conducive to creating a dynamic environment for participation or discussion.

In a room with a clearly defined front (board and projection screen permanently located on the same wall), my top-three arrangements are a modified semicircle or U shape (Figure 4.1) that allows everybody to see clearly while giving me quick, easy access to all students; a flexible plan (Figure 4.2) with worktables or grouped desks to the sides and a semicircle instructional area in the center; or pair share seating (Figure 4.3) for when I want students to work in pairs. To make teams, the pair share desks can be moved quickly into groups of four.

The flexible arrangement can be tweaked to fit a number of different classroom shapes and sizes to facilitate small-group instruction plus independent or group work at the same time. This is the most compatible arrangement for teachers who like to use differentiated instruction and independent assignments or projects. The teacher can provide direct instruction in the center of the room while students work independently in the side areas.

For small-group activities, I place the desks into clumps of three or four. I try to separate the groups enough to allow for private discussions and eliminate distractions from other groups. Some teachers ask their students to arrange the desks for group activities, which has the added benefit of giving students a bit of physical exercise and provides a perfect opportunity to teach students the procedure you would like them to use to prepare for group activity.

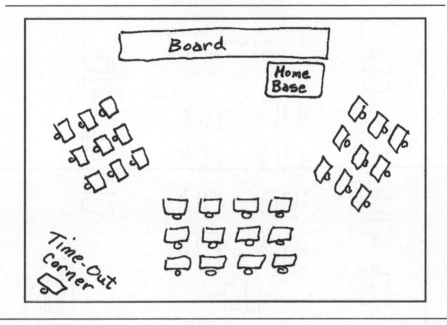

Figure 4.1
Modified U Seating.

Board

Home Base

Time-Out corner

Figure 4.2
Flexible Seating.

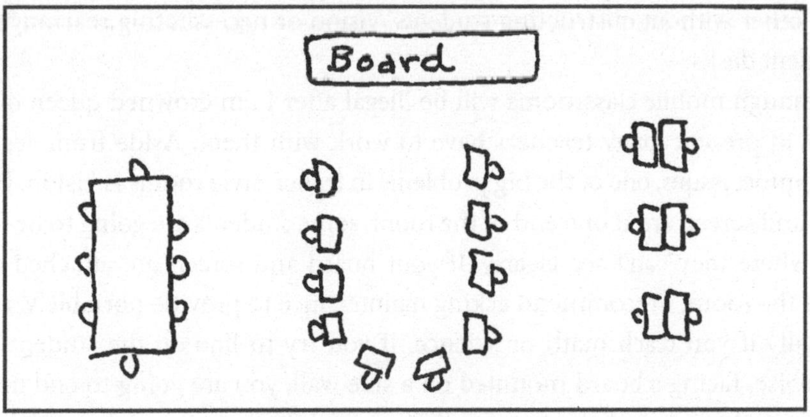

Board

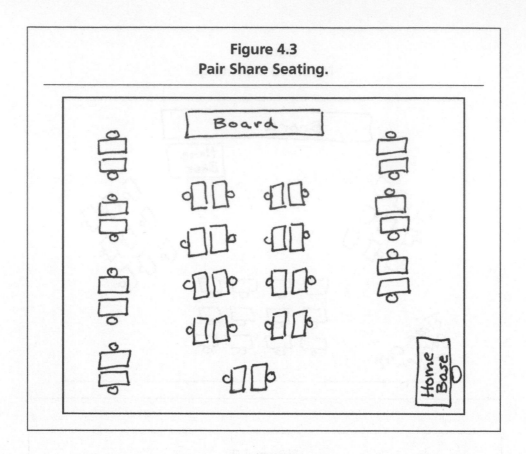

Figure 4.3
Pair Share Seating.

In a classroom with two possible fronts (boards or screens on opposite walls), I use a double semicircle formation (Figure 4.4), so the focus shifts from one side to the other without obstructing students' vision or necessitating rearrangement of student desks.

Although mobile classrooms will be illegal after I am crowned queen of education, at present many teachers have to work with them. Aside from aesthetic and comfort issues, one of the big problems in trailer-style rooms is vision. If your board and screen are at one end of the room, some students are going to be forced to sit where they can't see clearly. If your board and screen are attached at the side of the room, I recommend asking maintenance to provide portable versions, especially if you teach math or science. If you try to line up the student desks lengthwise, facing a board mounted on a side wall, you are going to end up with all your students crowded into a small space, and those on the ends won't be able to see well.

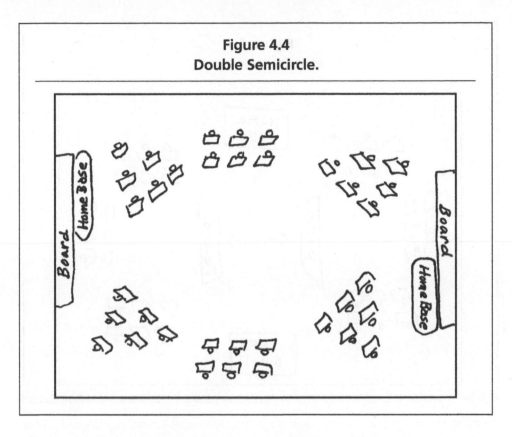

Figure 4.4
Double Semicircle.

My approach to trailer teaching is to divide the students into two groups, one at either end of the trailer (Figure 4.5). While one group of students works independently at desks, I instruct the other group using the overhead projector and board (moving the screen and board for each group so they are positioned where the whole group can see them). Although I have to present the same lesson twice, it doesn't deprive anybody, and it actually helps those students who process information more slowly, allowing them to tune in to both presentations as needed.

There are many other options for arranging desks, including getting rid of half of them and using conference tables, work centers, floor pillows, armchairs, futons, and the like. And even if you are stuck with a specific arrangement for some reason, you can still switch it up a bit. I read about one teacher who had trouble getting students to transition from one activity to the next. Her solution: she asked students to spin their desks 90 degrees or 180 degrees so they faced a different wall. This simple shift in visual input helped her students shift their focus to the new activity.

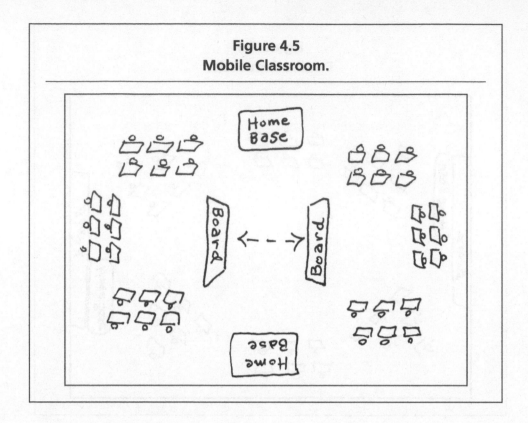

Figure 4.5
Mobile Classroom.

Open Seating or Seating Charts?

Some teachers swear by seating charts—and some students swear at them. Alphabetical seating is popular because it helps teachers learn names, take roll, and coordinate activities that require students to line up and move as a group. Alphabetical seating arrangements can be helpful to teachers, particularly if they work with very young children, but such charts can backfire with older students. Some become irritated or apathetic after years of being assigned to the front or the back of every lineup, and some will have been forced to sit year after year near others with whom they have serious personality conflicts. During high school years, conflicts can cause serious behavior problems.

I recommend starting without a seating chart. Here's why: when you use a seating chart, you give up a great power tool and miss out on an opportunity to learn more about your students. When students are permitted to select their own seats, you will find that some make a beeline for the back of the room. Some prefer an aisle seat, just as some airline travelers do. And still others choose to sit close to the teacher. Not all students who sit in the back are troublemakers—some people simply can't concentrate when there are people behind them, sort of like the poker player who likes to sit with his back against the wall. Students who choose the perimeter of the room may have private lives where they often feel a need to escape. They can't concentrate when they feel trapped. Front-row students may have hearing or vision problems—or they may be wary of sitting near somebody who has bullied or harassed them in the past. All of this information can help you understand your students better, and students may be more inclined to cooperate immediately if they feel comfortable.

The way students sit also gives you insight into their personalities and attitudes toward school. Scholars tend to sit up straight and place their books and notebooks quietly on their desks. Reluctant students will flop or slump into their seats and may drop their backpacks (if they bother to bring them) into the middle of the aisle, blocking other students. Those who distrust teacher may expand as they sit, stretching their arms and legs to take up the maximum amount of space. Think of the advice park rangers offer to hikers: make yourself appear as big as possible when threatened by a bear. A school bully may be the bear. Or it may be you.

Another advantage of beginning a class with open seating is that it leaves you holding a good power tool. If misbehavior becomes a serious problem, you can warn your students that you will have to create a seating chart, which might mean they won't have the option of sitting near their friends or in a favorite location. This puts the responsibility for their behavior squarely on their young shoulders, where it belongs. And if they haven't developed enough self-control to control their behavior, the assigned seating may help them. When behavior improves, allow them to sit in self-selected seats again as a test. This may take two or three tries, but if you use seating charts as learning tools instead of punishment they can be an effective method for nurturing self-control.

One year, I had a very unruly class, so I threatened to create a seating chart and eventually did. Instead of resigning themselves to the inevitable, as my students had done in the past, this group whined nonstop for days, until out of frustration, I said, "Fine! You don't like my chart? You create one where we don't have so much talking and disruptions when people are trying to work." Working effectively as a group for the first time, those kids came up with a complex arrangement that worked better than any of my plans. Here is the student-designed seating program, along with their justification for each step.

Some students find it boring to sit in the same seats every day, whereas other students prefer the emotional security of sitting in the same seat. So the students who need to sit in the same seat get to claim seats, and nobody else can sit there even when those students are absent.

Some kids who like to sit in the back cause a lot of problems by throwing stuff or saying things the teacher can't hear. So nobody gets to claim a seat in the back rows unless they have a B or an A in the class; anybody with a D or lower has to sit right beside the teacher's desk. If people bring their grades up, they can claim a new desk.

Finally, the students who get bored sitting in the same seats get to choose from the seats that are left every day. Every quarter or semester, we redo the entire plan so that students who didn't get to claim their first choice of seats will have another chance.

Because the student-designed plan worked so well, I made it my default. I follow that plan at the start of the semester or school year—but I explain to students that if self-discipline becomes a problem, I will give them one warning. Then, if they aren't working effectively as a group, I will create a seating chart that stays in effect until the end of that quarter or semester. I rarely have to create a new chart.

If you do decide to use a seating chart at the start of the school year or semester, I recommend taping name cards to the desks the first time students are to sit in assigned seats. Better yet, stand in the doorway of your room to greet your students as they enter and direct them to their assigned seats. Students are much more receptive to sitting in an assigned seat if they don't have to move after they have selected a seat. Changing seats after students are already seated can create confusion, animosity, and a poor rapport between you and your little scholars.

If students complain about their seats, ask them to come talk to you after school—not after class. If they care enough to stay after school, you might strongly consider changing their seats. Often students will ask for a new seat because somebody is bullying them or they don't want to sit near a former friend. Some students don't want to sit by their own best friends because they know they won't be able to concentrate or resist the temptation to whisper or pass notes when they should be paying attention. Once in a while, a student actually thanks me for separating her from her chatty friends because she couldn't do it herself without offending them.

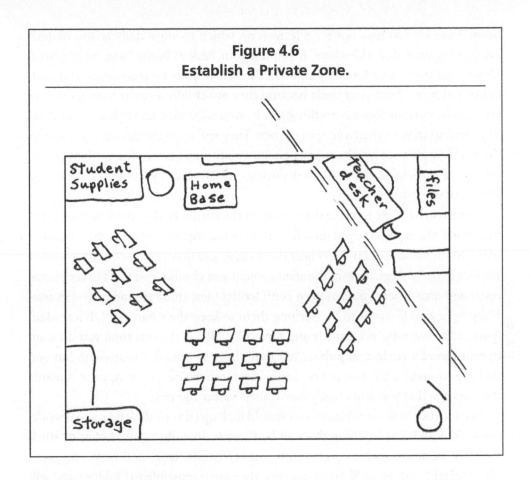

Figure 4.6
Establish a Private Zone.

Student Supplies

Home Base

teacher desk

files

Storage

Establish a Private Zone

Kindergarten and elementary classrooms usually have multiple cubbies and storage shelves. If you post pictures or photographs to show what goes where, children are usually delighted to retrieve their own books and supplies—and help you put things away. And many early-grade classrooms consist of workstations or activity centers instead of student desks or tables. How you arrange your classroom will depend on whether you share the room with another teacher, what furniture is already in the classroom or available from storage, the standard practice at your school (ratio of individual seat work to group projects, for example), and your own teaching style. But you will still want to consider making your desk and personal property off-limits to students.

Choose a spot as your home base—the spot you will return to before and after class and during breaks between activities. You may choose to put your desk at home base, or you may opt for a lectern on which to store daily lesson materials, leaving your desk elsewhere. If you use your desk as home base, be prepared. Unless you mark your territory and strictly enforce your no trespassing rule, students will buzz about your desk; because they are children (even teens), they are going to be curious about everything in, on, around, under, and behind your desk. They will sit in your chair and spin or rock. They will open the drawers and snoop. They will jingle your keychain and peer into your purse or briefcase. Many teachers sit at a work table or a small desk during class time, away from their desks and all those temptations.

Some teachers like to place their desks in the corner of the room farthest from the door. Others prefer to put their file cabinets and supply shelves in the far corner of the room but keep their desks near the door, where they can more easily monitor student activity. Regardless of the arrangement you choose, you need to create one restricted area where you can keep confidential files, student grades, and exams. Hang up a sign if you need to, warning them to keep their hands off. If a student ignores the warning, act quickly and forcefully. This is the one time you do want to reprimand a student in public. You don't have to punish the student, but you do have to make a big deal out of the incident; otherwise, you give your students the message that you don't really care if they snoop and pry.

Even if your desk is off-limits, you should lock up (if your desk has actual working locks and keys) anything that can be thrown, spat, flung, or shot at or stuck to other students, such as paper clips, rubber bands, tape, and tacks. Be especially careful with black Sharpie markers; they are irresistible to children and will disappear faster than most other supplies. If your desk doesn't lock or you don't want to worry about keys, buy a plastic bin with a solid latch to store extra staples, paper clips, rubber bands, markers, and so on.

I have tried both arrangements—using my desk as my home base and keeping my desk private and using a lectern or podium during lessons. The second method works better for me. I don't stand at the podium and lecture. I move constantly. But having a podium limits my space, which forces me to stay organized, and I can move quickly from one activity to the next. Each morning I place the lesson plan and necessary materials at the podium. Between activities and class periods, I may make quick visits to my desk; however, if students are present I stay at the podium so that they can ask questions or request my help.

My own desk is off-limits to students at all times. I place it diagonally across one corner of the room, with a file cabinet behind my chair to store student records, exams, and other confidential materials. As shown in Figure 4.6, one corner of my desk meets the wall, blocking access from that side. I place a visitor chair against the other side of my desk and allow an opening just wide enough for me to walk past to my chair. I place a computer workstation, another file cabinet, or a bookshelf next to my desk to create a narrow entrance to my personal area. This setup reinforces my no-trespassing rule by creating a physical barrier between my private territory and the rest of the room.

Supplies and Storage

Once you have situated your desk and storage units, find a small shelf or table for student supplies. Keep it near your home base so you can monitor student use and restock as needed. Supplies will vary according to your student needs, but I recommend a box of tissues, a bottle of hand cleaner, a small mirror (children get things in their eyes), and a box of Band-Aids. Ask students to use hand cleaner after they have sneezed or used a tissue to blow their noses, especially those who currently have a cold. Use it yourself between classes, especially after handling student papers. You will cut down on absences, including yours.

I also provide paper and pencils for my students. Although some teachers insist that parents or the school district should pay for all the paper and pencils, I believe we could save our energy for bigger battles and keep a package of lined notebook paper on hand along with ten unique pencils (sparkly, polka-dotted, engraved, and so on). For classes with older students, I also provide ten unique and easily identifiable pens. I keep the pencils and pens in a jar labeled "Writing Utensils to Borrow" and assign a student to be the official pencil counter for each class or instructional period. The pencil counter's job is to make sure ten pencils and ten pens are in the jar before students leave my classroom. This may seem trivial, but if you don't designate a pencil counter your pencils and pens will disappear; it's easy for students to forget they borrowed a writing implement.

Next, fill your supply cupboard (or buy a big plastic bin) with trash bags, antiseptic cream, disposable gloves, disinfectant cleaner, disposable antibacterial wipes, paper towels, a whisk broom, and a dust pan. When kids make a mess, unless they are very young, don't clean it up for them. Have them put on the gloves and get to work.

Set one wastebasket near the tissue box on your student supply table and another near the door to your room. (Buy an extra one if you have to; your room will stay much cleaner.) When wastebaskets are conveniently located, people are more apt to use them.

Post Your Agenda

You can train your students to check for certain information each time they enter your classroom. For example, if you reserve the upper right-hand corner of your chalkboard or whiteboard for the daily agenda and make sure you post the agenda well before students enter the room each day, you won't have early birds hounding you with incessant questions of "What are we gonna do today?" while you are trying to prepare for class. When students enter the room and ask you what they're going to do, point to the board and smile. Soon they will learn to look for themselves.

Make sure you post your agenda where everybody can see it. If you are very organized, you may choose to list details and specific times for specific activities. I prefer to make my agenda more. Sometimes students zip through an assignment I thought would present a challenge; other times they struggle with something I thought would be easy. So I make a simple list of general activities. Monday's agenda might read like this:

- Independent reading
- Spelling quiz
- Vocabulary review
- Journal writing or homework review

Usually I post the following day's agenda before I leave the classroom at night so it will be ready for the early birds. Some schools require custodians to clean all the boards, so if you post your agenda early be sure to ask your custodian not to erase it.

Another option is to buy a portable erasable whiteboard, write your agenda with dry-erase markers, and post it above the student supplies table. If your board is large enough, you might consider listing today's agenda, with a brief outline of the previous and next day's agendas for students who were absent or who like to plan ahead.

Having a daily agenda helps students focus, but some of them also need to see the bigger picture. Using poster board or giant construction paper, I create a classroom calendar big enough to be legible from across the room and hang it high enough so that it's clearly visible when students are seated. I mark all holidays, reviews, quizzes, exams, and special events. Quizzes are noted in blue marker and exams in red. (For each quiz or exam, I count back three school days and post a reminder on that day for students to study and review.) Special events such as graduation, picture day, and homecoming are marked in purple.

In addition to eliminating complaints from students that they didn't know about a test (no matter how many times you announce a test, somebody will forget), a classroom calendar provides a visual record of progress for students who feel overwhelmed by the length of the school year. Your calendar can also be a good motivational tool. One successful technique I have used is to place a star on the calendar for each day that I did not have to ask somebody to stop disrupting class; when a group earns fifteen stars, students earn a reward such as fifteen minutes of free time, a chance to play educational games, or a class visit to the library for thirty minutes of browsing. The only disadvantage of using stars to motivate classes is that you need a separate calendar for each class if you teach multiple classes. On the other hand, making separate calendars can inspire students in one class to work harder so that they don't fall behind another class. Although I don't like to focus on cutthroat competition, I do try to use positive peer pressure as long as students don't turn the process into a tool for humiliating each other. This is where your excellent teacher judgment comes into play.

Rules of Order?

My recommendation is to nix the rule list unless you are teaching kindergarten or first grade. Kids in second grade or higher know how they are expected to behave because they have already gone to school where every teacher has at least one rule. I think it's a good idea to create a behavior code or list of rules, but hang onto it. Don't hang it on the wall to remind students how to misbehave. Instead, give students a chance to show you how well they can behave. Welcome them to your classroom and immediately engage them in an interesting or challenging activity. If everybody cooperates, save your rules and regulations for later.

If you have one or two disrupters, quickly point out what you would like them to do—not what you don't want them to do. Instead of saying, "Don't talk when I'm talking," say, "It's my turn to talk right now. Please listen." Then immediately thank the students who are being quiet. If you have a handful of students who seem determined to disrupt your wonderful first-day plans, then go ahead and whip out your rules.

Some administrations instruct teachers to spend the first minutes of every class going over the rules and regulations. I urge you to disobey that order (and I spent nine years on active military duty, so I know the importance of following orders). Let me restate my recommendation here. I urge you to delay obeying the order to make rules your number-one topic of conversation with a new class of students. I don't suggest this out of pure orneriness or whimsy; I recommend holding back for a reason. My niece Lila explained it much better than I could. Excited about her first day of high school, she couldn't sleep for two days before classes started. She couldn't wait to be a freshman. I called her after the first day of school and asked how she liked being one of the big kids. She responded with a long, melodramatic, teenage sigh.

"It was so-o-o-o-o-o boring," Lila said. "All we did was listen to a bunch of rules six times in a row in six different classes. It was just like kindergarten. I thought it was going to be different in high school. Now I don't even want to go back tomorrow."

Lila speaks for most middle and high school students: needless repetition is boring and demoralizing. Reading the rules on the first day can cause other logistical problems. When new students join your class, you have to repeat the rules for their benefit, which will once again bore the other kids who have already heard fifty million rules. Or you could hand students a printed copy of your rules, which they may glance at before throwing it in the trash or stuffing it into their backpacks. You could ask the new students to stay after class, which will irritate them because they have better things to do and because they heard the rules yesterday from the other teachers before their room assignments changed. Or you could cross your fingers and hope they behave.

If you prefer research to anecdote, here's another good reason for delaying your discussion of rules. The June–July 2007 issue of *Scientific American Mind* reported the results of a study conducted by social psychologists from Harvard and the University of California wherein subjects observed 2-second video clips of professors teaching. The teaching ratings of those subjects accurately predicted the actual end-of-term evaluations of the professors' own students. The researchers reported that it takes 6 seconds or less to get a sense of somebody's energy or warmth. And another researcher spent twenty years conducting studies where he flashed images of faces and objects for just 0.2 seconds. People evaluated the faces and images within .25 seconds, supposedly due to pathways that connect the human eye with the brain's rapid-response emotional-control centers, bypassing the cortex, where thinking occurs. Apparently, we humans feel before we analyze; we get a gut feeling when we meet somebody new. Opening the conversation by telling students what they can and cannot do might not be the best choice if mutual respect and trust are your goals.

You have probably heard something to the effect that the first day of class sets the pace for the rest of the year. I have heard veteran teachers say (and I agree with them) that the amount of disorder you have on your first day of class is likely to be remarkably similar to the amount you will see on the last day. So on day one concentrate on grabbing your students by their overactive brains. Get a good grip. Focus on creating a classroom where good behavior is the norm. There will be plenty of time to talk about rules later on. In Chapter 6 we'll discuss discipline plans. But those things can wait. First, we need a plan for organizing the piles of paperwork every teacher has to shuffle, even in today's paperless world.

PREPARE YOUR PAPERWORK

Your classroom is looking good and smells nice too. Your supplies are stowed safely away, and your student desks are arranged to give you easy access to each little darling who will soon be sitting there, looking to you for knowledge and inspiration. Now it's time to get your paperwork in order and put out the welcome mat.

Paperwork problems can overwhelm a teacher who isn't organized. You can do much to prevent those problems, improve your efficiency, and save hours of time if you design a workable file system. Your individual circumstances will guide you, but I would like to offer some suggestions for techniques that have served me well.

Deep In-Basket

Place an in-basket on your desk that is deep enough to hold at least one hundred sheets of paper or thirty student reports or file folders. Instruct students to place all items for you in the basket—not on your desk, your chair, or on top of the file cabinet. (Any item too large to fit into the basket must be delivered to you in person.) Also enforce a strict policy that makes it a classroom felony for a student to remove anything from the in-basket, including his or her own paperwork. If students must retrieve something from the in-basket, they must ask you for assistance, which helps protect the privacy of other students and avoids the misplacement of important paperwork. At the end of each hour or class period, collect all student papers from your in-basket and stow them in the proper color-coded file folder until you have a chance to organize or grade them.

Daily Lesson Folders

Keep one brightly colored folder for each hour or subject with daily lesson plans, assignments to grade, graded papers, and personal notes for students. If you need to take papers home to grade, tuck them into this file folder. (If you teach multiple classes or subjects, keep your file folders in a binder that you use only for this purpose.) After you have graded papers at home, return them to the file. Add your lesson plans or notes for the next day, and you have everything in one place for easy access.

Your Own Emergency Plan

Accidents and illnesses happen, as do fires, earthquakes, and other disasters. Your school will have emergency procedures and instructions to follow during drills, lockdowns, or evacuations. Place this information in a three-ring binder that has pockets to hold papers and a place to store a pen or pencil. Put a copy of your roll sheets in the binder, along with your own contact information (address, phone number, and name and phone number of a relative or friend). When an emergency occurs or a practice drill is announced, grab your binder and lead your students to safety. And in the event that you are called away without notice, your supervisor can easily find information to contact your family or friends or to give to your substitute teacher.

Sub Folder

For use if you have an unplanned absence, create a folder that includes a copy of your roll sheets and three full days of lesson plans that focus on your subject and provide review of important skills and information but that are not going to make or break your students' learning. If you know you will be absent, you may choose to provide lesson plans that continue your present unit of study, with associated activities. But be aware that not all substitutes are created equal. Some of them will follow your instructions to the letter; others will do nothing or—worse yet—create their own lesson plans.

Once, when I became ill with the flu, I came into school one evening to write out detailed lesson plans for my remedial freshman English class, which was reading *Romeo and Juliet*. Reluctant readers, the students had agreed to read Shakespeare only because I promised they could watch the movie afterward. I provided the sub with page numbers, worksheets, journal-writing assignments, and a review worksheet. I specifically asked her not to show the movie even if they begged. When I returned after three days, I found that the sub had ignored my lesson plans and shown the entire movie during her first day. During the subsequent two days, she held discussions and ignored the worksheets and assignments. When I complained, the sub countered by saying that I was too controlling and that she should be allowed to design the lesson when she was subbing, although she had no teaching license and her major field of study was science, not language arts. Now I create a series of independent lessons that enable students to practice important skills but do not necessarily coincide with our current unit.

While we're on the subject of subs, know that some schools permit teachers to request certain subs. If you find a good sub, ask if you might have her or his phone number so that you can call and check his or her availability. Having one or two regular subs can be a real benefit. Students enjoy seeing a familiar face, and they often behave better for somebody they like and trust. And you can relax knowing that your students won't be wasting their time while you're away.

Beware that if you work with students who are not emotionally secure, they may act out while you are gone, even if they have an excellent sub and even if they are normally well-behaved students. Instead of punishing those students upon your return, hold a class discussion. Ask students to describe their feelings and think about why they misbehave when you are gone. Remind them that their behavior is a reflection on you; you are very proud when they can behave well for a sub. Suggest some alternative positive behaviors for students to use if they feel stressed or upset about your absence. They might ask to go visit with a familiar counselor, coach, secretary, teacher, or administrator for a few minutes. (You might want to discuss this with the adult staff members involved to prepare them.) They could write you a note or make an entry in their journals. They could offer to help the sub by taking roll, erasing the boards, or passing out papers.

Fun Lessons Folder

Do a little research and find some quick, fun, entertaining, or challenging lessons. Trivia quizzes, brain busters, riddles, word games, and IQ tests are big hits with students of all ages. When your students zip through a lesson faster than you expected, when they behave especially well, or when they do something to make you proud, take a few minutes at the end of the hour or day to reward them with a fun lesson. Every bookstore has a section of books with educational games and puzzles, or you can create your own. You can also find suggestions on the Internet.

Makeup Work Folder

Buy an accordion-style folder with alphabetical divisions and write MAKEUP WORK in large bold letters on both sides. If you teach more than one group, buy a separate accordion-style folder for each class. Whenever you distribute paperwork or an assignment, pencil in the last name of absent students on the assignment and place it in the folder under the appropriate letter. If you cover material in the textbook on that day, make a brief note of what you covered and make copies of the note for each absent student. When students return to class, their missing assignments will be readily available, saving you time that would otherwise be spent searching for copies and explaining what they need to read to catch up.

Elementary-level students may need help remembering to pick up the papers and may require help doing the assignments, but you should expect older students to pick up their assignments and get them done. Make clear that students are responsible for making up the work, although you will be happy to answer any questions they may have or suggest sources for information or assistance.

Prefilled Passes

Fill out the basic information (your room number, destination, and any specific instructions) on library, hall, and bathroom passes. Don't sign the passes, and be sure to number them so that students can't steal them. Keep the passes tucked or locked away in a folder with a simple tally sheet showing which numbers you have issued. When you need to send somebody out of the room, you won't have to spend much time filling out passes. Just fill in the student's name and the date, then sign the pass. With this system, you don't have to stop teaching to locate a pass and make everybody else wait while you fill it out.

Roll Sheet Copies

Make three or four spare copies of all your roll sheets as soon as you get them, and use them to create your own records for rewards, attendance, seating charts, teams for group projects, birthdays, field trips, fire drills, and other occasions for which you might need a list. I take a copy of my roll sheets home to use when I am creating lessons, such as vocabulary worksheets or quizzes, to use my students' names in sentences. They always perk up and smile when they read a sentence that contains their own or a classmate's name. (Be sure to check off names and use everybody's name at least once to avoid hurting feelings or giving the impression that you have favorites.)

Rolls sheets can also be used for parent public relations. At the start of each school year, I take copies of my roll sheets home to use for thank-you calls. I select three or four students for each class period who demonstrate extra wonderful behavior. Around dinnertime, I call the parents or guardians of those exemplary students to thank them for teaching their children good manners. I want them to know that I realize children don't behave well by accident. They were taught, and I appreciate the effort their parents and guardians have made. I call at dinnertime because I know that if I interrupt the evening meal, it gives the family a great topic of conversation and shines the spotlight on the students. And those students return the following day even more motivated to keep up the good behavior—and good behavior is contagious. The parents I call remember me fondly in the unlikely event that I need to call in the future to request their help adjusting student attitudes or behavior.

Crates for Student Folders

This is my all-time favorite time-saving organizer. I buy a different-color plastic file bin for each class I teach, and I label a file folder for each student in a particular class. For each class I use a separate color or folders cut on the same tab—all left one-third tabs, for example—so I can easily identify folders and match them with the proper bin. If I can't find any colored file folders and I have to use all manila folders, I use a marker to draw a colored line across the tab, all red for one period, blue for another, and so on. (Note: At the start of the year, the folders will be slim, so you may elect to store two or three different groups in the same bin until the folders fatten up. Then you can transfer them to separate bins.)

Using my roll sheets, I lightly pencil in student names on the folder tabs and keep a few blanks for students who may transfer into my class later. During the first days of school every term, I distribute the folders as students are taking their seats and doing their first work activity of the day. I quickly see who is absent and keep those absent students' folders on my lectern, where I can insert copies of any handouts or reading assignments for that period. Personal folders help students learn to organize their work and make it easier for them to locate study materials prior to exams. Because the folders are personal, many students like to decorate them. I allow them to draw or write whatever they like on their folders, except vulgar, obscene, hateful, or gang-related words and symbols.

At the start of each class, I distribute the folders for use that day. I can immediately see who is absent, and as the class goes on I can place worksheets or assignments into my makeup folder for students who are absent. When students return, all of their graded assignments are waiting for them inside their folders.

When I return their homework or assignments, students have the option of taking the graded papers home to show their parents or placing them in their folders. I always suggest that students keep important assignments, quizzes, and tests in their folders for future reference and as a record in case of report card questions. Some students take their paperwork home and keep their own records, but many students (and parents) are so disorganized that they will lose anything you give them.

Emergency Misbehavior Folder

Usually students wait until several days into the school year before they become truly disruptive. But sometimes you'll have an overachiever who will decide that the first few days of school would be prime time to act like a maniac. I'm referring to serious cases where a quick step out into the hallway for a private talk isn't an option because a student assaults or seriously threatens you or other students. You can remove the student who is out of control, lose the minimum amount of precious class time, and send a very clear message to the rest of your students that you will not tolerate outrageous behavior for even 1 minute in your classroom—if you have prepared an emergency misbehavior folder ahead of time.

Fill out one or two disciplinary referral forms with as much information as you can, except for the date and the student's name. Where it asks you to describe the incident, write: "Student disrupted class, interrupted my teaching, and made it impossible for others to learn. I will provide full details as soon as possible. I request a student–principal–teacher conference before the student returns to my classroom."

Place these partially completed forms in a folder labeled "Misbehavior," where they will be readily available at the first sign of serious disruption. The first time you pull out that folder, whip out the form, and send your obnoxious student packing, other students will get the message that you are prepared and serious about teaching. Your principal will require specific details, and you will have to follow up on the incident; however, if you have a form prepared ahead of time, you will have provided enough information to remove the student from your classroom quickly, preventing more serious problems and establishing your control without wasting time or losing face by engaging in a prolonged argument.

Assignments for Button Pushers

If you teach people who are old enough to walk to the school library or counselor's office without an escort, label a file folder "IA-Independent Assignments." Fill this folder with five or six lessons that are challenging and pertinent to your subject matter. Make sure the written instructions for each assignment are clear, so no additional instruction is required. Meet with your librarians and counselors and ask if you may send a student to work independently from time to time, but communicate that you do not expect other staff to tolerate any misbehavior. Fill out a pass with everything except the date and student's name and write "independent study" on the pass. Put your file away and hope you won't have to use it.

If the day arrives when a student repeatedly misbehaves just to trip your trigger or if you have a sneaky student who repeatedly instigates bad behavior in other students, a pupil whose parents have tried but failed to convince their child to act respectfully in your classroom, or a student who is perfectly capable of polite behavior but who intentionally ignores your requests, then you have a button pusher on your hands.

Don't argue or warn your button-pushing student. Simply select an appropriate lesson from your IA folder. Remove the other assignments and hand him the folder. He may make a big show of pretending he doesn't care. Ignore his antics. Show-offs hate to lose their audience. Show the student the library pass and inform him that he must return the signed pass and the completed assignment to you approximately 1 minute before the end of class. Explain that if he doesn't return at the end of the class period, you will be obligated to report him as cutting class and the school's disciplinary system will have to take over. Walk the student to the door of your room, wave good-bye, and shut the door firmly.

If the student returns with the completed assignment, say thank you and tell him you hope he will decide to remain with the class in the future. Most students stop their disruptive behavior if they lose their audience because they were either seeking attention or weren't capable of doing their assignments independently. (Better to be considered bad than dumb, in their young minds.) If you have a whiz kid who aces the assignments on her own and doesn't seem to mind being sent to work alone, you have identified the root of the misbehavior—boredom—and you can take steps to create lessons that will challenge her.

Note: If you can't use the library or counseling office, you may find another teacher who is willing to create a reciprocal agreement—on occasion, you may each send one student to work in the other teacher's room at a desk in the corner where other students won't be disrupted. And in the unlikely event that a student refuses to leave your classroom or won't accept the folder, simply return it to your file cabinet and take out your misbehavior folder. Fill in the student's name on the referral form and call your security office, or go to the nearest classroom to alert the teacher that you will be gone for a few minutes. Escort your student to the office and quickly return to your lesson without any further interruption or discussion with your remaining students. If they seem to be on the verge of an outbreak, look very slowly around the room and say, "Does anybody else need to leave?" My prediction is that nobody else will need to leave. If they do, repeat the procedure. (See Chapter 6 for a more thorough discussion of disciplinary techniques—and for creating an environment where such misbehavior is much less likely to occur.)

The Grade Book

Create a system for your paper grade book. (Keep a paper book for backup even if you use a computerized grading system because systems crash and some students are accomplished hackers.) Don't write in your grade book during the first few days—or weeks if you work at a disorganized school. Instead, make a couple of copies of the first page of your grade book and use that to keep track of students' progress until after the administrative shuffling has ended and you have had the same students for a few weeks. Then enter the names in your grade book in alphabetical order. Enter the same names in the same order in your computerized grade book so that student number one and student number fifteen are the same in each book. This will save you time later on.

With a little creativity, you can design a system so your paper grade book functions as a record of attendance, participation, and extra effort as well as a record of graded assignments. When students are absent, for example, you might outline the box for a specific graded assignment in red so that you can see at a glance which students were absent when you gave that assignment. (Some students will claim they were absent; if you don't mark it in your grade book you will have to track down your attendance sheets and compare them to your grade book. You don't have time for such silliness.) When absent students make up the missed assignment, you can enter the grade in the box and still have a record of the absence. If the student doesn't turn in the assignment by the deadline, you can enter a red zero to remind you that the assignment was not completed.

Some teachers assign each student a number in the grade book. If you teach multiple classes, it's a good idea to use a combination of letters and numbers to avoid mixing up student papers from different classes. Instruct students to write their assigned numbers in the upper left- or right-hand corner of all papers they turn in. You can then place the student papers in order as you collect them and identify any missing numbers immediately. Read out the missing numbers to alert students that you do not have their papers, and place all the papers in a folder, making a note of the date and any missing numbers on the inside cover of the folder. When students turn in a late paper, make a check mark and write the date, creating a record of all missing or late papers. This method prevents lost papers, avoids arguments about whether students turned in assignments, and makes it easier for you to enter grades or notations for missing assignments into the grade book. If you have a particularly argumentative group, you might consider stapling papers together after they are collected as proof that those papers were collected on time.

Master Lesson Plan Draft

My advice to new teachers is to make your lesson plans as simple and flexible as possible. If you need to structure each minute during your first few months (or years), do so. But as you develop more experience and confidence, shift your focus from planning to teaching, using your students' performance, instead of the calendar, as a guide.

Many education textbooks advise new teachers to make detailed lessons plans so that they use each minute of class time productively. That concept sounds good on paper. When I first began teaching, I planned each class to the second. I was so nervous that I didn't trust myself to remember what I wanted to cover during a specific time period. I imagined myself facing my students and not being able to think of a single intelligent thing to say. So I planned and outlined and made hourly, weekly, monthly, quarterly, and semester calendars, all filled in neatly and completely, down to the last spelling quiz. I also broke down each hour into 5-, 10-, or 20-minute blocks of time. I was prepared to walk into the classroom and be the super teacher I knew in my heart I could be.

Unfortunately, I hadn't planned time for the daily announcements, calls from the administrative offices, buses delayed by traffic, announcements over the squawking intercom, sick students, or an occasional spider dangling from an overhead light causing momentary chaos. I also hadn't planned—and nobody could—for the variances in student ability and behavior that drastically affect the speed with which a given class will grasp a new concept, master a new skill, or complete a given assignment. Often students would zoom through an exercise in 10 minutes when I had expected them to take 30, leaving me 20 minutes to spare. Or they would labor for an entire class period over what I thought would be a simple 10-minute activity.

At first I spent hours revising those detailed lesson plans, but something always seemed to happen to throw my classes off schedule. I finally realized that I was far more likely to lose my mind than create lesson plans that I wouldn't have to change or frequently adjust. Now I make a very rough schedule of what I want to cover during a given time frame and I alter the plan to fit the needs of my students.

My preferred method is to make copies of a monthly calendar template so I have one page per month. Then I consult the school calendar and mark every noninstructional day in red: holidays, teacher in-service days, state-mandated testing days, midterm and final exam days, open house, and picture day. I also use red ink to block out days on which many students are likely to be absent or obsessed with some important social event such as homecoming, prom, baccalaureate, pep rallies, band or chorale concerts, sports tournament, college day, or prearranged field trip. For these days I plan a flexible lesson that will count toward grade credit for students who are present but will not include essential information that absent students will need for future exams.

Next I highlight quarter, semester, and final exam days in green ink. One week before each major exam, I back up and schedule a day or two for review of material that will be on the exam. Then I plan two days without homework following the exam so that I will have time to grade and return exams quickly. Now I have a rough idea of how many instructional days are available for the various units in my curriculum.

At this point it's time to put away the pens and start using a pencil so that I can make changes later. On a separate sheet of paper, I make a list of all the elements I intend to teach during the year: journal writing, essays, reports, research papers, poetry, short stories, plays, novels, literary analysis, and so on. I break my master list down further by assigning each element to a specific unit.

Now that I have a rough outline of various units, I can figure out how much time to devote to a specific skill each day or week and how many weekly or monthly quizzes will be appropriate. Because some schools require a specific number of graded assignments during a given period, I can easily check to see that I will have enough. In my experience, students of all ages and abilities do better when practice exercises and quizzes take place on a regular schedule—vocabulary exercises every

Tuesday morning, for example, with a quiz on Friday. Regularly scheduled activities will also help you create plans when you are ill, overwhelmed, under stress, or exhausted. My daily and weekly plans are very general and flexible, with optional activities and exercises that I can add or delete as time allows.

Some schools provide a template and require teachers to use it to prepare lesson plans. If that is the case at your school, don't despair. Fill in the template. But don't work yourself into a tizzy if you can't follow that template every second of every day. Unless you are in a very unusual situation, you won't find somebody standing in your doorway, checking to make sure that you are giving a spelling quiz at exactly 9:15 a.m. on Thursday. If somebody does visit your classroom and you are not right on target, explain that you realized your students needed a bit of extra time on whatever they are doing at that moment. Offer to do the activity on your prepared lesson plan the following day at a specific time if the observer would like to return. In most cases, they won't. If they do, teach the lesson and consider yourself warned. I think that's highly unlikely. What is much more likely is that somebody is tasked with collecting (and perhaps reviewing) lesson plans to fulfill a directive from higher up. As long as your students are well behaved, you rarely send students to the office, your students' grades on standardized tests are reasonable, report card grades for your classes are reasonably good, and parents don't complain about you, nobody is going to be overly concerned about whether you are following your lesson plan to the letter.

Of course, I do include required curriculum in my plans, and when administrators or department chairs require standards and benchmarks to be specifically referenced on lesson plans I do a quick online search for "common core lesson plans." (You'll find them posted by helpful veterans for any subject or grade level.) I print the sample plans and post them over my desk. That way, I can quickly look up and see the name and number for a particular standard—small-group reading, for example, or identifying the purpose of a nonfiction article—and add that information to my plan. If the Common Core Standards info is not required I don't include it, but I am prepared to discuss the standards for each lesson upon request.

If you can't find lesson plans online that include specific numbers for your grade level or subjects, print out the standards you need and post them on a wall by your desk. Add the numbers to your existing lesson plans. Before long, you'll quickly make the association between the activities and lessons you create and the standards they address.

As you plan your activities, keep in mind the brain-based learning research. People can focus closely for approximately 1 minute per year of age, up to about 15–20 minutes. If you have very young students, don't expect them to focus very long without getting fidgety. Ten seconds of jumping jacks or marching in place every few minutes will help your little learners. Build in breaks for older students as well. A quick pair share after 15 minutes of instruction will help students refocus. People sometimes argue, "I can sit and work on something I love for hours at a time without stopping." That may be true. But their brains are taking breaks without them realizing. Think of student brains as a car engines. Run them too long at high speeds and they will overheat. You will have to stop driving until they cool down. But plan some stops along the way and you will reach your destination faster and in better shape.

Above all—don't distribute a handout if you want students to listen to you afterward. This is true for any group, from kindergarteners to adults. If you give people an object or something to read, their brains will focus on the new item and they will ignore what you are saying. So give your instructions first and your handouts or materials later. Or give your instructions and model the procedure. But know that once you place something in students' hands, they won't hear you for a few minutes.

A note about Common Core State Standards: As of January 2015, only thirteen states remain in the Common Core Consortium. More changes are on the horizon as No Child Left Behind is the target of reform among lawmakers from both parties. And the Partnership for Assessment of Readiness for College and Careers (PARCC) benchmarks and testing standards are under strong attack from all sides, especially parents and students. Before you start stressing about including standards on your lesson plans, talk to your mentor, colleagues, department chair, or principal. Find out exactly how detailed they expect your lesson plans to be. If they want specific standards tied to each activity, ask other teachers in your grade level or department if you can review some of their recent lesson plans. Take note of the standards they listed for activities and lessons you will be using. Somebody will probably have a simple chart you can post for quick references. If not, make your own. But it has been my experience that most administrators are as tired of the overabundance of demands and paperwork from misguided lawmakers. Mandating tests does not automatically improve student performance. Most teachers are already teaching the best they can. Adding more requirements for their lesson plans doesn't make better teachers. More requirements simply creates frustration and resentment. *If you don't trust that we know to teach, why issue us teaching licenses in the first place? And if you do trust us, then leave us alone and let us do our jobs as we have been doing them all along.* The general consensus among veteran teachers: if you are creating solid lesson plans and students are making noticeable progress in learning new information and skills, you are already incorporating the standards. So unless your supervisors specifically ask you to include more detailed data about standards, put your time and energy where it will be most effective—teaching your students.

Include Stakeholders

As you create your lesson plans throughout the year, keep in mind the many stakeholders who have a vested interest in the education of the children in your school: parents and families; businesses and potential employers; colleges and vocational schools; public and private agencies; and the local, state, and federal government. With just a little effort, we can incorporate input from all of these stakeholders into our lessons and activities. Family members can be called upon to give informal talks about their jobs and hobbies. College counselors can provide assistance and information about applications and scholarships. College and university professors will often welcome high school students to audit a class. Vocational school instructors can provide encouragement and inspiration for students who have excluded college from their immediate future plans. Local agencies often have extensive public relations campaigns and can provide reading materials and posters for student use. Local, state, and federal government employees are available to speak on a wide variety of topics and will invite students to visit their agencies as well.

If your students don't know the name of their local mayor, teach them. If they don't have library cards, help them apply for cards or host a field trip if possible. If they have never seen the inside of an executive office, a hospital, a jail, or a department store stockroom—show them. Invite local business owners to come into your classroom and conduct mock interviews with high school students who have written their resumes, learned how to fill out job applications, and now are ready to practice their interview skills. Adopt a local police officer and have your students map out his or her daily agenda. The high school where I currently teach has its own junior Humane Society, and students work with the local dog shelter in pet adoption and spaying programs.

Community service programs are mandatory at some schools, but even if your school already has a good program you can do more. Assign students the task of creating a mini-documentary about their community's history. Or ask them to come up with a list of the most serious problems facing their neighborhoods, brainstorm solutions, and put the best solution into action. An added benefit of initiating interactions with your community is that once you begin to invite the world into your classroom and begin sending your students out into the world to gather information and implement their ideas, more people will offer their services and students will come up with dozens of suggestions for more projects.

Welcome Handout

If you teach children who are too young to read, you might decide to write a short letter to send or give to parents and guardians that introduces you and provides your phone number and e-mail address along with some basic information about your classroom. It doesn't take much time to draft a welcome letter, and it can be a great public relations tool. You won't seem like such a stranger, which can prove helpful as the year progresses and situations arise that require you to contact the families of your students.

If your students are old enough to read, consider designing a one-page "Welcome to My Class" handout that includes a short course outline, truly important information, a few tips for success in your classroom, and an abbreviated overview of your most important rules and procedures. If you don't like that title, try something more formal like "Course Outline and Objectives." (Note: Please don't title your handout "Classroom Rules and Procedures." If you do, you will create a dynamic of teacher versus student from the start because so many students are resistant to rules of any kind.) Many students like to have something tangible that they can take home and read over (and maybe even share with their parents!).

Visual learners and students who are beginning middle school or who have multiple teachers for the first time really appreciate having handouts for their different classes because it helps them keep everything straight. One of the big fears middle schoolers and high school freshmen have is that they will forget where their classes are. Handouts from teachers can allay those fears. Handouts also serve as reminders of different teacher personalities. Some teachers are sticklers for legible handwriting. Others have a zero-tolerance policy on missed homework. It's helpful for students to have that information in writing for reference until they learn their class schedules and teachers' expectations.

For two examples, see the handout I use to welcome my high school English classes in Exhibit 4.1 and a sample handout for third graders in Exhibit 4.2.

Exhibit 4.1.
Miss J's Welcome Handout.

Welcome to Miss J's English Class!

The Official Plan: This class will focus on improving your language arts and communications skills through reading, writing, vocabulary, and grammar exercises; group assignments; and individual projects. We will read a wide variety of literature. Assignments will include timed responses, journals, essays, literary critiques, and creative projects.

The Rule: Respect yourself and other people. No insults based on ethnic background, skin color, native language, gender, sexual preference, religion, body shape, or body size will be tolerated. It is unfair to erase somebody's face. We all have the right to be treated with respect.

First Things First (FTF): Every day you'll find an assignment posted on the Student Agenda Board. I expect you to be seated and working on the FTF of the day when the bell rings. Not five seconds or a minute after the bell. Please don't be a ding-dong.

Be There or Be Square: My job is to make this class enjoyable and informative. I will never intentionally embarrass you. Your job is to come to class. Be there or be square.

Be on Time: Don't you hate waiting for people? I do. Let's be on time.

Be Prepared: Imagine how you would feel if you made an appointment to have your car fixed and when you took it to the shop, the mechanic said, "Oh, whoops, I forgot to bring my tools today. Sorry." Not cool. Bring your learning tools to school.

Homework: We won't have homework every night, but when we do, it's your job to do it—by yourself, using your own personal brain (it is perfectly acceptable to get help or share ideas with friends). If you have problems or questions, call me at 555–1212.

Makeup Work: When you return to class after any absence, it is your responsibility to check the makeup folder on my desk. You will have three days to complete the work. If you need more time, talk to me.

Please Behave: I prefer to deal directly with you instead of calling your parents. You are responsible for your own behavior. You behave yourself, and I'll behave myself.

Fun: We will have the maximum amount of fun allowable by law. Please bring your sense of humor to class. If you forget yours, I'll be happy to share mine.

Exhibit 4.2.
Third-Grade Welcome.

Welcome to Mr. Bob's Super-Duper Third-Grade Class!

Hello! Hello!

I'm Mr. Bob Witherspoon—welcome to my Super-Duper
Third-Grade Class.

I believe every student (that means *you*) is super-duper in
her or his own way.

Here is our class mascot, Digby the Dancing Dog.

What we are going to do this year? Dozens of things, including:

- Create exciting, fun projects to use our incredible brains.
- Spiff up our spelling skills. (We'll even spell supercalifragilisticexpealidocious!)
- Refine our writing skills by writing *our own books*!!!
- Make reading really, really, really, really interesting and fun. (I promise.)
- Watch some spectacular movies about things going on in the big wide world.
- Learn interesting facts about people, places, things, critters, caterpillars, and so on.
- Have *huge* amounts of *fun*!

My job as your teacher is to:

- Do my best teaching every single day.
- Be my best self every day.
- Make sure you are safe in my classroom.
- Make sure everybody in our super-duper class feels respected.
- Teach you what you need to know to rock in grade four.

Your job as a student is to:

- Be your best self every day.
- Do your best work on every assignment.
- Be respectful to yourself, to me, and to your classmates.
- Bring your learning brain to school with you every day.

Ready? Set? Let's rock and roll!!!!!!!!!!

PREPARE YOURSELF

With your room and your paperwork organized and ready and your philosophy of teaching fresh in your mind, you can now focus on physically and mentally preparing yourself to grab your students by their brains when they walk into your classroom. Don't worry if you feel nervous: almost all teachers get nervous before the start of a new semester or school year, even experienced teachers. (Sometimes the veteran teachers get more nervous than newbies because they know exactly what they are walking into!) Don't panic. Most of the time, students will cooperate if they know exactly what you expect them to do. Therefore, *you* must know exactly what you expect them to do.

Plan Your Procedures

If you are underprepared and are therefore forced to create procedures as you go along, students will follow your example and create their own. So brainstorm every routine activity that will occur in your classroom, and establish a procedure for performing it. Sit in your classroom as you brainstorm so you will be reminded of physical obstacles or space limitations. For example, how do you want students to request permission to do the following: use the bathroom, ask or answer a question during your lectures, or request help during classroom activities? How should they turn in late assignments, line up when the entire group needs to leave the room together, and conduct themselves in the hallways? Make brief notes or use index cards to remind yourself of each procedure so that you can quickly teach it to your students. You may have to repeat some procedures many times before students catch on, so it's a good idea to have written instructions to help you remain consistent.

Decide how and when you are going to teach your procedures. (For a more detailed discussion, see the section titled "Establish Routines and Rituals" in Chapter 5.) Some teachers like to teach all of their procedures, a few at a time, at the start of the year and add a short refresher course when it's time to implement a specific procedure. If you teach your students your procedure for walking to the library as a group, for example, but don't take them to the library until three weeks after school starts, many students will have forgotten what they are supposed to do. Some will forget the instant after you tell them, which is another good reason to write your procedures down. You can copy your procedure cards individually or as one list and distribute a copy to each student to keep in his or her folder as a reminder. Or you can practice them until students become familiar with them. Either way, be prepared to patiently repeat your instructions several times—especially for students who have multiple teachers. A middle or high school student may have five teachers, all of whom have different requirements for asking questions or requesting bathroom breaks.

Smooth Transitions

A key element of a successful classroom—and one that new teachers may overlook—is the art of the smooth transition from one activity or subject to another. You can lose many valuable minutes and a lot of momentum as you gather or distribute required materials. Students may lose focus as they chat and dawdle. You can avoid lost time and focus by teaching students your standard procedure for each specific transition—moving to the reading rug, getting books from a class set on a shelf in the corner, putting away their math books and preparing for the science lesson.

How long should you allow for a given transition? It depends on the age and personalities of your students. Sit down in a student desk and imagine that your teacher wants you to stop doing what you are doing and begin something else. What do you need from the teacher to motivate and guide you?

I watched a video clip where a class of elementary students got up from their seats and marched around their room in single file, singing their class song as they made their way to the storytelling area, where they quickly seated themselves and quietly waited for the teacher to begin reading. It took them less than a minute to make their way around the room, and during that minute every child was smiling and had the opportunity to expend some energy before sitting down to listen. That teacher faced a group of happy, receptive students. What a brilliant idea!

If you teach older students, you can use a variation of the singing march by playing the same musical passage to signal that it's time for everybody to finish up what they are working on and turn in their papers or get out their textbooks or find their art supplies or retrieve a calculator or a dictionary or a workbook from the storage center. Use the same music to signal the same activity every time, and students will soon know the cue. Musical transitions create energy and enthusiasm without creating the resistance that often accompanies verbal instructions and requests.

I read about a teacher who used a similar strategy to signal cleanup time in her classroom following art projects involving materials that needed to be gathered and stored for the next group. She played the first seconds of the *William Tell Overture* (DAH DAH DAH dum) as her signal. Her students responded with delight to such a dramatic cue.

Practice your transitions, but expect that at least one student will forget the instructions. Model what you want students to do. Show them each step. Even older students may need to be reminded several times about things they should already know.

Design Your Discipline Code

Write down your discipline code. If it's too long or complicated to fit on an index card, you may find it difficult to communicate to students and even more difficult to enforce. When I first started teaching, I did the rule thing. Sometimes I created rules; sometimes I included students in the creation of rules. But every time I used a list of rules, I also had to make a list of consequences and then a list of increasingly punitive consequences for the students who broke the rules. I had to figure out a system for keeping track of offenses, consequences, follow-up conferences, and referrals to the office. Quite often I found myself bending a rule because of special circumstances; for example, a boy missed school to attend his grandfather's funeral, so I broke my zero-tolerance policy on late assignments and allowed him to turn in a project two days late. Other students then appealed for extensions based on their own "emergencies," which were very real to them. A sister went to the hospital. A toilet overflowed. Their requests put me in the position of deciding which emergencies were important and which weren't. Everybody was upset and nobody was happy, including me.

After that incident I read more books, but I couldn't find the perfect discipline plan. So I branched out into psychology books and into books on salesmanship, leadership, and the art of persuasion. I tried different tactics with different groups and finally settled on one universal approach that has served me well with every group of students I've taught, from at-risk high school freshmen to university graduate students. After our welcome and get-to-know-you days, I lay out the ground rules for student conduct in my classroom. I make the following speech:

> You are individual people with individual lives and needs. And life
> presents surprises and obstacles to us all. So I am not going to create
> a set of rigid rules and then argue with you about enforcing them.
> I reserve the right to make judgments as needed in my classroom. But

I do have one rule that applies to every person in the room, including me, and it is absolutely unbreakable.

Respect yourself and everybody in this room—no put-downs of other people based on their race, religion, ethnic background, skin color, native language, gender, sexual preference, intelligence, body shape, or body size.

Those characteristics are not chosen by people; we are born with them. You can change your religion when you are an adult, but most children are required to accept their parents' religion; to criticize them for respecting their parents is wrong. Criticizing or insulting people for things that are beyond their control is not fair. It is not respectful, and I will not tolerate it in my classroom. You may comment on people's behavior as long as you voice your observations respectfully. If you believe somebody is being cruel or insensitive, for example, you may say, "I think your behavior is cruel," or "You are being really rude." You may not, however, call the person a *stupid jerk* or blame bad behavior on gender or skin color—which brings me to the subject of prejudice.

There are many, many forms of prejudice. You are entitled to believe and think whatever you choose. You are not entitled, however, to express your opinions in a manner that may insult, degrade, embarrass, hurt, or humiliate other people.

I always ask if anybody believes my rule is unreasonable. Nobody ever has. And since I have started using my one-rule policy without a list of specific offenses and consequences, I have had far fewer discipline problems. Again, the connection between expectation and reality proves true: I expect students to take responsibility for their behavior, and, barring the occasional inevitable exception, they do.

We'll discuss discipline at length later on, in Chapter 6, but for now if you can distill your discipline plan or behavior code down to one or two sentences that will enable you to communicate it clearly to your future students you will be way ahead of the game.

Rehearse Your Serious Speech

I hope this exercise will be a waste of time and you won't have to warn anybody to stop misbehaving. But just in case, it's a very good idea to know what you plan to say, should you decide you need to say it. If you can find a willing volunteer, it may be helpful to rehearse the warning speeches you will deliver to mildly disruptive or defiant students (those who are in fifth grade or higher) who may need a quick trip to the corner or to the hallway outside your classroom for a brief one-way discussion. You will do the talking, saying something along the lines of, "Your present behavior is not acceptable in my classroom. You have the right to fail my class, if that is really what you want to do. But you do not have the right to interrupt my teaching or somebody else's learning. And you do not have the right to waste my time trying to get me to argue with you about your behavior. You are an intelligent person, and I know you know how to behave. So why don't you take a minute out here to consider your options? When you are ready, please come back and take your seat. Thank you." (Some teachers prefer to have students return when they are ready, while others insist that students remain outside or in the private conference spot until the teacher decides it's time for them to return.)

Younger students—up to about fourth grade (you'll have to make this determination based on the intellectual and emotional maturity of your students)—may not have the self-control to monitor their behavior for more than a few minutes after a quick chat. So you will probably want to come up with some catchphrases that you can use to remind younger students of your expectations. If you explain right from the beginning that you want everybody in your classroom to make good choices, you can ask a student, "Are you making a good choice right now?" That question fits a wide variety of behaviors and gives a student the option of discussing his or her behavior and then getting back on track without suffering negative consequences.

Create Some Call-and-Response

Call-and-response is a very popular activity with students of all ages. The first day of class, you teach students the responses to your calls. For example, with young children, you teach them that when you say, "one, two," they are to respond, "eyes on you." You say, "three, four," and they respond, "talk no more." And so on. If you teach older students, try using the call, "W-W-W dot," and students respond, "zip-those-lips dot-com." You can also use a nonverbal rhythmic call-and-response, such as clapping your hands two times. Students respond by clapping three times. You initiate the clapping and stop when students are paying attention. I have seen this work quickly for an entire cafeteria filled with noisy students.

When you notice a student on the verge of straying off-track in your class, you can initiate a call-and-response to interrupt the behavior cycle—and then praise all your students for their quick response and good behavior. Keep an eye out for the student who had started to become disruptive. When he is behaving himself, stop by his desk and quietly praise him for his good behavior. This positive reinforcement is much more effective than repeatedly issuing individual or whole-group warnings.

Check Your Wardrobe

Make sure that you have at least a few changes of clothing that are comfortable, easy to launder, and somewhat attractive because students have to look at you all day long every weekday. At various times during discussions of what makes an effective teacher, students have suggested that teachers pay more attention to their clothing. You don't have to be a fashion plate, but as one student put it when he was describing a teacher he did not like, "It's a drag to have to look at somebody who looks like they just keep all their clothes in a pile on the floor." When I mentioned that I often speak to new teachers, he said, "Tell them not to wear the same outfit every Monday. It's like having those stupid underpants with the days of the week on them. School is boring enough without having to look at the same shirt every single Monday of your life." That's one young man's opinion, for what it's worth.

I've already suggested comfortable shoes, but your feet are important enough that I'm going to repeat the suggestion. If you are twenty-one and still indestructible, your feet may not notice the stress, but most teachers welcome as much comfort as they can find when it comes to shoes. Sore heels and achy arches can really ruin your day.

Find a Friend

Make a reciprocal chill-out pact with a teacher whose room is near yours. (If you can't find a friendly teacher, find an administrator, counselor, or secretary—but find somebody.) Occasionally you will have a student whose behavior doesn't warrant a referral to the office or an official warning but who nevertheless jangles your nerves beyond your breaking point. And unfortunately, once in a while you may find yourself having a bad teaching day. Make an agreement with your ally that either of you may send a student to sit in the back of the other teacher's class for a short time (10 to 15 minutes) to allow you and the student a break from each other.

And if you realize that you are about to slip over the edge, you might ask your chill-out buddy to supervise your classroom for a moment while you supervise hers, if she is a teacher, or take a brisk walk, if the person is not a teacher and can spare a few minutes. You may never have to make use of your chill-out option, but if you need to those few minutes can save the day with a minimum of fuss and paperwork.

Meet the Admin and Support Staff

If you haven't had a chat with your principal and vice principal, request one. Find out how they handle discipline problems. Ask for information about the local community and how local politics affect the school. Let the principals know that you plan to send students to the office only if you are at your wit's end. Ask if you can call on them for support if you need it during the first days of class. I once had a very large principal who offered to come and scare my belligerent freshmen boys. It was very effective. The same boys acted out every morning, so the principal and I preplanned his visit. On the appointed day, when one of the boys began to disrupt, I called the office. The principal burst into the room and said, "Who needs to come with me?" I indicated the boy who had been acting out. The principal glared at the boy and then looked around the room. "Anybody else want to go?" he hollered. Nobody did. And after that, the boys toned down their behavior because they knew the principal and I were on the same team.

Don't forget the support staff. Seek out and introduce yourself to the maintenance crew, the audiovisual and computer gurus, the attendance monitors, the detention coordinator, and the custodian who is responsible for your classroom. Also, take time for a quick chat with your school librarian, classroom aides, and all the many secretaries who keep your school running. Recognize that these are valuable people without whom your job would be much harder. Ask if they require specific things from you or if you can do things to make it easier for them to respond to your requests. Not only is it the right thing to do to get to know your classroom custodian and to treat him or her with respect, but you also will find that a good custodian can provide advice, assistance, and an occasional miracle during the school year. And incidentally, it makes an incredible difference when stress levels rise to walk into the school building and find yourself greeted with smiles and encouragement from the adults on staff.

Check Your Classroom

Sit at your desk in your classroom and take a good look. Close your eyes and sniff. Make sure that everything is in place for the first day of school. Review your checklists and the index cards containing your procedures and discipline code; give your supplies and student folders a final inspection. Then turn off your teacher brain. Go home and try to be a regular human being.

Take a Break

Give yourself a break, even if it's only for a few hours the night before school starts. Go out to dinner, rent a video, take a long, hot bath—do something that is not connected with teaching. You may be tempted to stay at school as long as your security office will allow, but if you spend the weeks before school planning and preparing and the few days before school arranging your room, shuffling roll sheets, grade books, curriculum outlines, textbooks, and file folders you will need at least a short break if you expect to greet your students with a genuine smile on the first day of school. You deserve the break, and they deserve the smile.

Three Checklists

Here are condensed versions of the three checklists to help you get ready.

Exhibit 4.3.
Three checklists.

Your Classroom

- ☐ Sensory details
- ☐ Seating arrangements
- ☐ Supplies and storage
  - Home base
  - Private files
  - Teacher desk
  - Student supplies

- ☐ Student information
  - In-basket
  - Agenda
  - Calendar
  - Student-supplies table

Your Paperwork

- ☐ Place in-basket on your desk.
- ☐ Create daily lesson folders.
- ☐ Create a personal emergency plan.
- ☐ Prepare a sub folder.
- ☐ Fill a folder with fun lessons.
- ☐ Create a makeup work folder.
- ☐ Fill out library, hall, and bathroom passes.
- ☐ Copy roll sheets.
- ☐ Buy plastic crates for student folders.
- ☐ Prepare a misbehavior folder.
- ☐ Create independent assignments for button pushers.
- ☐ Copy a blank page from the grade book.
- ☐ Draft a master lesson plan.
- ☐ Design a welcome handout and make copies.

Yourself

- ☐ Plan your procedures.
- ☐ Design your discipline code.
- ☐ Rehearse your warning speeches.
- ☐ Check your wardrobe.
- ☐ Find a chill-out friend.
- ☐ Meet your admin and support staff.
- ☐ Inspect your classroom.
- ☐ Take a break.

WHAT DO YOU THINK?

1. Which seating arrangements did you prefer as a child? Which do you prefer as a teacher?
2. For nonreaders, what might teachers do instead of distributing a welcome handout?
3. Which classroom procedures are most important to teach on the first days of class?
4. What can new teachers do if they have mild personalities and want to develop an air of authority?
5. What can teachers do to counteract the emotional and physical stress that accompanies teaching?

Start with a Smile

We all know what's supposed to happen on the first day of school. You take roll, cover a few basic school-wide ground rules, and get on with the task of teaching. Usually, what actually happens on day one is closer to this: the bell rings and students continue to trickle in, late because their parents couldn't find the car keys or had to drop off three children at three different schools. Somebody got lost in the labyrinth of high school hallways or spent 10 minutes rummaging through a backpack in search of the elusive class schedule. Somebody else needs to use the restroom this very minute, and where is that bathroom pass? Perhaps a very small person hides in the corner where he throws up and cries because school is very scary indeed. Meanwhile, back at the office, the counselors are still juggling numbers and test scores and parental requests, wondering if you have room for one more—perhaps two or three?

Teachers are trained to carry on in the face of challenge, so you finally get everybody seated. You begin your introduction. But the intercom interrupts your introductory remarks several times to announce changes in the bus schedule and to remind students that free lunch tickets are available. Your students stop being scared and start to fidget. You rush through the safety instructions and the procedures for your classroom. Halfway through procedure number one, somebody knocks on the door to explain that two of your students are in the wrong classroom. They should be in B103, not C103. You send them on their way and start again. You're on procedure number two when there's a knock on the door. You open the door to find a tongue-tied girl who blushes and stammers that she just moved here and somebody, um, told her she is supposed to be in your room. You hurry to your desk to retrieve your roll sheet and find that her name is missing. You direct her to an empty seat and call the class to attention. They respond reluctantly, and you resume your recitation. Another knock. This time it's a boy and a girl; neither child is blushing. They glare at you and thrust their schedule cards in your direction as though it were your fault that the computer goofed and they won't be in the same first-period class with their best friends. Again you check your roll sheets, hoping the names of the two disgruntled newcomers won't be there. But they are. And so it goes.

Regardless of how chaotic the first day of school may be, my advice is: Smile. And keep smiling. The chaos will pass, eventually. But the opportunity to create a good first impression, to connect with your students, will pass very quickly. Research consistently shows that the human brain takes just a fraction of 1 second to evaluate an unfamiliar face as friend or foe. And our brains are naturally inclined to respond to a smile with a smile in return. So use biology and psychology to your advantage. Make those first seconds count. Don't worry that your students will interpret your kindness as weakness. They know the difference. You can project a positive, friendly demeanor without sacrificing your authority or your students' respect.

DON'T KEEP YOUR DISTANCE

For years, teachers were warned: Don't smile until Christmas. Keep your distance. Familiarity breeds contempt.

Ignore that advice. Don't widen the gap between teacher and students. Close it, instead. Distance, physical or psychological, plays an important role in human interactions. If you stand behind your desk or podium, you will be placing a double barrier between you and your students from the start—the last thing you want to do if your goal is to develop a quick rapport and an environment of mutual trust and respect in your classroom.

My recommendation is to stand in or near the doorway as students enter your room. Standing just outside the door is more of a power position, if you are looking to establish your authority. Welcome each student to your classroom, and ask him or her to sit down (be specific—should they choose a seat or find the seat that has their file folder or name on it?).

Standing near the doorway has several advantages. It establishes that students are entering your territory as they cross the threshold of your room. It sends a clear message that you are in charge of your territory and that you are allowing them to enter. This helps students understand that entering your classroom is a privilege and not a right. Your physical presence forces students to slow down and enter the room individually, which greatly reduces chattering and focuses their attention. One teacher, rather small and slim, told me he not only stands in the doorway but also shakes the hand of each student who enters his room. He introduces himself by name and welcomes the students to his room. "They know right away that I am the boss and it is my classroom," he said, "but they don't feel threatened."

If shaking hands feels comfortable for you, consider emulating this teacher's method. You can learn a great deal from the way a student shakes your hand. Sweaty palms could mean the student is nervous about school—or she ran to get to class on time. Calloused hands might indicate that you've got a gardener, a martial artist, or a manual laborer in your classroom. A limp handshake may mean the student is shy or unused to being offered a handshake or uncomfortable touching a teacher. A very strong grip could indicate an athlete, a leader, or a student who may decide to test your authority. And so on.

Whether or not students make eye contact as they enter your classroom also gives you information. Those who don't look at you may have been taught not to look directly at an adult as a sign of respect. They may be shy, nervous, or uninterested in school. Pay attention to those who do make eye contact and how long that contact lasts. You'll soon learn to recognize signs of interest, intelligence, energy, humor, curiosity, fear, distrust, aggression, and all the emotions that students bring to school along with their books.

CHOOSE AN ENGAGING OPENER

You can do much to ensure that your first day goes well, regardless of accidents, delays, and interruptions, by putting the focus on your students and not yourself. Instead of starting with a teacher-centered activity that requires students to sit and listen to you, begin with a student-centered activity. Choose an opening activity that is simple but engaging. For example, provide large index cards and markers and ask students to create tent-style name cards for their desks. This activity is good for difficult or very talkative groups, and you can learn a lot about students from the way they write their names on their cards. Big, bold letters usually indicate an attention seeker who either has confidence or would like to. Tiny letters may indicate shyness or lack of self-esteem.

You have unlimited options for your opening activity, including:

- Place name cards or file folders labeled with students' names on desks before they arrive, along with colored markers or crayons placed randomly on desks. Ask students to find their names, take their seats, and decorate the cards or folders. Sharing markers or crayons will help them bond in a nonthreatening way. (This will also give you a good opportunity to remind them to say please and thank you if they need such reminders.)

- Distribute a fun questionnaire. Provide pencils.

- Design a bingo-style game where students must find other students in the class to match the squares on the bingo cards (Who has a puppy? Who can tap dance? Who likes pizza?).

- Provide art materials and ask students to draw cartoon characters that reflect their personalities (then tack the characters to a wall in your classroom and admire them).

- Create a treasure hunt game for students to complete inside your classroom.

- Provide old newspapers to make crazy hats.

- Write a definition on the board, such as "the anatomical juxtaposition of two *orbicularis oris* muscles in a state of contraction" (a kiss) and see if they can figure out the word.

- Supply a sample "I am a person who ... " poem (on the board or on a handout) and ask students to create their own versions. Give them the option of reading their poems, tacking them to the wall, or leaving them on their desks and then walking around the room to read each other's poems.

- Group students into threes or fours and give them a short, fun project to complete, such as completing a jigsaw puzzle, matching pictures with words, or putting together strips of paper that contain your classroom rules which you have cut up in advance.

- Place different objects on tables spaced around your classroom (sports equipment, games, books, comics, electronics, and so on). Ask students to enter the room, look at the objects, and go to stand near the table that holds the items that interest them the most. This will help them look at ways they are similar instead of viewing each other as strange and different.

- Ask students to draw a picture of their favorite animal, and then ask them to share and tell why they chose that particular animal.

- Create a crazy quiz that consists of unusual questions: How many times does a hummingbird flap its wings in one minute? How much does a butterfly weigh? How long do baby kangaroos live in their mothers' pouches? How fast can an ostrich run? Have students work in pairs or teams to answer the quiz. Give the winners a round of applause or special pins to wear for a day.

- Distribute air-filled balloons and see who can keep his or her balloon in the air the longest using just noses, elbows, and knees.

- Have students form a circle. Say your own name, and then toss a bean bag across the circle to a student. She says her name and tosses it to another student. Continue until everybody has participated.

Remember that older students may have six or seven classes during one day and several teachers may ask them to write, so if your opening activity involves writing keep it short. Your goal is to get to know your students' personalities and general abilities, not to intimidate or bore them.

A good opening activity reduces the chances of misbehavior because students won't be bored and won't feel put on the spot, as they often do when they file into a quiet classroom and sit facing an unfamiliar teacher. A student-focused activity also gives you a chance to check out your students while they are otherwise engaged. You will immediately get a sense of which students are shy or unsure of themselves, which are gregarious and inclined to socialize, and which are reluctant to cooperate.

PROVIDE CLEAR INSTRUCTIONS

How you deliver your first set of instructions is very important. Your students are going to form their opinions of you and your teaching style within the first few minutes of your first meeting. You will project a very different persona depending on whether you are seated at your desk, perched on a stool, roving about the room, or standing in the doorway. Students will respond to the pitch, volume, and tone of your voice; your choice of words; and especially your facial expressions and body language. Arms crossed over your chest is a sign of defensiveness, for example.

Since this is the first day of class, some students will be eager, and some will be anxious or nervous. Make sure you provide clear, simple instructions for your opening activity. Don't forget the visual learners: it's a good idea to write the instructions on the board as you give them. And many students, especially kinesthetic learners, will respond faster and better if you model the activity for them.

While your students complete their first activity, you can take roll and handle any last-minute tasks. Then it's time for you to greet your class. But don't distribute your "Welcome to My Class" (see Chapter Four) handout yet or jump right into your second activity. Talk to your students first. Walk around. Give them the opportunity to look at you without appearing to be rude. Tell them how much you look forward to working with them. Tell them how much you like your subject (or grade level) and why you chose to teach it. Tell them what they are going to learn during this school term, but don't go into great detail. Keep your introduction short and simple.

GRAB YOUR STUDENTS BY THEIR BRAINS

Once students have completed the opening activity and the first-day frenzy has had time to fizzle a bit, it's time to grab your students by their brains. Literally. Scientifically. According to Kevin Dutton, a research fellow at the University of Cambridge and author of *Flipnosis: The Art of Split-Second Persuasion* (Heinemann, 2010), certain behaviors will disable the brain's cognitive security system—the brain does a double take that leaves it open to suggestion. When something unusual happens, brain activity increases in the amygdala (the brain's emotion center) and the temporoparietal junction (the novelty detector). For a split-second after something unexpected occurs, cognitive function is disabled, which provides a perfect opportunity for a persuasive person, such as a teacher, to introduce a suggestion. Surprised brains are far more likely, biologically, to follow the suggestion.

Students may expect you to go over your rules and discuss the consequences for misbehavior. Your school administration may instruct you to discuss the school's disciplinary code during the first day. This is one time when I would risk ignoring their instructions, because most students already know how to behave. Even in the unlikely case that they haven't been to school before, their parents or other adults have repeatedly told them to sit down, be quiet, stop hitting or teasing each other, mind their language, and behave politely in public. Most schools require parents and guardians to sign a legal liability statement when they enroll their students. Teachers are responsible for the safety of their students in their care, but I don't believe it's fair or right to make the teacher the traffic cop when what they need to do is bond with students. So I hold off on talking about rules until the second, third, or fourth day of school. (If you simply can't bring yourself to ignore instructions from your administration, find an entertaining way to present the rules. According to Dutton, humor is one of the most effective tools for disarming people and persuading them to cooperate with you.)

I usually begin by saying something like, "We are supposed to go over the rules and regulations today, but I would like to save that for later this week because right now I'd like us to get to know each other." Then I do something to grab the students' attention. I entertain them with a slide show or a film excerpt, shock them with statistics about things that affect their lives, tempt them with a brain teaser puzzle, engage them with a goofy game, ask them to draw a picture of a dog that likes to eat poems, challenge them to beat me at a game of Scrabble—the entire class against me and they can use the dictionary. If they win, they all get an A for their first assignment (so far, that hasn't happened, but if it did it would be a good thing. They'd all be A students, temporarily at least). I do anything except what students expect me to do, which is talk about rules, requirements, objectives, standard procedures, the importance of education, upcoming standardized tests, and ZZZZZZZZZZZZ.

What you choose to grab your students' brains with will depend on your subject, your personality, and your students. Whatever you choose, tweak the assignment to add an unexpected element. I am not suggesting that you use novelty for novelty's sake or that your job is to entertain students. But the first days of class are important—just as the first dates in a romantic relationship are important—because they set the tone for the long term. We can use science to our advantage in setting that tone.

For a scientific but accessible explanation of how brain chemistry affects students' attention and how stress affects learning, I highly suggest reading Eric Jensen's book *Teaching With the Brain in Mind* (Association for Supervision and Curriculum Development, 1998) or David Sousa's *How the Brain Learns* (Corwin Press, 2006).

NO MORE TEACHER VERSUS STUDENT

There's an old Navy saying: "Kick butt now; take names later." Boot camp instructors use that approach to keep new recruits on their toes and quickly establish control. I use a modified, gentler version of that strategy, but my purpose is the same: I want students to understand immediately that they are welcome in my classroom but that it is my classroom and I am in charge. Also, I want to establish an environment in which students are working with me and not against me. I do not allow students to manipulate me into a teacher-versus-student stance. (I did let that happen during my first year of teaching, but after I figured out how to make them respond to me instead of me responding to them, I stopped letting them manipulate me.) Instead, I try to show them that we are both on the same side and that we can work together to tackle the curriculum and have as much fun as possible while doing so.

If you can show that you share the same feelings as your students, they will mentally put themselves on the same side of the desk as you, so to speak. They stop viewing you as the enemy or the adult or the rule enforcer and start seeing you as a fellow human being (not a pal, but a human all the same). Until we have students on our side, we can't teach them anything; we will be too busy trying to establish discipline and enforce our rules.

Getting students on your side isn't that hard. I have yet to meet a child who wanted to be a failure or who wanted to be disliked. But many children, especially teenagers, act obnoxious and unlovable when they are afraid, and children are afraid of a great many things. In school they have two particular fears: people won't like them and they might get bad grades. Even smart kids worry about those two things, so I address their fears in my welcome. My speech goes something like this:

> Welcome to my classroom. My name is Miss Johnson, and I'm very happy to have you in my class. I want to help you become more effective students, which will help you be successful people. I'm not here to pick on you or try to flunk or boss you around. I was in the military for nine years when I was young, and I got very tired of people telling me what to do all the time. So I try not to be bossy, even though my job is to be the teacher. Somebody has to drive this bus, at least until we get out on the road.
>
> I promise not to embarrass you or humiliate you in my class because I know how that feels—it doesn't feel good to be embarrassed, does it? But I will expect you to think. If anyone dies from overthinking, I take full responsibility for your death.
>
> Now, how many people would rather go to the dentist than read out loud? Raise your hands please.
>
> *(There are always hands.)*
>
> Relax. I was very shy when I was young, and I was afraid to read out loud. You never have to read out loud in my class if you don't want to, so quit worrying about that right now. I don't want you to hate reading. I want you to enjoy reading and discussing the books and stories and articles on our agenda. I hope you will relax and volunteer to read out loud later on, but you won't have to.
>
> Here's what I really want you to learn: I want you to be able to analyze other people's ideas, compare different ideas, and express your own ideas in an intelligent, articulate, and logical way. The more command you have of your language skills, the more successful you will be in school, in your work, and in your personal life—especially your love life.
>
> *(They giggle. They think I'm joking, but I'm not.)*
>
> I'm serious. Think about it. We use words to get many of the things we want in life. Of course, you use words to answer questions in school.

But you also use words to ask somebody for a date. Or to explain why you don't want to take drugs or take off your clothes—or to convince your parents to let you get a tattoo or borrow their car. And later on you'll use words to make your future mother-in-law like you—and if you don't think that's important, you're in for a big surprise. And speaking of surprises, it may surprise you to learn that everybody starts my class with an A. Whether you keep the A or not is up to you, but I will do my best to help you keep it. And I promise you that if you come to class regularly, cooperate with me, and work hard, you will pass this class.

For years, I used the everybody-starts-with-an-A technique without understanding why it was so effective. The first time I used it, it was an accident, but it worked so well that I made it standard practice. Recently, as I delved into some research reports about effective leadership, marketing, and persuasion, I realized why that tactic is so effective. It has to do with people thinking they are getting something for free. Once they have something, they don't want to lose it. Marketing professionals use this technique all the time. Two-for-one sales, for example, may convince you to buy something you wouldn't have purchased in the first place, but since you are going to get a free second item you buy the first one, which you already see as yours. Coupons and memberships give grocery store shoppers the feeling that they are getting something free, even if prices on coupon items are higher than normal. Car salespeople will often place the keys to a car you haven't decided to purchase on the desk in front of you. Then they slide the keys toward you and say something about "your keys." They aren't your keys, but they feel like your keys, which makes you more likely to buy the car.

Starting students with an A isn't really giving them anything. They don't have any grades. But that A is there in the grade book, in ink, so it's real. And most students will make an effort to keep the A. Conversely, if they feel they are beginning with a zero and must work their way to an A, they feel as though they are starting with a debit. The debit doesn't exist any more than the A does, but sometimes reality takes a back seat to persuasion.

What you choose to do and say to create empathy between you and your students depends on your personality. But I urge you to tell them a bit about yourself and present a nongraded activity that allows you to get to know each other as people. You don't want to be their pal and you may want them to know you have strict standards for behavior, but you also want them to know that you are a compassionate, caring adult.

Sometimes I like to follow up on our opening activity by distributing index cards and asking students to provide some information. (I use a different color card for each class so that I can easily identify where a card belongs and can take that group's cards home with me for phone calls or parent communication activities.) Because so many kids are visual learners, I write the information prompts on the board:

Name:

Full mailing address:

Phone number:

Birthday:

Name of parent/guardian:

Student ID #:

Be sure to keep extra blank cards on hand for students who transfer into your class later so you can add them to your files.

As my students fill out their index cards, I write the names of any absent students on blank cards for them to fill out if and when they show up. Then I walk around the room between the aisles, with my roll sheet in hand. I mentally test myself to see whether I can remember the students' names. If I get stuck, I sneak a peek over students' shoulders to check the names on their cards. When they finish filling out the information I requested, I ask them to turn the card over and write a little bit more on the back of the card.

I explain, "I want you to tell me anything I need to know to be a good teacher for you. If you have dyslexia or a speech problem or epilepsy or you just hate reading, let me know. If you have a job, I'd like to know where you work. If you have favorite hobbies or sports, please tell me so I can try to include those things in our lessons."

I give students a few minutes to make the notes on the back of their cards (and for me to memorize more names). Instead of letting them pass the cards to me, I walk down the aisles and take each card individually. This serves three purposes: it brings me closer to them, which makes them nervous and more likely to behave; it gives everybody a bit of personal attention, which may prevent the attention seekers from demanding extra attention; and it gives me another chance to match student names and faces. As I accept each card, I say thank you and repeat the student's name aloud. Once I have collected them all, I go to the front of the room and flip through them quickly, mentally testing myself. If I can't identify a particular name, I ask the student to raise his or her hand. After a quick review of all their index cards, I tell the class it's time for our first test. Invariably, they gasp and groan and mumble.

"Relax," I say, "this test is for me. I am going to go down the roll sheet and see if I have learned everybody's names. If I get them all right, I win. If I miss one name, you all get an automatic A on your first test, and you don't even have to lift a writing utensil."

Of course, I have no test prepared for them, but they don't know that. And I have grabbed them. Even the kids who are too cool for school are intrigued. They are certain that I will make a mistake and they will receive that freebie A. Sometimes a sharp student asks what I will win if I remember all the names correctly. My response, "I win everything," delights them. They can hardly stand the excitement as I work my way down the roll sheet, identifying them one at a time. (If you decide to try this and your first activity was making name cards, be sure to have kids turn their cards face down so no one can accuse you of cheating.)

So far I have managed to pass the name test every time. Sometimes I forget half the names as soon as one group of students leaves my room, but they don't know that and it doesn't matter. I have another chance to relearn their names the next day. When I do make a mistake and forget a name, as I know I will someday, it won't be a disaster. The students will be delighted at earning a freebie A and even more delighted at having caught a teacher making a mistake. It will be a good lesson for them to see that adults make mistakes too yet the world goes on.

You may be thinking, "What a waste of time! My job is to teach, not to show off my memorization skills." I would argue that you will be able to teach much more effectively (and much faster) if you take the time to know your students before you begin your lessons. Names are much more than words; they represent us. In many cases children come to school empty-handed. All they have to bring with them are their names.

Or perhaps you're thinking, "But I could never learn a hundred names in one day!" If that's the case, tell students you have a terrible memory but it's important to you to learn their names, so you're going to give it a shot. They will be thrilled when you make a mistake. And they will like you even more.

Taking time to learn student names is worth the effort because it eventually pays off. First, it demonstrates that you care about your students enough to be willing to take the time to get to know them. Second, people are much more apt to misbehave if they are anonymous members of a crowd.

At the end of our first meeting, I stand in the doorway and smile as my students file out. I wave and drawl, "Y'all come back now." Some of them laugh and wave; others roll their eyes and shake their heads at my silliness. But they leave my room smiling, and a group of laughing children is a lovely sight.

TEACH YOUR PROCEDURE FOR ORAL RESPONSES

Even if you plan to teach a lesson on procedures later, now is the time to teach your procedures for answering questions in your class. There are endless variations on the theme of student responses, but students have three basic options:

- Students must always raise their hands before speaking and cannot interrupt people.
- Students may spontaneously respond to your questions or to each other's comments.
- Everybody must wait for a specific period of time (10–60 seconds) before responding.

Some of us believe we want students to raise their hands before speaking—until we actually start teaching. Then we realize that sometimes we want students to speak out quickly, such as during brainstorming sessions or when we are trying to generate enthusiasm or excitement about an idea or activity. During other activities, especially exercises that involve complex or abstract concepts, we might want students to take 2 full minutes to consider any question before making a response. Even if you opt not to use this method, I recommend trying it as an experiment. If you allow time for students who process information more slowly and for your quick responders to consider their comments before speaking, you will find that the complexity and intellectual level of student responses rises and that you will hear from students who normally don't volunteer an answer.

If you begin with just one hand-raising option and teach that as your standard procedure, students will soon learn to respond as you have taught them. If you then decide you want them to respond in a different manner, they may not be able to make the switch. Therefore, I recommend teaching all three methods, using a variety of exercises, and then announcing which method you expect students to

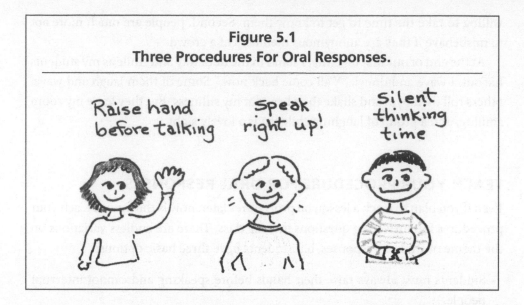

Figure 5.1
Three Procedures For Oral Responses.

Raise hand before talking

Speak right up!

Silent thinking time

use as you begin any new activity. One easy way to alert students (and remind them) is to make three posters like the images shown in Figure 5.1.

If you are creative, you can draw illustrations yourself, or you can ask an artistic student to make the posters. When you begin an activity, prop the appropriate poster against the board or tack it to a wall where everybody can see it. For younger children, you might turn this into a fun project: students can make the three posters and store them in their desks so that they can put the appropriate poster on their desktops during a given activity.

BE PREPARED FOR TEST THE TEACHER

So many factors affect student behavior that it's impossible to predict how students will respond to you. If you can get them engaged in doing something challenging or fun, most students will forget to misbehave, which is your goal. But sometimes students may begin to test your tolerance during the first few minutes of the first day of class. A couple of kids seated farthest away from you may begin to pass notes or talk loudly while you're addressing the class. A student may sit directly in front of you and start writing his name on his desktop. Somebody else may get up and boldly stroll across the room to talk to a friend or pull out a cell phone and start texting.

What will you do if those things happen? Your reaction will set the tone for the rest of the school year. Remember: you are still establishing your teacher persona. Don't let students draw you into a confrontation over trivial misbehavior, or they will all realize that they can distract you any time they choose. Of course, you have to respond to their challenges, but you don't have to let them dictate your behavior. They expect you to yell at them, send them to the office, threaten to call their parents, or ignore them. Do something unexpected. For example, draw in your breath loudly so everybody hears you, and then freeze in place and stare at the student, wide-eyed. Hold that pose for as long as you can (or for as long as the other students stay quiet, awaiting the outcome). If the student stops the misbehavior, exhale and say, "Thank you so much," as though you just averted a major disaster.

If the same student disrupts the class again, walk right up to the student. Stand very, very close. Look very serious. And wait. If the student quiets down, you are good to go. Depending on your personality, you may wipe your brow, cross your eyes, and give the misbehaving student a goofy look that nobody else can see, hurry to the window (if there is one in your classroom) and look outside, march to your desk, and pretend you are looking for something important. The idea is to break the tension and disrupt the behavior cycle. If you can distract students even for a second, you can often derail the disruptors. For example, you might choose to share a knock-knock joke or a riddle—when people laugh together, it actually creates positive chemicals in their brains, thus making them more likely to cooperate. You might smack your forehead and say, "Yikes! I forgot to bring my Taser."

You might move away from the disruptive student and then turn to somebody else and say something such as "Oh, I love the first day of school, don't you? It gives me goose bumps!" You might announce, "I forgot to tell you: if you don't want to do the activities I have planned, we can always jump right into our textbooks and get to work studying for our first test." Or you might say, "Everybody gets a little nervous on the first day of school. Who's nervous?" If anybody raises a hand, engage her or him in a conversation. If nobody does, just go on with your instruction or activity. Don't worry if students snicker at you or exchange glances that say, "What a weirdo!" You are a teacher. It's a given that you come from a different planet.

If you have a persistent troublemaker (or several of them) and the disruptions are minor, ignore them. Focus on the students who are cooperating, and thank them for their excellent behavior. But if the disruptors are determined to stop you in your tracks, you need to act. Don't react. Try to make your behavior your choice and not a response to theirs. If students can make you react to their behavior, they win. And because they aren't worried about covering the curriculum, they have an endless list of misbehaviors to share with you. You need to choose a behavior from your own preplanned repertoire of student motivators. Your goal is to get students to respond to you, not the other way around. If you have serious problems, see Chapter Six for specific discipline techniques and suggestions.

Don't let one or two rotten apples ruin your appetite for teaching. Remember your basic psychology: in a given group, the odds are good that at least one strong personality will challenge the leader just to see how the leader responds. If the leader demonstrates self-control, confidence, and courage, the challenger will usually back down—if given the opportunity to back down without losing face.

Don't Take Student Misbehavior Personally

Don't take student misbehavior personally, especially at the start of a new school year or term. Children act in unacceptable ways for a lot of reasons, but you are very probably not the reason. Often, when students express anger, even if they express it in your direction, you aren't the real target. Following are just a few examples of student misbehavior in my own classes, along with the reasons that the students misbehaved:

- A boy leaped out of his seat, overturned his desk, and started shouting and shaking his fists, and then he ran out of the room. He refused to explain his behavior, but one of his friends told me in confidence that a girl had been sitting across from the boy, crossing and uncrossing her legs seductively while staring directly at the boy, and he wanted out of the room because he was embarrassed and physically uncomfortable.

- A girl jumped up and hit the boy seated next to her, and then she refused to explain her behavior. He told me to forget about it. Thinking that perhaps the boy had taunted her, I told her to sit down and behave herself. Her response was to hit a different boy in the head. I saw no choice but to call the office and ask somebody to come escort the girl out of my room. Later the girl confided that she had wanted to be sent home from school that day because she had to make a bowel movement and was afraid she would be assaulted in the school bathroom. (Older girls had twice assaulted her in the restroom.)

- A boy threw a dictionary at my head. He wanted out of my classroom because he couldn't read; he was afraid I would find out his secret and embarrass him in front of the class.

I could go on, but I'm sure you get the picture. Don't take your students' behavior personally, especially when they don't know you well enough to hate you. Don't assume that every challenge to your authority is an intentional sign of disrespect to you as a person. Assume it is your status as teacher, adult, or authority figure that is the target. Continue to demonstrate the respect you want your students to show to you—and to themselves.

CREATE A DAILY DO-NOW ACTIVITY

Your do-now activity (or bell ringer or warm-up or whatever you choose to call it) is one of the most important and effective strategies you can use to eliminate time wasted trying to get students settled and focused. It is also one of the best deterrents to misbehavior. Instead of letting students enter your classroom and mill about, waiting for the bell to ring, a do-now activity requires students to begin working on something as soon as they enter your room. When the bell rings, they should already be busy (or immediately upon entering the room if you have a bell-less schedule). If you start your school year or semester with a good do-now every day, in just a few days your students will be in the habit of settling down to work right away.

Students must know exactly what you expect, so it's very important that you provide clear instructions for the first few times they perform do-nows. Print your instructions on the board, project them onto a screen, print them on individual handouts, or present them verbally as you demonstrate the task. Simply presenting verbal instructions is not a very effective way to teach do-nows because so many students are visual or kinesthetic learners and will forget or misunderstand verbal instructions. The key is consistency. If you post your instructions on the board one day, post them there every day. Likewise, if you project them on a screen, project them every day. Many teachers have found that it's easier and more effective to use a special location such as a portable whiteboard, a bulletin board, or a handout located near the entrance.

Obviously, the content of your do-now activity will depend on your subject, grade level, and students, but all good warm-up activities share some of these common traits:

- They can be completed quickly—in 5–15 minutes.
- They can be accomplished independently, without assistance.
- They are interesting, fun, or challenging.
- They are educational, not just time fillers.
- They are not graded as such, but do contribute to student grades.
- They are collected and corrected or discussed.
- They change periodically to add interest and avoid boredom.

Since one of the goals for do-now is to form a habit, it's a good idea to do the same kind of activity for at least a week to avoid having to provide different instructions every day. Once your students are in the habit, you can change the activity once a week or at the start of every month, to maintain student interest and engagement. As students become experienced at different tasks, you can mix them up for more variety. If you teach science, for example, you could start with a week's worth of unusual animal photos. Each day students will find a photo posted in the room. Their task is to name the animal, spell its name correctly, and list three or four characteristics of the animal. The following week you might post photos of plants or try a completely different activity.

It's important to follow up with do-now work after it is finished. Discuss it as a class or in small groups as a springboard to the day's first lesson. Ask volunteers to share their finished products. Collect papers or have students compare answers and self-correct them, if applicable. For example, if you teach math and you ask students to do a few math problems as their do-now, go over the answers with them or have them self-correct before they turn them in. If you teach science and your do-now requires reading a short selection about a specific animal or plant, hold a short discussion about the reading. If you assign a do-now and don't do anything with it later, students will quickly learn that it isn't important and may stop cooperating.

The possibilities are endless, but just to spark your imagination here are some popular activities from different grade levels that I have used or observed. Most can be adapted for older or younger students.

- Place an object on a stand in the front of the room. Students must come up with a list of ten unusual ways to use that object.

- Three math problems are projected on a screen. Students must solve the problems and compare their answers—the class as a whole must submit the same answers.

- A yes-or-no question about something the class has studied is posted or projected. On one wall of the room, a large sign reads YES. On an opposite wall, a sign reads NO. Students must read the question and then stand on one side of the room or the other. The teacher moderates a brief discussion without revealing the correct answer, and students have the opportunity to change sides before the teacher shares the answer.

- Project a photo of a person. Ask students to draw a picture of something that person might have in his or her living room.

- Challenge students to find out whose pulse in the room is the highest and whose is the lowest. They must figure out how to take their pulses and how to time them.

- Post a single word on the board. Students must write down as many smaller words as they can, using only the letters in the posted word.

- Repeatedly play a short film clip that shows somebody performing a physical action. Students have 3 minutes to try to learn to perform the same action.

- Place three small bean bags on each desk—or on each pair of desks. Students have 10 minutes to learn to juggle the bags (or at least try). When class begins, they must explain what factors are involved in learning to juggle (balance and timing, for example).

- Project a set of images on a screen or board. Students have 2 minutes to memorize the images before they disappear. They will be asked to say or write the names of everything on the list.

- Write an unusual word such as *flatulence* on the board. Students must figure out the meaning of the word and write a sentence using that word properly.

- Post the name of a city on the board. Students must find out the country where that city is located and tell approximately how far away the city is from their own location.

- Project a close-up of a section of an object on a screen. Students must figure out what the object is.

- Post or project a question for students to discuss: Do people ride zebras? How much does a camel weigh? Can puppies hear when they are first born? After 2–5 minutes, ask students to share their answers with the class.

- When students enter the gym, they find a circuit course like the ones used in military boot camps, with a sit-up station, a jumping jack station, a squat-thrust location, and so on. Each station has a picture and written instructions for the exercise to be completed and the number of repetitions. After they complete the circuit, students may jump rope or shoot baskets until everybody completes the course and is ready to begin class.

As you read this list, you probably thought of other ideas for good activities for your students. If you run out of ideas, ask your students for suggestions. They often come up with more difficult and challenging tasks than teachers do, and when student input is incorporated into tasks they often become more interested in doing the activities.

INTRODUCE STUDENTS TO EACH OTHER

Choose your method of introduction carefully. Students are much more likely to treat each other well if they know each other's names, but many of the popular games designed to help people get acquainted are more effective with small children and adults than they are with older elementary, middle, and secondary school students. Why? Little kids are usually too innocent to be intentionally cruel, and adults are usually too polite. But preteens and adolescents are experts at humiliating and tormenting each other. Another consideration, which breaks my heart, is that many children are targets of gangs, cliques, or bullies. What may seem to you to be a simple game designed to give students a chance to become acquainted may create an uncomfortable or even dangerous situation. I do not recommend pairing students or forming small groups until you know the students in a given class well enough to be sure that your grouping won't cause problems.

Another consideration is shyness. Some people are naturally introverted. That is not a bad thing. We can't all be extroverts. Just as actors need an audience, leaders need followers, athletic competitors need spectators, and classrooms need listeners as well as talkers. Some teachers believe it is their duty to help shy people overcome their shyness and become comfortable speaking in front of groups. Others believe it is our duty to create a safe haven where students feel comfortable and then provide opportunities for them to naturally come out of their shells. The feedback I have received from shy people indicates that most prefer the second approach. I can't say which is correct, but I believe it's best to err on the side of comfort. I was a very shy child, and although I have learned to overcome my anxiety enough to allow me to speak in front of groups it still makes me very nervous. So I do not force shy students into the spotlight for more than a few seconds at most.

A popular introductory game is two-person interviews. You've probably played this game more than once. The instructor asks students to pair off and interview each other and then to introduce their partners to the class. This exercise appeals to teachers because it's quick and simple. But for many students this activity is an exercise in embarrassment and agony. Here are just a few reasons why so many students dread these peer interviews:

- Unless the teacher assigns pairs, a few students are always left out, often by accident. They feel rejected and unlikable. If the teacher forces people to join them, they feel even worse. And they never forget that nobody wanted to be their partner.

- Children are quick to pick up on differences such as lisps, accents, stutters, and blushing. They may tease or torment other students.

- Preadolescence and puberty cause all kinds of physical situations that embarrass children: budding breasts, acne, sudden voice changes, random facial hair, uncontrollable physical responses to stimuli. Sometimes the worst thing teachers can do to students is make them the center of attention.

- Poverty, religious rules, or strict parents may force a child to dress differently from the norm. Their clothing may embarrass them or lead classmates to ask questions that they would prefer not to answer in public.

Please don't abandon the idea of using a get-acquainted activity. A number of games and activities don't require students to address the class or stand in front of the entire group.

Don't be put off by older students who shake their heads at your efforts to generate enthusiasm. If they have enough sense of humor to laugh at you, they'll probably go along with whatever game you prose. But if you have a truly tough class, as I have had, and you see that the ringleaders are going to ruin the game or refuse to play, you'll have to make some quick choices. You can ignore the party poopers and play with the kids who cooperate, which sends the message that students who cooperate are going to get more attention from you than the ones who don't—not a bad message. You can nickname all those who refuse to play as "Taking the Fifth Amendment" and show that it doesn't bother you if they can't play well with others. You can ask the nonparticipants to step outside until the rest of you are finished, which is risky because they may refuse to go, which will force you into a confrontation—not a good precedent to set. You can stop the game without explanation and move on to the next item on your agenda, preferably a challenging worksheet or reading assignment, which might be a good choice because you will have made it clear to everybody that if they don't want to play you have plenty of work up your sleeve—another good message. Trust your instincts.

ESTABLISH ROUTINES AND RITUALS

Standard procedures are probably the number-one way to eliminate wasted time. You may have to spend a few minutes each day reviewing your procedures until students can follow them without supervision, but once students learn them you're set. Every teacher has his or her own teaching methods, curriculum requirements, and classroom logistics to consider, but many procedures are common to any classroom. For example, at times we all need to quickly get students' attention, collect papers, distribute materials, approve or disapprove requests for bathroom visits, check for understanding, clean up after projects, and transition from one activity to another. If we design and teach procedures for accomplishing those tasks that we must perform repeatedly during a school day or week, we can save time, prevent frustration, and make our classrooms more efficient, happy places to be.

If you are at a loss about what procedures you should use and how to teach them, try to find a successful, happy teacher to observe. You'll notice that students in those classes know what to do when it's time to start an activity, collect papers, and line up to go to the library. If you can't find a teacher to observe, check the books, videos, and DVDs in your school district staff development library. Ask your fellow teachers. Do an Internet search for "classroom procedures," and visit Web sites hosted and designed specifically for teachers to share best practices and experiences.

Attention, Please!

Another key to successful teaching is finding a way to get students' attention quickly. Kindergarten and elementary teachers are a great source for ideas. They often use call-and-response chants, nonverbal hand gestures, unusual sounds, or large colorful manipulatives posted on the walls at the front of their rooms. These methods also work very well for older students if you alter them a bit. Some teachers shout. If that works for you, fine—but shouting tends to lose its effectiveness after a while and also gives the impression that you are losing control. We have all seen parents who stand and repeat a child's name over and over while the child blithely ignores them. Children tune out adults who shout. Calm people don't shout. Calm assertive authority is much more effective than panic or anger. If you find yourself shouting a lot, it means your students are not listening to you. Time to switch tactics.

Chants or signals are usually much more effective and far less irritating than shouting. Some teachers can silence a classroom by clapping their hands three times. Others may blow two toots on a whistle. The idea is to produce a sound that stands out from the voices of your students, and let them know they are to stop what they are doing, face you, and listen quietly.

British teacher Andy Bell, whom I observed in a video clip online (schoolsworld.tv and titled "Sharing Expectations") used a rain stick that produced a sound very similar to gentle rain. The first time he held up the stick and students heard the noise, his students all became quiet and looked at him. He said, "Sometimes I need everybody to look at me and listen to me. That's what I want you to do as soon as you hear this sound." The students were intrigued, and the rain stick worked very well to get their attention without creating a loud, startling noise. I have since used a rain stick with my college and high school students: they love it, and it works. (Most rain sticks are made from dried cactus and pebbles. You can find them online at very reasonable prices or make you own from a piece of plastic pipe and some pebbles and duct tape.)

Bell made a noise meter in the form of a vertical strip with self-stick material at three distinct points—Quiet Time at the bottom, Partner Work in the middle, and Group Talk at the top. He placed a large easy-to-see ball to indicate which level of noise he wanted for a given time period. Then he gave his students the opportunity to engage in three short activities, one at each noise level, so he could provide feedback to let them know when their voices were at acceptable levels. Such feedback and practice are key steps to teaching any kind of procedure. We can't expect students to automatically understand what we mean when we say, "Talk quietly with your partner." What seems quiet to them may sound like shouting to us. It's so important to remember that students' failure to comply with our requests may be due not to lack of respect or unwillingness to cooperate but rather to lack of clarity about exactly what is expected.

Silent Signals and Nonverbal Cues

Sometimes a silent signal or nonverbal cue is more appropriate than a voice or sound signal. Students who need to make a quick bathroom visit, for example, can give you a prearranged signal such as three fingers raised, palm facing forward. They can give the signal even while you are speaking, without interrupting you. This allows you to nod or mirror the signal to give them permission. Some teachers hesitate to allow students to sign themselves out for bathroom visits, but many teachers report that even young or so-called difficult students respond favorably to being given the trust and responsibility of signing themselves in and out. They usually work very hard to maintain the trust and freedom that you give them—because they don't want to lose them. Students who abuse the privilege lose the privilege.

At any time during your instruction, you can check for understanding by making a thumbs-up gesture and looking at your student questioningly. Those who get it also raise their thumbs. Anybody who is confused gives a thumbs-down. This gives you the option to back up and rephrase what you were saying, try a different approach, or put students to work individually or in pairs or groups while you circulate and assist.

Students can also silently initiate checks for understanding if you teach them to tap their index fingers against their heads anytime they become confused during instruction. If only one student keeps tapping his head, you know that you will need to spend some time with that student while others are working independently. If you have more than a couple of finger tappers, then you can slow down or vary your instructional method. This method prevents you from continuing to give instructions when nobody needs them or realizing later that you have lost students along the way.

Some teachers opt for a hand signal instead of verbal cues when they want students to stop talking and pay attention. The teacher may stop and cup his or her hand behind one ear while giving students a meaningful look. Students then stop talking and cup their own hands behind one ear. The teacher waits until every student complies, then says, "Thank you for listening," and proceeds with the next instruction or activity. Likewise, the teacher may simply raise one hand and wait for everybody to raise one hand in response before proceeding.

Bell, the teacher I mentioned earlier, used what he called "Give Me Five." He displayed a chart on the wall that showed five things he expected when he held up his hand: look at the teacher, stop talking, keep your hands to yourself, hold your feet still, and listen. Each expectation was numbered. During his lessons, if a student strayed, the teacher quickly and quietly got the student back on track by saying, "Jenny, number two, please. Thank you." It worked brilliantly. The teacher didn't have to stop the lesson and the students responded without being put on the spot. This method can work with any age of student as long as you tweak the expectations to suit your class.

All Aboard?

An important factor to consider when using verbal or nonverbal cues is the percentage of student response you require. During regular lessons and activities, I think it's best to ignore minor misbehaviors and avoid being what students refer to as a *control freak*. But if you use a verbal or nonverbal cue to check for understanding or to correct behavior, ideally you want 100 percent response. For example, if you ask for a student hand signal in response to your hand signal cue (you raise your hand and wait for everybody to stop talking, and they raise their hands in response), you should probably insist on a 100 percent response. If you proceed with only 95 percent, it may seem as though everybody is on board, but soon more and more students begin to opt out. Before long, you may find yourself back where you started—or even trying to regain lost ground. Young children are usually very responsive to hand signals, so getting 100 percent participation is easy. Older students will be very cooperative as well. But if you have some noncooperative souls in your classroom, you might choose to begin with verbal cues. That way if you have a few nonresponders in the group it won't be so obvious and you can ignore them since they'll be swept along with the flow.

Don't make an issue of singling out the one or two students who are not verbally responding to your cues. Most likely they are testing to see whether they can manipulate you into a showdown. You have far better things to do than engage in arguments with childish people. But if the same one or two students continue to flaunt their noncompliance, they may be begging for your attention. I suggest giving it to them—but not when you're in the midst of teaching. Find a time to give them your undivided attention when it's convenient for you and highly inconvenient for them. A good time might be when the other, more cooperative students are enjoying 5 minutes of free time to socialize as a reward for their good efforts at the end of an activity or class period.

End-of-Class Procedure

Once you begin designing procedures, you'll find yourself creating new ones as needed. Be sure to create clear instructions for each new procedure and allow students the opportunity to practice until they get it right. Don't punish them if they require several practice sessions. If they aren't doing what you want, they may not understand exactly what you want. Don't worry about wasting time. The few minutes you spend teaching procedures will come back to you tenfold as you save time by not having to repeatedly request that students settle down and focus on their assignments or use their indoor voices or neatly stack their books on the bookshelf or clean up their messes or stand quietly beside their desks while they wait for the dismissal bell.

That reminds me of one of my favorite and most necessary procedures: the end-of-class, or EOC, procedure. I learned the hard way, during my first year of teaching, that if I didn't stop one or two students from edging (or thronging) toward the exit 5 or 10 (or even 15) minutes prior to the dismissal bell, I'd soon have an unruly horde on my hands. And hordes are very unattractive.

During my second teaching year, I began teaching my EOC procedure to every class on the first day. It made a tremendous difference. You may choose to have students stand at their seats or line up along the wall. (You can use the first places in line as a reward for good behavior—but be sure to rotate this privilege.) Younger children are much less conscious of time and are more receptive to learning a song or chant and a routine for getting ready to leave. Older students often watch the clock. So my policy is: class ends when the bell rings. No early backpack zipping and paper shuffling. I give a 3-minute warning, at which time they can prepare to leave. They can talk to each other, but they must stay within arm's reach of their seats. No edging and elbowing toward the door. If I see edging, elbowing, shuffling, and disorder, then they receive an additional homework and a quiz the following day. If students cooperate and follow the EOC procedure all week, their reward is 5 minutes of free time during class on Monday.

TAKE TIME TO THINK

A psychologist who works with dyslexic students shared an experience that completely changed my attitude about time and my approach to class discussions. The psychologist told me about a teenage boy who came to her treatment center and asked her to give him an IQ test so he could prove to his father that he wasn't retarded, as the school claimed he was. The psychologist administered a standard IQ test under normal conditions, as requested. The boy earned a very low score—but he insisted that the score was incorrect and asked to be retested.

"Normally, a child who has been told for years that he is not intelligent will believe what he is told, especially if the parents believe it, too, "the psychologist said, "but this boy wasn't having it."

So she administered a second test. The second time she allowed the boy to take as much time as he needed to answer the questions. He spent more than triple the amount of time normally allowed—but he scored in the genius category!

After hearing that story, I wondered how many little geniuses had been sitting in my classroom feeling stupid because I didn't give them sufficient time to process information. Those slower thinkers may have had better ideas, but they rarely got a chance to share them in my classroom. I realized I had inadvertently been teaching slower thinkers not to bother thinking because I had been encouraging students who offered quick answers to my questions, regardless of the accuracy or depth of their answers. I liked a fast pace. It made misbehavior less likely, I thought, because students were engaged. But while I was busy racing along, encouraging the quick responders, I was teaching the slower thinkers not to bother, because by the time they arrived at an answer to the first question the rest of us had already moved on.

So I instituted a new policy that required a mandatory thinking period (10 seconds, then 20 and eventually a full 60 seconds) before anybody could offer an answer to a question, and the results were amazing. Students who normally didn't respond began raising their hands, and their thoughtful comments inspired deeper thinking from the quick thinkers. My own thought process improved as well. We didn't use the mandatory thinking time for every class discussion, such as informal chats about school activities, but when we did take more time to consider important questions it really changed the dynamic in that classroom.

If you have been rewarding faster thinkers in your class for raising their hands immediately, it might take you a few tries to teach your students to slow down and think. You may have to start with 5 or 10 seconds and work your way up to a full minute of silence. Sometimes teachers find it hard to be quiet for 10 or 20 seconds themselves. (Go ahead and try it now. Ask yourself a question and think about it for at least 10 seconds. If 10 seconds feels like a long time, you are probably a fast processor. If you didn't have time to really think, you are a slower processor. You may be smarter than you think you are!)

I strongly suggest trying this technique in your classroom. Students are usually very receptive to experimenting with longer thinking times, especially if you allow them to take turns being the official timer. That way they feel they are challenging themselves against the clock instead of being forced (by you) to be quiet.

DO SOME DIAGNOSTICS

Give the counselors a day or two to straighten out student schedules before you distribute your one-page welcome handout. During those two days, give your students a diagnostic exam or create assignments that will let you judge their skills and abilities, their strengths and weaknesses. (Don't quench their enthusiasm by grading these assignments. Ask students to do their best, but don't assign grades. Another option is to give every student who sincerely tries to complete the assignment full credit so no one is punished for making mistakes.) Diagnostic exams and exercises enable you to adjust your lesson plans so that you don't bore students or frustrate them by giving them work that is too easy or too hard. On my diagnostic exam I include sample questions from chapter tests, semester reviews, and final exams to find out how much my students already know. If the results show that the majority of the class needs to back up and cover some old ground, we back up. On the other hand, if nobody misses more than one or two grammar questions, I eliminate the easiest lessons I had planned in that area.

For younger children, you might play games or do activities that will show you where students are on the learning spectrum for various subjects. Math games, science projects, and spelling or writing activities will give you a good idea of who knows what. For students in third grade and higher, responses to reading are an excellent way to find out what your students know about a given subject in addition to giving you a good look at their logic and writing skills. Find an interesting or controversial essay, editorial, movie review, or feature article in a newspaper or magazine and make copies for your students. Have them read the article silently and write a response to the content. (For younger students, I require a paragraph or half a page; for high school students, I require at least one full page.) This gives you information about students' analytical thinking and composition skills and gives them good practice for the kind of writing they will be expected to do if they go on to attend college.

At one time I taught freshman composition at a four-year university. My freshmen, all high school honors students, had a terrible time coming up with their own theses; they wanted me to tell them what to say. When I returned to the high school classroom, I added many more open-ended writing assignments to my lessons, and my former students have reported that they were better prepared than many of their college classmates to produce the kind of writing that professors expected from them.

WELCOME HANDOUTS AND FOLDERS

Once you are reasonably sure that the students in your classroom will be there for a while and you won't have ten new students the next day, it's time to distribute your one-page welcome handout and cover your ground rules. Read your handout to the class to ensure that everybody has seen and heard exactly what it says. After you read one section, stop and ask students if they have any questions or comments.

After you have read the entire handout together, ask again for questions or comments. Tell your students that this is their chance to argue with you, if any of your rules or procedures seem unreasonable to them. If anybody has a complaint or suggestion, you can make a decision on the spot or tell them you will consider their ideas and let them know what you think at the next class. If you are an experienced or natural teacher or you have an unusually cooperative and well-behaved group of students, you may choose to open your rules to student input. If you don't have much teaching experience or are feeling at all insecure about establishing your authority, you will probably want to keep the rule making in your court. Giving up control of the rules may sound positive and democratic on the surface, but you may find yourself giving up control of your classroom, which is not a good idea, even with intelligent or mature students. Somebody has to be the boss, and that's your job. Of course, it doesn't hurt to consider your students' comments and opinions. Listening to their ideas is a good way to avoid future misbehavior or mutiny.

If you have a well-behaved, cooperative group, you might reward students' good behavior by giving them a fun practice exam on your rules. Here are two sample questions from my quiz:

1. If you arrive to class tardy, you should

    a. Make lots of noise so everybody notices you

    b. Gasp and pretend you just ran 5 miles to school

    c. Slap all your pals on the back as you pass by

    d. Take your seat quietly and get to work

2. What materials should you bring to class every day?

    a. Candy, gum, toothbrush, spiders, and assorted bugs

    b. A pen or pencil, paper, and your textbook (if applicable)

    c. Your dog, a pair of smelly socks, and two sodas

    d. A coloring book, a comic book, and a note to Santa

Students enjoy the exam and everybody laughs, which is very good because it dissipates tension and creates an immediate feeling of bonding among your students. I have said this before, but it bears repeating: groups that laugh together develop a quick rapport, and they tend to cooperate more quickly and efficiently.

If you haven't already created individual folders, distribute them on the same day you distribute your welcome handout so students have a place to keep the handout and any other paperwork you may distribute. A blank folder beckons to many students, so be prepared to answer the question, "Can we decorate our folders?" This is one of those small things that some students will try to enlarge into an argument to derail the teacher train.

If you find it difficult to tolerate immature or mildly defiant behavior, then it might be a good idea for you to insist that students not write anything on the folders except their names. I allow students to decorate their folders with anything except gang insignias, racial slurs, or obscenities. I explain that the primary purpose of the folders is to act as an organizational tool, not for them to display their talents and political beliefs. Folders make it easier for me to communicate with students, they save time for everybody, and they help students store important paperwork.

DELEGATE SOME AUTHORITY

Teachers tend to be nurturing souls. We like to help other people. But we also like to be in control, and many of us find it difficult to delegate any of our authority. Sharing your authority can reap huge dividends, however. By assigning jobs to students, you can conserve your precious time and energy for more important tasks. Student jobs also boost tender young egos, teach children how to handle responsibility, and encourage students to cooperate with you and each other. Some elementary teachers assign every student a specific task, with an important title to accompany the job: President of Pencil Sharpening, Official Attendance Taker, Certified Paper Collectors, Guest Greeter, and so on. High school teachers often take on student clerks or assistants who earn credits for providing administrative support during a particular class period each day. Even when a school doesn't have a formal clerking program, I often request that the office approve such arrangements; my requests have never been denied.

In my classes I always assign a student helper to take attendance, but since attendance records are legal documents I always check to make sure the report is accurate (so students can't be pressured by others to record incorrect data). For each class period, I have an attendance monitor and a backup for days that the monitor is absent. Here's your chance to recognize the memory skills of one of your students who remembered everybody's names. I also assign a door monitor for each class period to answer the door during class time. Instead of allowing people to walk in and interrupt our lessons, the door monitor greets anybody who knocks and accepts any notes, messages, or paperwork that doesn't require my immediate attention. I have taught at schools where two or three student messengers knocked on the door each hour to deliver notes from parents about after-school pickup times, birthday balloons, informal school surveys, and club meeting notices. Having a door monitor cuts down on disruptions and sends a message to your students that their work is too important to interrupt for trivial reasons.

The student cleanup crew is one of the most important student posts. I always request volunteers first. If I don't get at least four volunteers, I split the students into teams of four and rotate their assignment. The cleanup crew is responsible for making sure that no debris remains on the floor or desks when the dismissal bell rings. Students occasionally complain about being expected to do what they consider to be "the janitor's job," but when I explain that the custodial crew's primary responsibility is to create a safe and hygienic environment, not to clean up after slobs, they get the message. And when they are responsible for cleaning up their own or other students' messes, they encourage each other to be neater and more considerate of classroom furnishings and materials.

REVIEW MASLOW'S HIERARCHY

Perhaps you are thinking, "Oh, right. I need one more thing to add to my already overcrowded curriculum. Between school holidays, pep rallies, assemblies, and administrative busywork, I don't have time to cover my textbooks, much less try to teach psychology." If you are thinking along these lines, you are absolutely right. Teaching psychology isn't your job, so you may decide to skip this section. But if you have problem students who sometimes make you want to change professions, then you might consider discussing Abraham Maslow's theory with your classes. Young people are more interested in themselves and in each other than in any other topic. Introducing this theory will take only a few minutes, and it may save you many hours or months of aggravation.

At some time during your teaching training, you probably had a survey course, maybe two, in child or adolescent psychology. You've probably read at least one interpretation of Maslow's Hierarchy of Needs. I first discussed this idea with a class of students who had serious problems resisting the lure of gangs, drugs, shoplifting, and sex. One day we began talking about why people do what they do, and I told them that during my college studies in psychology, I learned that we often do things because we need to belong to something. No matter how many times we promise ourselves that we will be independent and stand our ground, we end up giving in and doing things we regret.

"That's me! That's me!" One of my students waved her hand in the air. "I'm always going shopping with my sister and her friends, and they always steal stuff from stores and I say I'm not going to do it. But then I go right ahead and do it again, and I always wish I didn't. I swear I won't go with them again, but the next time they ask me, there I go, doing what I said I wasn't going to do. And I feel so bad, like I'm a horrible person."

I assured Tyeisha that she wasn't horrible; she was simply human, because human beings need to belong and be accepted by a group of people. That's why we join clubs and social organizations, including gangs.

"How many of you have a family, people who love you, but you still feel like you don't really belong?" I asked my class. More than half the students raised their hands. I explained that many people feel disconnected, even when their families love them. But we need to find someplace where we feel we belong because people who feel part of something are less inclined to join negative groups such as gangs, vandals, and shoplifters.

My students were so attentive that I decided to introduce them to Maslow's theory. I outlined his theory briefly, and we discussed it. That night I made a chart for them to take home and keep where they could check it periodically to remind themselves to keep growing and moving up the ladder of happiness and self-fulfillment. Many students reported that knowing about human needs helped them make better choices.

Depending on students' age and maturity, I may use more or less sophisticated vocabulary and more complicated examples than those shown in Exhibit 5.1, but I've never had a group who didn't understand this theory. In fact, the "worst" classes are most interested in discussing these ideas.

Exhibit 5.1.
Maslow's Hierarchy of Needs.

Level 1: Physical. You need food, water, and sleep every day. If you're starving, you don't care whether you're wearing cool shoes—you care about finding something to eat. Until these level-one needs are met, you will spend your time and energy taking care of them. If you don't have these basic things, ask for help. Don't be embarrassed. Teachers can refer you to people who will help.

Level 2: Safety. Once your basic physical needs are met, you start to think about things such as keeping warm, avoiding harm, and staying healthy.

Level 3: Social. People—and lots of animals, like wolves—need to belong to a group and feel loved. You can have a family and still feel unloved. Sometimes this is why we hang around with people we don't really like or do things we know are wrong. Instead of doing these things, try finding something to belong to: a team, a club, maybe just a couple of kids you eat lunch with every day. Find somebody who likes you just the way you are. It doesn't have to be somebody your age—somebody older or younger will do just fine.

Level 4: Ego. Once we feel like we belong, we start to look for ways to increase our self-respect, because we all need to feel important and appreciated. We want other people to respect us, too.

Level 5: Self-Fulfillment. You have food, shelter, people who love you, and self-respect—now you're cooking! You know who you are and you want to become your best self. You are strong enough to walk away from a fight, but you stand up for your principles. You nurture your talents and learn just for the fun of learning something new. You follow your dreams!

INTRODUCE METACOGNITION

Sometimes students don't realize that an "easy" assignment is actually one that requires higher-level thinking. A few years ago, a high school junior challenged one of my classroom assignments. He wanted to know the point of doing the work. I asked him what he thought the point might be. He said, "To waste our time and give you something to grade." I was tempted to hush him up but decided to give him such a complete explanation that he'd never ask such a question again. As it turned out, the explanation blossomed into such a lively discussion of Bloom's Taxonomy that everybody in class sat up and paid attention. The next day I presented the same lesson to my other classes, who all responded positively.

When I write "Bloom's Taxonomy of Cognitive Domains" on the board, I always hear whispers and a few groans. They don't know what taxonomy means, but it sounds like taxes and nobody likes those.

I ask my students to try to figure out the meaning of the phrase. Usually they recognize the word *domain* as a kind of kingdom, but *taxonomy* stumps them. I grab a thick dictionary from the shelf and announce that I am going to "look it up in my handy-dandy pocket dictionary." Freshmen usually giggle; older students roll their eyes and make disgusted tsk-tsk sounds when I grab my dictionary. I ignore their ridicule.

Somebody usually says, "That's not a pocket dictionary."

I wink and say, "You gotta have big pockets."

(I don't do those things just to be a clown but to model the behavior I want my students to practice. It works. Before long, students start grabbing their handy-dandy pocket dictionaries or smartphones and making a big show of looking up words they don't know during class.)

After we define the terms, I tell the students that I'm going to share with them a lesson that teachers learn in college. I tell them I think they should know why we ask them to do the things we ask them to do. So we're going to try some *metacognition*—thinking about thinking. I explain the different levels of thinking, giving one or two examples. I ask them to think of additional examples from different academic subjects for each thinking level, and I distribute a handout on Bloom's Taxonomy (Exhibit 5.2).

Bloom's Taxonomy has, of course, been updated, and some versions use different terms—*create* instead of *synthesize*, for example, and *understand* in place of *comprehend*. I prefer the original words because I think they more accurately describe the actions. I don't think the specific terms are as important as comprehending and applying this information in our lesson planning.

Exhibit 5.2.
Bloom's Taxonomy of Cognitive Domains.

School Applications

Recall. Remember information: recite your ABCs, identify different colors, list the fifty states, name all the planets.

Comprehend. Understand things: know that words are made up of letters, subtraction means to take away, fifty states make up our country, skating requires balance, mixing red and blue paints will give you purple.

Apply. Use things you understand: spell words correctly, add or subtract numbers, write a sentence, draw a picture of the solar system, pass a football, perform a skateboard stunt, or select the correct paints to mix a specific color.

Analyze. Compare and contrast information or ideas: compare two different characters in a story, identify the parts of an engine, find the misspelled words in a sentence, or state the differences between the human rights policies of three different countries.

Evaluate. Make judgments based on knowledge: conduct three science experiments and decide which one gave the best result, choose the most convincing of three different arguments on the same topic, state your opinion about why a certain book is worth reading or not, choose the best solution to a problem, decide whether a country's nuclear arms policy is good or bad for the rest of the world.

Synthesize. Use knowledge and skills to create something of your own: write a story or poem, design and build a model, create a math problem, draw a picture to illustrate a scene from a play, form a theory about why something happens, or make up your own test for a class at school.

Using Bloom's Taxonomy in Your Own Life

Recall. Remember all the words to a song or all the items on your grocery list, recite the stats of a sports team, or name the parts of an engine or stereo system.

Comprehend. Understand the difference between a receiver and an amplifier, know how a gasoline engine or computer works, or realize that some people are more sensitive than others.

Apply. Hook up stereo speakers, copy a music CD, change your car's spark plugs, use a recipe to make guacamole, fill out a job application, fix a toaster or a bicycle, or ask a shy person for a date without scaring him or her.

Analyze. Compare two different jobs; list the pros and cons of getting married, having sex, having a baby, sending your kids to private or public school, joining a gang, or quitting smoking.

Evaluate. Decide whether your present job offers the kind of future you want, listen to all the candidates and choose the one who will get your vote, discuss with your partner various options for disciplining children, or determine whether you contribute your fair share to doing household chores.

Synthesize. Make a plan for your life and put it into action, start your own business, write a song, build a doghouse, create your own secret barbecue sauce recipe, or design and implement a budget based on your income.

My students are amazed to see that all the "boring, useless stuff" they are learning in school may help them when they begin their "real" lives. Incidentally, after I teach my students to recognize higher-level thinking skills, they often point out the level of thinking skills required for a specific task and are more receptive to challenging assignments.

One final note on this topic: Please don't assume that your students aren't smart or mature enough to grasp these concepts. I have discussed them with very low-performing students, disenchanted teenagers, and adults who don't speak English well, and they all understand at least the basic ideas—and they appreciate being treated as intelligent, capable people.

SHOW YOUR GRATITUDE

Thank your students every day for coming to class and cooperating with you. They won't get tired of hearing how wonderful they are. If we expect young people to behave well and to continue doing so, we need to acknowledge the good behavior. And we need to take every opportunity to shake their hands, pat them on the back, and encourage them to continue demonstrating their growing maturity and self-control. Like it or not, the children we teach are going to grow up to be just like us. They will treat other people the way adults have treated them. Since most children spend more time around teachers than they do with their parents and families, we teachers really do play a significant role in shaping their values and behavior. Therefore, we have an obligation to teach our students, by our own example, to be articulate, ethical, compassionate, and honorable people.

THE HARD PART IS OVER—WE HOPE

Not bad—by the end of the first week of school, you know the names of all your students, they know your rules and expectations, you have a good idea of what you have to work with, students understand that you hold them personally responsible for their actions, and they know what they will have to do to pass your class. Students know some of your procedures, and you are prepared to remind them if they forget. You have kept them so engaged and occupied that they have forgotten to misbehave—or they have learned that cooperating is much more enjoyable than disrupting. With a little luck, they also understand themselves a little better and have at least a basic understanding of the different levels of thinking and how they will need to develop the highest-level thinking skills. So your second week should be easier than your first, and your third should be easier than your second. And so on. At least that's the general idea.

Now you can create lesson plans that suit your classes, but don't get too specific just yet. If you plan your teaching days down to the minute, the administrative tasks and unavoidable interruptions (inoculations, club photos, field trips, career counseling, college days, armed forces information day, and so on) will drive you crazy, and driving you crazy is your students' job. You wouldn't want to spoil their fun.

WHAT DO YOU THINK?

1. Is there any value in the old advice, "Don't smile at students until after Christmas?"

2. Share some good first-day activities you have observed or heard about.

3. Should teachers force shy students to stand up and speak in front of the class? Does this really help them in later life? Or does it traumatize them forever?

4. Design three nonthreatening introductory activities for students of various ages.

5. What are some specific things teachers can do to assess students' prior knowledge?

6. Create a one-page welcome handout for students in a specific grade level.

Discipline Is Not
a Dirty Word

Mention the word *discipline* to most students, and they immediately think *punishment* because they focus on one facet of that multidimensional word. In the military, however, discipline has a more positive connotation because personnel understand that discipline allows them to function as an efficient team. It allows them to accomplish things together that they could not accomplish alone. From a personal perspective, they see how discipline helps them develop self-control and strength of character.

Classroom teachers can use the principles of military discipline to help students develop self-discipline and respect for others. Of course, I'm not suggesting that we order kids to hit the deck and give us fifty push-ups when they step out of line, but I do believe children need and want strong guidance and leadership. The world can be a scary place. Young people may protest, but they want us to set limits and establish boundaries for behavior. As they gain maturity, we relax those boundaries, but young students—including teenagers—thrive when teachers set and maintain limits.

Fear is the enemy of learning. In a safe haven, people relax and cognitive functioning flourishes. But in a danger zone, learning stops because our brains switch to survival mode. Schools so often become danger zones for students because they feel overwhelmed, threatened, or vulnerable. I believe fear is the biggest obstacle to learning—bigger than all the assorted learning disabilities combined. In spite of the many books and newspaper articles and TV programs warning us that modern children are likely to be apathetic, learning impaired, developmentally delayed, unwilling or unable to pay attention, and impossible to reach or discipline or teach, I don't believe those things for a second. I have taught too many "unteachable" students. Time and again, those students taught me the same lesson: they can and will learn in a classroom where they feel safe—mentally, physically, and emotionally.

All children are teachable. Humans are born students. We are naturally curious and eager to learn. Sadly, though, when many children begin formal schooling their natural curiosity and enthusiasm are replaced by fears: their teachers won't like them, they can't live up to the standard set by their older siblings, they will fail their classes, they will be unpopular and lonely, they will be assaulted by bullies, their developing bodies are ugly or unlovable, they won't be smart enough to graduate or go to college, their parents will get divorced, they are destined to go to jail or die from AIDS or a random drive-by shooting or a drug-crazed loner on the streets outside their school.

We can't address all of children's fears, but if we can create an oasis of calm and order in our classrooms where students feel safe and protected, where they know what we expect of them and that we will not permit other students to hurt or torment them, their natural enthusiasm for learning will resurface. Positive discipline is the key to creating that classroom oasis.

DEFINE YOUR PHILOSOPHY

Perhaps you have observed those "lucky" teachers who don't seem to have any discipline problems. Luck does play a part, but preparation has a lot more to do with effective classroom management. You can prevent most discipline problems if you lay the groundwork. I like to think of classroom rules as scaffolding. Our rules provide support and safety. They keep students from falling and seriously injuring themselves. As children grow older, we can relax or remove the rules one at a time until the children stand alone, making their own decisions, taking as much risk as their confidence and abilities allow. If we make reasonable rules, enforce them fairly, and adjust them to meet children's changing needs, we teach children that, instead of restricting them, rules actually can create more freedom.

As you design your discipline policy, keep in mind your purpose. Be honest with yourself. What is your true goal when you discipline students in your classroom? Do you want to punish them for misbehaving? Do you want to scare them or teach them a lesson? Do you want them to accept responsibility for their behavior? Do you want them to learn to make better choices in the future? Do you want payback? Do you want to flex your authority muscles? Do you want to feel powerful? Do you want to get even with them for disrupting your brilliant lesson?

In my discipline workshops, I ask teachers to do this brief journal assignment:

1. Quickly, in one or two sentences, articulate your goal when you discipline a student in your classroom. What do you hope to achieve?

   _____

2. Now, imagine that you have just been stopped by a traffic cop who says, "I have pulled you over because _____."
   [fill in the blank with your reply from step one].
   How would you respond to the police officer? Would you be cooperative and grateful for the correction, the warning, or the ticket you just received? Would you be inclined to change your attitude and be more law abiding in the future? Or would you become defensive, argumentative, determined to be sneakier next time, or intent on going to court to prove the officer wrong?

3. Let's go back to your reply in step one. If you honestly believe you would respond positively to what you originally wrote, you're fine. Otherwise please rephrase or revise your goal so you would be more receptive if a person in authority repeated those very words to you.

The goal of this exercise is to come up with a statement in which your words match your intentions. Your goal should be the same in every situation where you discipline a student. You should be able to articulate your goal clearly and repeatedly so students know what that goal is. You want your goal to be reasonable and, most important, something that a student would agree with and accept in a positive way. For example, if you say, "I am asking you to stay after class because I want you to make better choices," some students would argue, "I think my choices are just fine." If you say, "I am giving you lunch detention because I want you to accept responsibility for your behavior," the student may argue, "But it wasn't my fault. Jimmy hit me, I told him to leave me alone, and then you yelled at me for talking."

On the other hand, if you say, "I want you to know that you are responsible for everything you say and do, and you can change your behavior and thoughts any time you want to," your student may try to argue, but he or she cannot win the argument. If you say, "I am asking you to change your seat right now because I am trying to help you be a successful student," or "I would like you to stay after school and chat with me because I want you to pass my class," very few students will argue with you. Even if they said, "I don't want to be successful," it wouldn't be true. Nobody wants to be a failure—unless failing will somehow achieve a personal goal, such as upsetting parents. That occasionally happens, but for the most part students want to succeed. It's human nature.

My personal goal is this: I want my students to be successful. Whenever I discipline a student, I include those exact words as part of every request or direction. "Because I am trying to help you be a successful student, I want you to do X." After a few weeks in my classroom, students begin finishing my sentences for me. Sometimes they pull a face and parrot my instructions for the benefit of their classmates. They pretend they are making fun of me, but we all know the truth: they got the message.

You don't have to be able to articulate your discipline goals perfectly right now, but it is important to spend some time thinking about it because once you start teaching you may find yourself so busy implementing your discipline plan you won't have time to think about making adjustments. It can be very difficult to think quickly and effectively on your feet when trouble is brewing or boiling away in your classroom.

PUNITIVE OR POSITIVE

We tend to teach the way we were taught unless we make a conscious effort to do otherwise. If you can recall your own childhood, you may remember that standing in the corner or sitting in detention did not inspire you to turn over a new leaf. Instead, it made you vow to be sneakier in the future—and perhaps you spent the time plotting revenge against the teacher who doled out the punishment. Perhaps you can also recall a teacher who made you accept responsibility for your own behavior and who rewarded your efforts with a handshake, a pat on the back, a complimentary note in the margin of a paper, or a phone call to your parents.

Do an Internet search for "classroom discipline" and you'll find thousands of different approaches—all of them guaranteeing success. But you may find that what works for somebody else does not work for you. That's why I suggest that teachers create their own personal policies and tweak them as needed until they arrive at their own perfect policy. Where to start? First, sort those thousands of ideas into two categories: *punitive* and *positive*.

Punitive discipline policies involve sanctions, demerits, referrals, detentions, suspensions, lowered grades, reduced privileges, confinement, withdrawal from sports or arts or music programs, and so on. Punitive discipline techniques are meant to punish, embarrass, frighten, or restrict student freedom as a result of some transgression. For some teachers and some school districts, punitive policies are effective. But research suggests that those successes are the exception. As a rule, punitive methods may temporarily change student behavior, but they do not encourage students to take responsibility for their actions or motivate them to cooperate with adults. Purely punitive disciplinary methods often result in a cycle of misbehavior and punishment that escalates, causing more classroom disruptions and declining grades. Look at the high number of high school students who are repeatedly sent to detention or suspended from school. Many of these students end up in dropout prevention programs because they miss too many critical classroom lessons. They blame their teachers or parents or schools for their problems and become less and less motivated to achieve with each punishment.

Positive discipline techniques, on the other hand, are designed to make students think about their behavior, accept responsibility for their actions, make amends when possible, understand the effects of their behavior on others, solve problems, and learn how to make better choices. Instead of relying on humiliation or threats, positive discipline provides an opportunity for students to discuss the reasons for their behavior and helps them learn new ways to behave. Instead of blaming teachers or parents for their own misbehavior, students realize that they can control their behavior and affect the way they are treated in school and in the world.

If you use humiliation as a tool for embarrassing students, don't be surprised if they follow your example and try to humiliate each other. In my opinion, using humiliation to control children is not just unprofessional, unethical, and unfair but also psychologically abusive. Perhaps you can't remember how you felt as a child when an adult intentionally embarrassed you. Perhaps you are among the fortunate few who were never subjected to humiliation. You may be able to empathize with your students if you imagine yourself in the following scenario:

> Your principal has forwarded an important fifty-page report to all teachers. You find a copy in your mailbox on Friday with a note from the secretary saying that the principal expects all teachers to read the report before the staff meeting on Monday. You put the report in your bag and take it home, but between chaperoning your son's birthday party, doing the laundry, driving your daughter to a soccer match, visiting your mother in the hospital, and trying to squeeze in a few minutes for your spouse you don't get a chance to read the report. You do glance through it, though. At the staff meeting on Monday morning, the principal asks how many people read the report. You raise your hand because, technically, you did read a bit of it. Imagine that the principal then looks directly at you and asks you to stand. She says, "Please summarize the main points from the report." Clearly, she thinks you are lying. She senses that you haven't read the report, and she is going to make you do one of two things: try to fake your way through this experience or admit in public that you lied when you said that you had read the report.

> You now have the choice of discussing details of your home life in front of your peers or looking like a liar. The principal's point in asking you

to summarize the report is to embarrass and humiliate you. Perhaps she believes this tactic will scare the rest of the teachers and make certain you will read her next report to avoid being embarrassed. Her tactics may work. You may read the report, but at what cost? Your principal will have lost your trust. Or her tactics may backfire. You may skip the next staff meeting or call in sick that day.

There are far better ways to supervise and motivate people than using humiliation and punishment—and far better ways to teach.

COWBOY PHILOSOPHY

One year, at the Southwestern New Mexico State Fair, I had the unforgettable experience of watching Craig Cameron, the cowboy professor, in action. I was struck by the similarities between breaking wild horses and taming wild students. Cameron worked with two wild horses that afternoon—one that had never been ridden at all and one that had resisted being forcibly saddle broken. In both instances Cameron was able to mount and ride the horses within an hour without raising his voice or using any force whatsoever. As I watched Cameron tame those horses and listened to him explain his actions, I realized that I was in the presence of a master teacher. I took copious notes.

"Many people set out to break the spirit of a horse," Cameron told the crowd that had gathered outside the round pen where he worked the horses. "The last thing I want to do is break down the spirit of any horse: I'm out to build it up so that I can utilize it. I want to relate to the horse on his own level and on his time schedule. If you want a horse to have a good attitude, you can't force things on him. You have to give him time to decipher what it is you want him to do."

As he spoke, Cameron picked up a saddle blanket and took a step toward the horse he was breaking. The horse took one look at the blanket and started running in the opposite direction (just as our students try to escape from difficult lessons). Instead of chasing the horse or trying to corner it so that he could place the blanket on its back, Cameron stood still and waited until the horse stopped running and, overcome by curiosity, approached the unfamiliar blanket to investigate. He allowed the horse to sniff and nibble the blanket, and then he brushed it gently over the horse's legs and belly before placing it on the horse's back. Immediately the horse bucked the blanket off and ran away. Cameron picked up the blanket and waited until the horse returned to inspect it again. Satisfied that it posed no danger, the horse finally stood still and accepted the blanket. Cameron could have saved time by hobbling the horse and tying the blanket to its back, but he would have faced the same struggle every time he wanted to saddle the horse.

"People bring me all sorts of 'problem' horses," Cameron said, as he placed a saddle on top of the blanket and let the horse run until it realized that the saddle wasn't going to hurt it.

"Usually the problem is the way the horse was taught in the beginning," Cameron explained. "Somebody tried to force a lesson on him, or he was punished harshly for not doing right. If he doesn't do the right thing, he knows you're going to jerk harder or spur harder or get a bigger mouth bit. So now he's nervous, scared, and defensive. He is just flat-out turned off to learning."

Again, the horse circled the pen several times and then slowed down and walked to Cameron and allowed him to tighten the cinch on the saddle.

Students, like horses, resist having their spirits broken or being forced into performing uncomfortable or unfamiliar actions. If we give them time to get used to us and time to understand what we want from them, they are much more apt to cooperate. We can beat, scare, or bore children with endless repetitions when they don't cooperate. Children, like horses, may cooperate temporarily out of fear, pain, or exhaustion, but unless we gain their trust we will fight the same battles over and over again.

One comment that Cameron made during his training session struck me as particularly applicable to classroom teachers who must deal with students who resist accepting authority. "Horses naturally understand a pecking order," Cameron explained. "Your horse can accept the fact that you are the leader of the herd and he is the follower. That doesn't mean that a horse won't test you from time to time. He's going to test you. But you can establish that you are the leader, number one in the pecking order, without causing your horse pain or fear. The way you do that is to control your horse's mind instead of his body."

If you back a student against the wall and demand respect or obedience, you are not apt to receive either one. Children's natural instinct is to escape when they feel frightened or threatened or to fight if escape is impossible. If you make clear from the start that you are the leader in your classroom and that your leadership is necessary so you can teach and your students can learn, you allow students to accept your authority without feeling any loss of dignity. Instead of demanding cooperation, effective teachers make it a choice.

After seeing him work, I bought Cameron's videos, *Gentle Horse-Breaking and Training* and *Dark into Light,* to watch at home. The longer I watched, the more I became convinced that teacher-training programs should assign his videos as required curriculum. If you'd like to read about Craig Cameron, you can find archived articles about him online or in equestrian magazines such as *Western Horseman* or the *Quarter Horse Journal.* For information about his videos and workshops, visit www.craigcameron.com.

RULES VERSUS PROCEDURES

Rules and procedures are two very different things. Rules are rigid and inflexible; procedures can be adapted as needed. Rules are not made to be broken. Like laws, rules make no allowance for individual differences or circumstances. If you establish a list of rigid rules for your classroom, you may regret it later. For example, you may make a rule that you will not accept late work or that one missing homework assignment will preclude a student from earning an A in your class. What if a student cannot complete an assignment because of a true emergency, such as a serious illness, accident, or death in the family? You have two choices: stick to your rule or bend it. Either option has disadvantages.

If you adamantly stick to your rule, innocent students will suffer and you may earn a reputation as a harsh and heartless person. If you bend your rules for one student, other students will quickly line up to ask for special consideration because they too have emergencies (some of which may seem trivial to you but very important to young people). No matter where you draw the line, some students will feel that you have wronged them, that you play favorites. That's why I suggest making rules only about things that you will *never* tolerate, things that cannot happen by accident—hitting, kicking, biting, racial insults, or sexual harassment.

Procedures, on the other hand, don't legislate behavior; they provide guidelines for completing specific activities, such as using the restroom, completing makeup work, requesting permission to miss class, requesting admittance to your class when tardy. Establishing procedures for your classroom provides clear guidelines for student behavior while also allowing you more options. If special circumstances arise, you will be able to make changes without causing a lot of complaints or confusion. You will be able to make decisions based on individual circumstances. If students complain that you treat them differently from each other, respond by pointing out that you treat them individually because they are individuals. One-size-fits-all does not apply to education because each student has unique talents, abilities, goals, challenges, and circumstances.

One teacher reported that the first time a student complains about being treated different from another student, she says, "Sweetheart, you *are* different from each other, and I am not going to treat you all the same. Same doesn't necessarily equal fair. I will always be fair. And you can take that to the bank."

You can reduce the amount of disorder in your classroom if, early on, you establish a procedure for distributing and collecting papers, grading papers in class, turning in homework, collecting makeup work, dismissing class, issuing hall and library passes, allowing visits to other teachers, and so on. Instead of reviewing all your procedures during the first few days of class when students are often too excited or overwhelmed to remember them, cover each procedure as it arises. Remember that many students learn by seeing or doing, so don't just talk. Show them what you want them to do, and then practice each procedure until your students know the routine, especially with young children. You may opt to give students a copy of your procedures in writing. You may feel like you are wasting time at first if you spend 5 minutes at the end of each class for 2 weeks discussing the procedure for leaving the room after the dismissal bell, but you will save yourself a lot of time and heartache later. Kids know that if they can get you to ignore their behavior once or twice, they can ignore your procedure.

Don't create procedures unless you think they are important, and if you make them make sure you demonstrate and follow them. Otherwise you weaken your authority and lose students' respect.

RULES FOR CREATING RULES

You may have to experiment to find the best discipline methods to fit your unique personality and your students, but you are much more likely to succeed if you focus on these three key concepts as you create your classroom rules:

- Limit the number of rules.
- State rules positively.
- Consider the consequences.

The more rules you create, the more time you must spend enforcing them, the more complicated your list of consequences, and the more likely students are to misbehave out of defiance. Long lists of rules box in everyone, stifling creativity and hindering your efforts to develop a strong rapport and an environment of mutual respect.

My preference, after testing many methods, is to create one overarching rule for my classroom: *Respect yourself and everybody in this room*. This one simple rule covers any situation that may occur. For example, it is not respectful to text on your phone, stick chewed gum on desks or books, hit or insult people, carve obscene words into a desktop, arrive late to class, throw litter on the floor, interrupt other students who are trying to work, and disrupt the teacher's efforts to teach.

State your rules positively whenever possible. Remember the old joke that instructs, "Don't think of an elephant"? The same idea applies to rules. Don't give kids more ideas than they already have. Negatively stated rules—such as no gum chewing, no shouting, or no running with scissors—provide a list of suggested misbehaviors for students who crave attention. Negative rules also provide a challenge for students who want to distract you from teaching or simply want to push your buttons. And, finally, negative rules can inspire further negative behaviors. For example, if you make a rule that no gum chewing is permitted in your classroom, some students are going to forget they have gum in their mouths or may risk breaking your rule because they really like gum. When those students believe they are in danger of getting caught breaking your no-gum rule, they may hide their sticky wads under their desks. But if you have a positive rule, "Dispose of all gum properly," you leave it up to the students to choose their own behavior, and they are far more likely to cooperate.

Sometimes you won't be able to state a rule positively. Or you may have to add an addendum using negative words to avoid creating a mouthful of gobbledygook. My own one-rule policy, for example, includes a list of prohibitions for students who require specific information. The addendum specifies: no put-downs of other people based on their race, religion, ethnic background, skin color, native language, gender, sexual preference, intelligence, body shape, or body size. Because I state the main rule positively, the overall rule doesn't have a negative connotation and students don't feel compelled to break the rule just to show they can.

Consider the consequences of your rules on everybody, including you. Doling out demerits, for example, requires that you keep records of student offenses and spend time assigning punishments and consequences. Assigning lunch or after-school detention may seem like a good idea, but it punishes you as well as the student because you have to spend your time supervising your detainees unless you want their detention time to become a social hour. Making students write essays or reports is a popular punishment, but using writing as a punitive tool may backfire on everybody—you, the student, and the other teachers at your school—by teaching students to hate writing. Sending students to the principal, another popular tactic, may remove the student from your room but sends a clear message to students that you feel incapable of handling the situation alone.

ELECTRONIC INTERVENTION

Phones and tiny electronics are a growing problem in classrooms around the world because they are so distracting to students. But trying to detach children from their electronics creates drama and trauma and headaches for everybody involved. Teachers are in a delicate position. We may try to incorporate technology into our lessons, but sometimes we need human-only performance. We need student brains to be free from electronic interruption. However, we face some serious challenges in trying to detach students from their electronics. First, those little gadgets are expensive and delicate. We don't want to damage them. We don't want to contaminate them with our germs. And we don't want to set ourselves up for verbal assaults from parents who insist (reasonably) that in today's dangerous world they must be able to contact their children at all times.

It's no wonder that many school districts establish a no cell phone policy and leave it to teachers to try to enforce it. Or that so many teachers pretend they don't see the phones because they don't have the time or energy to battle their students. Upon demand, some students will hand over a phone and smile—because they have another one in their pocket. Some kids pout and refuse to participate after you confiscate their phones. Some are willing to put up a physical fight or be sent to the office to keep their beloved electronics. And sometimes if you confiscate a phone and turn it in to the office, the parents will arrive on campus, sign the required documents to retrieve the phone—and immediately give it back to the student. I have even had parents who repeatedly text their children during class for nonemergency reasons. Yikes!

I have tested various no-phone policies myself. I have tried taking away phones when they were clearly distracting students. I tried collecting all the phones in a box at the start of class. Once I even invested in dozens of 6 x 9 manila envelopes and instructed students to place their phones into the envelopes during instruction time. I have even tried ignoring the phones use in the hope that students would realize they couldn't learn if they were texting. None of those plans worked.

This year, by accident, I hit upon a plan that works—so far. One of my students kept fiddling with the cell phone in her lap. Whenever I approached her desk, she would hurriedly shove the phone into the pocket of her jeans and insist that it had been there all along. Her lie was so blatant that I had to laugh. So did she. Still smiling, I threatened to put her cell phone into detention if it didn't stop distracting her.

"If that cell phone can't behave itself, I guess I'll have to force it to stop distracting you," I said. The student laughed out loud.

Bingo! The light bulb hovered above my head. I needed to stop punishing students and start punishing their phones! That night, I bought three more small manila envelopes. Placing the flaps against the wall so the openings were facing me, I stapled the envelopes to the wall near the whiteboard. I wrote, **CELL PHONE DETENTION!!** in thick black marker and drew a cartoon of a cell phone with a very sad face on each envelope. The following day, I announced to each of my classes that I was going to be putting their phones into detention if the phones couldn't behave politely.

"I hate to do it," I said, "but I will. I'll be ruthless. I'll be cruel to those phones so you can be successful students. I don't care if they cry their little hearts out. I don't love your phones. I love you. I don't want you to get bad grades because of your selfish phones. And I don't want you to have to spend your money in therapy years from now because you are addicted to electronics. So if your phone distracts you I'm going to put it in detention for the rest of the class period. I'll give it one chance to shape up. If I have to put it into detention a second time, I will know that your phone has an attitude problem and I'll expel it for the rest of the grading period. After report cards are issued, I will give your phone another chance to behave itself."

My students giggled. They laughed when I confiscated the first phone and slid it into the detention envelope. They laughed again when I sent a second one to join the first. They stopped laughing when the third phone was sent to detention. Within a few days, the cell phones began behaving themselves. Now, occasionally, I have to put one phone in detention, but I rarely have to confiscate two during the same class period. As soon as I pick up one phone, the others disappear.

So far, so good. I did have to make one adjustment. One day, I slipped a phone into the envelope and it tore through the bottom and landed on the carpet.

Fortunately, the phone wasn't damaged. So I taped the bottoms and sides of my envelopes with strong packing tape to reinforce them. No phones have broken out of jail since then. And nobody has argued with me about my policy.

ID YOUR BULLIES AND OUTCASTS

Bullies are nothing new. However, whereas bullies used to use their fists to blacken an eye, today they are apt to use any number of weapons to cause serious, sometimes even fatal, physical injuries. Many schools have successfully implemented antibullying and character-building programs, but it's still not unusual to encounter a bully or two in any modern classroom. Usually it's difficult to catch bullies in action or even to identify them. Even harder to identify are the instigators who don't do the bullying themselves but who are experts at manipulating other students into insulting or assaulting each other. At one high school where I taught, students seemed to enjoy setting each other up. One student would confide to another, untruthfully, that a third student had been talking trash about her. The second student would confront or attack the innocent third student, who would end up being disciplined, sometimes suspended, along with the second student despite her innocence. Nothing happened to the first student, of course, because she was not involved in the confrontation.

One day, by accident, I hit upon a way to identify the bullies and instigators. In preparation for assigning students to small groups for projects, I asked students in every class period to take out a sheet of paper and write their own names at the top. Then I asked them to list the names of three or four students they would like to work with in small groups. As an afterthought, I added, "And if there are one or two people you never want to work with, please list their names. No details, just names."

When I reviewed the student lists later that night, at home, I realized that in every class, the same names appeared on the "Do not want to work with" lists. I realized that I was looking at the names of my bullies, my instigators, and my outcasts. Of course, I wasn't able to magically fix everything, but knowing who I was dealing with helped me monitor my classes better and significantly reduced friction among students. I tried to find adult mentors for the bullies. I kept an eye on the instigators and intervened when I suspected they were stirring things up. And I did my best to befriend the outcasts and help them develop social skills and self-confidence.

A quick Internet search for "antibullying" will bring up hundreds of Web sites with resources for teachers and parents. I wish there was as much help available for teachers who want to help the outcasts in their classrooms. Aside from the fact that some students suffer humiliation and cruelty every single day of their lives for years at school, ignoring students who are bullied can be dangerous. The bullies are not the ones who bring weapons into schools: it's the outcasts who can no longer tolerate being tormented by their peers.

Teachers are the first line of defense. We may not be able to eliminate bullying, but we certainly can reduce it by refusing to tolerate verbal abuse of any kind in our classrooms—and by making sure that we don't lapse into bullying ourselves.

CHARACTERISTICS OF SUCCESSFUL DISCIPLINE POLICIES

You can find any number of courses, books, workshops, and journal articles that offer keys to effective classroom management. Much of their advice is contradictory and confusing. Experts disagree vehemently about whether rewards have positive or negative effects on long-term behavior and motivation. Some insist that assigning consequences is the key to molding behavior; others believe that consequences equal punishment. So many different approaches exist that you may be tempted to throw up your hands and wing it or just pick a policy and hope it works. I suggest creating a policy that incorporates these characteristics of effective discipline plans:

- Consider cultural differences.
- Model the behavior you expect from students.
- Separate the child from the behavior.
- Make the student accept responsibility.
- Allow the student to back down gracefully.
- Seek solutions instead of simply assigning consequences.
- Assign consequences that address specific behaviors.
- Clearly state your expectations for future behavior.
- Provide positive feedback when behavior improves.
- Wipe the student's slate clean.
- Identify the reason for repeated misbehavior.

- Focus on rewarding good behavior.
- Teach students how to take control.
- Send students to the principal as a last resort.

Consider Cultural Differences

In today's multiethnic society, it is essential that teachers consider cultural customs and differences before assuming a student's behavior is rude, defiant, or disruptive. In my own experience, for example, I have had students from countries where children are taught to avoid making eye contact with adults as a show of respect. In other cultures, students were discouraged from asking questions because to do so might imply that the teacher had made a mistake. And one boy surprised me by explaining that in his country touching a person on their head was the ultimate insult—something I never would have guessed.

One of my online students posted a thought-provoking comment on the class discussion board: "I actually had an experience a few years ago with a Korean exchange student who smiled when disciplined in class. I was initially enraged until it was explained to me that that was his method of showing shame under chastisement. It was this newfound understanding that opened my eyes to individualization of discipline and the concept of respecting the individual student. I now make more of an effort to understand the context from which every single one of my students is emerging before I wade into classroom discipline."

Model the Behavior You Expect

No matter how brilliant your plan, it won't work if you don't set the example. You cannot mandate respect, for example. If you want students to treat each other with respect, you must show them how it's done (and in some cases, show them and show them and show them because this will be a new experience for some of them). If you want students to use a logical approach to solving problems, you must demonstrate the techniques for them by modeling the behavior when you encounter problems during the school day and explaining how you work through each step.

Yes, modeling behaviors takes time, but spending that time at the start of the school year will save you hours of time later: your students will cooperate with you, and you won't have to waste so much time on discipline.

Note: Do not let other adult staff members disrespect your students. Often adults will insist that they are just kidding when they insult or intentionally embarrass students, but because teachers hold positions of power students may be afraid to protest or admit that the teasing is offensive or insulting. Even when students do protest, some adults persist. Of course, you can't dictate adults' behavior, and it's hard to criticize them without stepping on their toes in front of students. You can't very well say, "Please stop abusing your authority," but you can call the adult aside and say, "Please help me out here. We have had a problem with teasing in my classroom, so we don't engage in that behavior at all. Sometimes students don't understand when teasing crosses the line, so we just don't do it. It's hard for me to enforce that rule when they see adults teasing students." Even if the adult isn't as receptive as you had hoped, pretend that he or she agrees with you. Smile and say, "Thanks for helping me out."

(I know, I know. You want to keep your job. You don't want to make enemies. But if you see adults bullying children and you say nothing, you are giving your tacit consent. Ignoring bullying is the same as ignoring sexist or racist jokes or child abuse. It's just not acceptable.)

Separate the Child from the Behavior

Sometimes a child will intentionally misbehave just to irritate a teacher, but most misbehavior is a result of immaturity, impatience, frustration, or the desire to fulfill some imagined or real need. Children act like children because they are children (and many teens are still children); as imperfect human beings, students are prone to making mistakes. Don't take your students' behavior personally unless it is clearly a personal attack on you—and even then you may simply represent authority. When we take children's behavior personally, we limit our ability to assess a situation objectively and choose the best response, but if we can separate the child from the behavior we can follow the excellent advice, "Hate the behavior; love the child." This attitude helps us focus on solving problems and helping students learn to make better choices instead of simply punishing the student or assigning meaningless consequences.

Make Students Accept Responsibility

When we assign consequences and dictate behavior, we take control of and responsibility for a given situation. If we place the responsibility squarely on the student's shoulders where it belongs, we create a completely different experience. For example, if a student disrupts your class and you immediately reprimand him and assign a consequence, you focus everybody's attention on you, and some students will automatically sympathize with the culprit just because he is in the less powerful position. If you ask the student to stop and think about his behavior and decide whether he wants to continue or make a change, the focus shifts to the student, and he now controls the outcome of the conflict. He cannot blame you for his behavior or any resulting consequences.

Recently, I had a class of advanced placement high school juniors whose good behavior deteriorated over a period of weeks until it became impossible to teach them. They were in the midst of a project based on Ernest Hemingway's short story "Hills Like White Elephants." After reading the story, students wrote informal essays in which they predicted the future of the couple in the story. Then, we watched four short video adaptations of the film online. For their final assignment, students had to design their own projects: write and/or act out the scene that took place before the story began or after it ended, produce and show their own video adaptations, or design their own writing or art projects. One day, while showing a video, I ran out of patience. Students were on task only if I was standing beside them. As soon as I looked elsewhere, they went back to texting on their cell phones, working on their math assignments, taking extra-long trips to the bathroom, and roaming around the room to chat with friends. I felt as though I was playing one of those games where moles pop up unexpectedly and you have to whack them on the head with a plastic mallet to win the game. I decided to try one last tactic before I gave up on them. I stopped the video and switched on the light. Twenty surprised faces turned my way.

"I am not angry with you," I said, "but I am very frustrated. I work hard to create challenging, engaging lessons that will help you learn the information and skills you need to be successful in this class, in your senior classes, and in college or on the job. But we can't do college-level work if you are going to act like high school freshmen. So it's up to you. I am going to take a walk. While I'm gone, you decide whether you want to be advanced placement juniors or whether you want worksheets and quizzes every day. I won't be angry. Maybe I expect you to act more mature than you are. Maybe you need more time to develop the self-control required to do project-based assignments. Discuss it among yourselves and decide. When I come back, you let me know what you want to do, and we'll move forward. I will create the assignments you need—but I refuse to be a babysitter."

I walked out the door and strolled around the hallways for about 10 minutes. When I returned to the classroom, the lights were off and the students were watching a video based on the story. After the end of the video, a girl turned on the lights and said, "We want to continue our projects, Miss Johnson. Everybody agreed except two kids, but we told them they were just going to suck it up because everybody else wants to do the projects." Those students did a good job, even the ones who weren't thrilled about the idea. And the class voted, unanimously, to do another project.

Allow Students to Back Down Gracefully

When students have the opportunity to retreat gracefully, many of them will decide to cooperate with you. But when you back them up against the wall, most will become stubborn and defiant; many will lash out. This holds true even for very young children, who often have a stronger sense of dignity than many adults realize. When we allow a student to back down the first time he or she engages in a specific inappropriate behavior, we teach that student and any observers several lessons: we are all responsible for choosing our own behavior; everybody makes mistakes; most mistakes are not permanent; and a good leader exhibits compassion, forgiveness, and respect. Our students imitate our behavior whether or not they like us, so it behooves us to set high standards and a good example.

When a student acts disrespectfully, you may ask, "Do you believe your present behavior shows self-respect and respect for others?" At this point, the student has the option of behaving different without losing face. Because it is his or her choice, the student may be more inclined to choose an alternative behavior and will not feed a need to exact revenge on you for meting out punishment if you must assign some consequence to restore calm to your classroom. When I give students the option of choosing to behave, I don't assign consequences if they do choose to cooperate. Instead, I thank them for making such a mature and responsible choice. Then we go on as if nothing happened.

The first time I tried that technique, the obnoxious student said, "That's it?" I said, "Yep." He said, "That was easy." I said, "Yep." He shrugged and sat down. By the way, his behavior improved. It's hard work to hate somebody who truly likes and respects you, and it's really not fun when they refuse to fight.

Seek Solutions Instead of Merely Assigning Consequences

Sending a tardy student to detention does not address the problem of tardiness and will most likely result in a worse student–teacher relationship and possibly in academic problems. Requiring a student to spend 10 minutes helping you clean your classroom would reduce the amount of effort and paperwork involved. Better yet, require the student to use a problem-solving model to brainstorm possible solutions to his problem. Then discuss his solutions and help him choose and implement the best course of action. In addition to addressing the current problem, you'll be teaching that student how to solve future problems.

Assign Consequences That Address Specific Behaviors

If you do assign consequences, try to select ones that actually address the misbehavior you want to discourage. If a student draws a heart with black marker or scrawls obscenities on her desk, sending her to detention just leaves you with a dirty desk. Making the student clean her desk—or all the desks in your classroom—would be more appropriate. Likewise, sending a disrupter to detention doesn't teach him to be quiet and respectful. Asking him to stand outside your door or stand at the back of the room until he feels able to control his behavior will give him an opportunity to practice self-control; if he makes an effort but fails at first, he may succeed if you provide a few more chances to practice.

Clearly State Your Expectations for Future Behavior

One year I had a student who repeatedly interrupted my lessons by standing up, loudly clearing his sinus cavities, and walking across the room to spit in the trash can. Because he was a well-behaved student otherwise, I opted to warn him to be more polite instead of assigning punishments. Finally, I called the student aside. He insisted, "But I am being polite!"

I asked, "Do you think walking across the room and spitting in the trash can is polite when I am trying to talk to the class?"

"Yeah, "he said, earnestly. "I'm not spitting on the floor."

That conversation taught me to be more specific in my instructions to students. My warnings no longer leave any room for misunderstanding: Now, I might say, "Keep your hands on your own desk," or "Throw things only in appropriate places, such as the gym."

Provide Positive Feedback When Behavior Improves

Everybody responds to positive feedback, and students are especially responsive. After any incident that results in a private conference, consequences, or punishment, watch for an opportunity to praise the student who misbehaved. When she behaves appropriately, let her know you noticed and that you appreciate the improvement. Youngsters often believe that the teacher no longer likes them after a confrontation, even a minor incident. I frequently remind students that I still like them as people, even if I don't always like their behavior. Note: Some students prefer not to have their good behavior recognized publicly in front of peers, but they will not object to a positive phone call to their parents, a quick note, a handshake, or a comment on the margin of a paper.

Wipe the Student's Slate Clean

In addition to providing positive feedback, make sure your students understand that a mistake is not a permanent condition. Just as we release criminals who have served their time, we must allow students a second chance. Of course, the more serious the offense, the longer it will take for a student to regain your complete trust; however, if you make clear that you don't hold any grudges, the student will be much more likely to cooperate in the future. After I invite an unruly student to step outside for a private chat, for example, we shake hands before we reenter the room. Then I make a point of making eye contact and making a positive comment to that student a few minutes later. The following day, I greet that student when he or she enters the room. I want it to be clear to that student, and to the rest of the class, that we all make mistakes and that when we do we need to address them, learn from them, and move forward.

Identify Reasons for Repeated Misbehavior

If you keep assigning the same consequences for the same misbehavior, nobody is gaining anything from the experience and everybody is losing valuable time. When a problem recurs repeatedly in your classroom, the student is sending a clear signal that he or she needs help in some specific area. Identifying the reason for a behavior may take some time and effort, but the time will be well spent if a casual conversation, a brief nonpunitive conference, an exchange of comments in a journal, a phone call, a confidential chat with close friends, or some similar method can help you figure out why a student is behaving in a certain way. Often students misbehave repeatedly because they want the teacher to send them to talk to a counselor or psychologist or they want you to inquire about their home situation. If you can't communicate with the student, ask around. Most students have a favorite teacher, coach, secretary, bus driver, security guard, school police officer, custodian, or counselor.

Focus on Rewarding Good Behavior

For some reason, looking for negative behavior seems to be our default setting. Unfortunately, if you look for bad behavior you will find it, but we can train ourselves to look for good behavior instead. When you focus on rewarding good behavior instead of punishing bad behavior, you create a different dynamic in your classroom. Rewarding or praising students for being considerate people is not the same as bribing them. A bribe is intended to entice somebody to do something for the sole purpose of earning a reward. Of course, we don't want to teach children that they will receive a reward every time they cooperate or work—because they won't. That's not the way the world operates. They certainly will be rewarded, though, for behaving responsibly and considerately as citizens and workers. We all respond to positive feedback, which may come in the form of verbal praise, high marks on our assignments in school, good performance appraisals on the job, promotions, monetary raises, certificates, employee-of-the-month awards, or some other kind of acknowledgment. Sometimes adults say, "We shouldn't reward children." And I ask, "Would you go to work every day if you never got paid?"

Teach Students How to Take Control

Feeling out of control can be thrilling—on a roller coaster ride, for example. But in the classroom, loss of control is frightening. There is too much at stake for the student. Punishment. Bad grades. Failure. Humiliation. After losing control and acting out, most students panic. Their panic may manifest as belligerence, defiance, or apathy, but their underlying emotion is fear, so their brains switch to survival mode. Cognitive function slows, and emotions hijack their brains. They switch to fight-or-flight operational status. They want out of the room. Or they want the teacher to go away. Unfortunately, the opposite usually occurs because students cannot think logically or make sound decisions when they are in a state of panic. So what's a teacher to do? Try to avoid the panic in the first place. Teach students quick, simple techniques to calm their minds so they can control their behavior. Deep breathing is one of the simplest, most effective ways to reduce tension and calm the mind. Teach your students to stop and breathe often during the school day.

If you are unfamiliar with deep breathing, meditation, and stress relief techniques, you will find easy instructions online after a quick search. Teach your students the easy movements: shoulder rolls, clenching and unclenching fists and arms, tilting the head slowly from side to side, massaging the back of the neck, flexing the fingers and shaking the hands, standing up and jiggling their feet to relax the ankles.

Encourage students to monitor their own emotional states and use these techniques to calm themselves down as needed. Build opportunities for developing self-control into your lessons. For example, establish a 10-second rule for thinking—nobody raises a hand or shouts out an answer for at least 10 seconds after you ask a question. Work to increase the thinking time to a full 30 seconds. Don't worry about wasting time. You will gain more time than you lose. A few seconds of relaxation can prevent hours of frustration and confrontation.

Make Office Referrals Your Last Resort

A hundred years ago when I was young, being sent to the principal's office was a very big deal. The principal would paddle you, your parents would paddle you, and your siblings would shun you for embarrassing the family. If you send a student to the principal's office today, there is a good chance that the student will refuse to leave your room or will leave campus entirely. Even if the student cooperates, he or she may spend an amusing hour trading jokes with other students in a waiting area or sit in a detention room reading comic books, doing word search puzzles, or staring at the walls.

When your wayward student arrives at the principal's office, the result may be very different from what you intended. Principals don't always support their teachers. Most do, but some simply don't. Students don't always care whether they pass your class or graduate. Parents don't always accept reality or the responsibility for raising their children. And in the worst cases, students or their families may raise legal issues—valid or not—to avoid the real issues of personal responsibility.

In addition to the obvious reasons, my primary reason for not sending students to the office is that I don't like the cycle of behavior that usually results. What we hope will happen rarely does: the student doesn't accept responsibility for his or her actions, learn from this mistake, and resolve to cooperate with you in the future. What usually happens is more like this: the student misbehaves; you send the student to the office; the student becomes angry or embarrassed and blames you for causing those feelings; the student also blames you for whatever punishment the principal metes out; the student misses hours or days of valuable lessons in your class and other subjects; the student returns to your class amused or still angry or ashamed or eager for revenge; and you're back to the beginning of the cycle, ready for another round.

With compassion and creativity, you can break this destructive cycle and offer alternative solutions. Again, I suggest sitting for a moment in your students' seats to change your perspective. Imagine how you would feel if your supervisor at work objected to your behavior and—instead of explaining the objection, discussing the problem, and giving you a chance to change your behavior—marched you past your coworkers to the company president's office for a reprimand. That may sound silly, but an office isn't so different from a classroom. You're the company president, and your students are your employees whose job is to learn their lessons and complete their assignments in exchange for credits toward an academic promotion or a diploma. When they make mistakes or become ineffective workers, your task is to correct them quickly and without damaging their dignity any more than is necessary. Of course, just as employers do, you must deal with serious offenses different from everyday problems such as tardiness, inefficiency, forgetfulness, and general bad attitudes.

TWELVE STEPS TO BETTER DISCIPLINE

"Theories are great, but I need practical advice," one young teacher told me during a workshop. "Tell me exactly what to do and say." The following sections list my twelve-step response to her question. I have experienced success using these techniques with a wide array of students, from troublesome teens to overachieving scholars. These steps are listed in order of power—beginning with the subtlest and least forceful responses from you. After you gain some experience, you will want to add your own variations, but this list will give you a good start and will provide opportunities for you to practice and evaluate different techniques.

1. Ignore the Offender

Often, students act out just to gauge your response. If you are easily upset, flustered, or angered, they will take advantage of your short fuse. On the other hand, if you ignore mild misbehavior, it often goes away. A student may whisper the F-word under her breath, for example, just to see your response. If you pointedly ignore the behavior, you send the message: *This is my classroom, and I will decide when and how I respond to student behavior*. If the student doesn't get the message, you have plenty of other options. Read on.

2. Send Nonverbal Messages

Everybody responds to body language. In fact, about 80 percent of our communications are nonverbal. Take advantage of this powerful tool by using eye contact, changes in your voice and posture, and gestures. Practice in front of a mirror to learn how to use your eyes to communicate a warning. Think a powerful thought as you practice: "You are going to be very, very sorry," or "Go ahead—make my day."

Silence is much more effective than shouting. Trying to shout over rowdy students makes them only more excited—and it makes you look weak. However, if you suddenly lower your voice and slow your speaking pace, students immediately pick up on it. If you stop talking in midsentence and look fierce, it's very likely that a student sitting near you will draw in her breath or otherwise communicate her concern through a change in posture. Within seconds, that concern will be communicated to everybody else in the room. You will actually be able to feel the change in the energy. Let that energy percolate for a few seconds. Then continue as though nothing had happened. Your students will get the message.

You can also use movement to alert students that their behavior is approaching a danger zone. Some behavior experts divide the classroom into three zones: red, yellow, and green. When you are across the room from a student, he is in the green zone and free to act. As you move closer, the zone becomes yellow: caution advised. (Consider your own response when a police car pulls up alongside you on the highway.) When you are near enough to touch a student, she enters the red zone and will control her behavior until you move away. The lesson here is to keep moving. Teachers who rove around their rooms experience far fewer behavior problems because students automatically react to the distance between them and the teacher. If this distance changes at random, students are much more likely to monitor their own behavior.

3. Use Humor to Defuse Tension

There is a reason that so many effective public speakers begin with a joke; it changes the entire dynamic of a room. And you may be able to make use of that fact to defuse the tension between you and students. I discovered by accident just how useful humor can be. I was trying to get my high school juniors to write haiku. One tough boy refused to try. He didn't respond to coaxing. I knew that warning him was unlikely to inspire creativity, so I gave up. I dropped to my knees and clasped my hands. "I'm an old woman," I said. "Please don't make me beg.

It's so unattractive, and it hurts my old knees." The boy shook his head and rolled his eyes at his classmates, but he couldn't resist smiling. And after I gave up and walked away, he wrote a haiku.

Another time, two Hispanic gangster wannabes strolled into my classroom wearing sunglasses. I knew they expected me to order them to remove the glasses; they were prepared to argue. Instead, I walked behind them and started singing *"Lo mucho que te quiero* (How Much I Love You)" softly in Spanish. They started laughing, which totally destroyed their tough image. And later on, I looked up and saw that they had both removed their sunglasses.

4. Drop a Behavior Card

Because so many students are visual or kinesthetic learners, or because they are simply stubborn, they may not respond to verbal requests. Or they may forget a few seconds after you have reminded them to be quiet or sit down. Create some behavior cards. Use colorful card stock so you can easily find them.

For young students, write this message: *Be polite.*

For older students, write this message:

Your present behavior is not acceptable. Please be more polite.

Return this card to me—in person—after class.

The moment a student begins to disrupt your class, walk over and drop a card on his or her desk. Don't say anything. If you are in the midst of talking, keep on talking. Stand near the student for a few seconds. In most cases the bad behavior will stop. Leave the card on the desk as a visual reminder to the student. Collect the cards after class or at the end of an activity with younger children. When you collect the card, thank the student for choosing to stop the inappropriate behavior. (If you drop a card and the student ignores it or throws it on the floor, see the next step.)

5. Have a Quick Chat

If nonverbal signals, humor, and behavior cards fail to motivate your student, ask him or her to step outside the room (or to the back of your room if you have small children or a strict policy that would prohibit having a student stand in the hall temporarily). Don't worry about the other students. They will be interested in seeing what happens. They may make a little noise while you are in the hallway, but they will be quiet when you return.

Ask your student if there is a reason for his or her disruptive, defiant, or disrespectful behavior. If there is a sensible reason, figure out a way to address it. If the student can't offer a reason, ask the student if you have somehow offended or insulted him or her. If you have, apologize and offer to shake hands. If you haven't, tell the student it is time to think. Here's the warning speech I make—you may choose to change the wording for younger students, but the gist of the message should be the same:

> You have the right to fail my class. If you truly want to fail, then I would like you to put that desire into writing and sign it so that I can keep it in my file to show you and your parents in the future if you question your grade. If you don't like the activity I have assigned, I'm sorry, but I am the teacher and I chose that assignment because I believe it will teach important information and skills. You don't have to do the assignment. You have the right to sit and quietly vegetate, but you do not have the right to interrupt my teaching, stop anybody else from learning, or waste everybody's time with obnoxious, selfish, or disruptive behavior.

Ask the student if he or she feels ready to come back to class and cooperate. If so, shake hands and ask the student to give you his or her word of honor that they will not disrupt your teaching or anybody else's learning. (Don't skip this step. Most students take their word of honor very seriously. And if a student starts to disrupt again, you can often stop that behavior dead in its tracks by quietly reminding the student, "I thought you gave me your word.") Then get back to business. Forget about the incident. If the student behaves well for the rest of that class period or activity, offer a word of private praise. He may shrug and act as though he doesn't care, especially if he is a teenager, but teens do care. They just hate to admit it.

If your disruptive student opts *not* to rejoin the class, it's time for the next step.

6. Give a Time-Out

Just as adults sometimes need some time alone to clear their heads or regain their composure, sometimes students need a break from the pressures of school (or life). If your disruptive student chooses not to rejoin your class the first time you issue the invitation, don't push. Leave the student standing outside your door. Remind her that if she runs off you will have to refer her to the office as being truant and then the matter is out of your hands. Be firm, but kind. Tell her you are trying to help her be a more successful student who has excellent self-control. Leaving your disruptive student alone gives her time to think about her behavior.

Go quietly back into your room and continue teaching. Thank the other students for waiting and tell them you appreciate their patience and cooperation. (You want them to realize they will receive more attention from you by cooperating than by disrupting.)

Occasionally, when it's convenient and other students are occupied, you can step outside to see whether your disrupter is ready to talk to you. If not, leave her there. If necessary, leave her there until the end of the class period or activity period or school day. Often students will pretend the entire incident never happened. You can then do the same. Once or twice, I have had students who stood outside the classroom for an entire period, disappeared the moment the bell rang, then returned the following day and behaved like little angels. Okay, maybe not angels, but definitely not devils.

7. Rewire Your Connection

Sometimes a teacher and student get off on the wrong foot for one reason or another and end up at odds with each other. You may not even know why you and a particular student don't seem to click. But if you find yourself repeatedly having to correct the same student for this or that, before you blame the student step back and assess your relationship. You can't be expected to love every student you meet, and not every student will like you. But you do need to get along, for both your sakes. If you realize that you dislike a particular student or just don't have a good connection, then it's up to you to change it. You have the grade book and the authority. You can afford to be kind and generous. Assign the student to be your classroom aide or helper and get to know each other a bit. Use a private journal to make a written connection. Send a positive note to the parents or ask a counselor to meet with you and the student so you try to learn to communicate better. Tell the student you'd like her to visit your room during lunch hour and surprise her with a cookie and a chat. She won't expect the gift or the conversation, and it may break the ice. When you do meet with your student, don't rush. Take your time. Often students will try to wait you out if they know you only have a few minutes to spare because it's uncomfortable to have an honest conversation. Talking makes you vulnerable. Don't expect immediate results, and don't be dismayed if the student shrugs off your attempts to talk and acts like he doesn't care. Trust me, they care. Even teenagers.

Another option, if you enjoy a good rapport with your students, is to discreetly ask students you trust if they know why your disruptive student misbehaves. Once a girl confided that a boy in our class had started acting out after his twin brother was killed in an accident. The girl said. "He didn't used to be like that." My awareness of the situation didn't change the boy's behavior, but it certainly changed my perception and my attitude toward him.

8. Call the Culprit

One evening after a particularly trying day, I called the father of a student who had tried to drive me crazy by whistling softly at a very high and annoying pitch for 90 minutes in my classroom. The father wasn't home, and Junior answered the phone.

"You know who this is?" I asked.

"Yes," he whispered.

"I was very disappointed in your behavior today," I said. "I like you, but I don't like the way you acted. It was very annoying, and it disrupted my teaching. I don't want you to do that again. All right?"

"All right," he said.

Junior never whistled again, and I realized I had happened upon an effective deterrent. I began calling students directly to discuss their behavior. In most cases those phone calls were much more effective than calls to parents because the students were entirely responsible for their behavior. Often when the student behavior improved, I did call the parents—to tell them how much I enjoyed having their child in my class. The students didn't know what to think, which kept them on their toes—which is a good place for them to be.

9. Create a Contract

Just as behavior cards serve as an effective visual reminder to students who forget verbal instructions, student contracts serve as effective written reminders to students who have promised to cooperate. Your contract doesn't have to be elaborate, and it doesn't have to be a form. Some teachers use a form on school letterhead to make the contract look official; all they have to do is fill in the blanks. Other teachers ask the student to write out an agreement about specific behaviors and consequences.

Just as positive reinforcement produces quicker and more lasting results in behavior, positively stated contracts result in quicker cooperation and a better relationship between student and teacher. Instead of listing things the student won't do, list things the student will do. If possible, also incorporate some reward (not a bribe)—for example, if the student does not break this contract for 30 days, the student will earn ten points for good conduct and the contract becomes null and void. Think about how much more responsive you would be if a traffic officer gave you 30 days to prove you could drive safely instead of issuing you a ticket.

In my classroom, I prefer a verbal contract and a handshake. Some students perceive contracts as forced confessions.

10. Send for Reinforcements

Sometimes even the best teacher runs up against an immovable student. If the first nine steps fail and the student still causes major disruptions, don't blame yourself. Clearly, the problem is bigger than a simple personality clash or routine misbehavior. Don't quibble. Send for reinforcements. Ask your principal for suggestions and support. Request a meeting between you, the principal, and the student to see if you can come to a resolution. Call the parents and request assistance or a conference. If parents or guardians are unhelpful or if you suspect after speaking to them that they may be contributing to the student's bad behavior, see if you can find an adult relative or older sibling. Check with the student's bus driver and your school security personnel; sometimes school staff members enjoy good relationships with students who don't respond well to teachers. Consult your school counselors and psychologists. Ask a coach to counsel the student. Ask until you find somebody.

11. Request a Student Transfer

Ask a counselor if your troubled student can complete assignments in the counselor's office. Once I had a principal who agreed to take my chief troublemaker under his wing and supervise the boy during my class period. If these aren't viable options, perhaps you could find a fellow teacher who would be willing to accept your disruptive student. Of course, teachers can't make this transfer themselves; however, if both teachers agree, your administrators will be much more likely to grant your request. At small schools where a transfer is not an option, you may be able to find a fellow teacher who also has a problem student. You can agree to switch students for a specified period of time each day to give yourselves and your students a break from each other.

12. Remove the Perpetrator

If you have an incorrigible student and you have exhausted every possible avenue, tried every intervention you can think of, and the student continues to disrupt your teaching and other students' learning but your administration won't remove the student from your classroom, then you need to remove the student yourself—unofficially. I have used this method successfully, and I have recommended it to other desperate teachers who report that it worked for them as well. It's best to keep this procedure to yourself, however.

First, create an assignment folder. Include the next two or three assignments that you intend to complete during class and a brief but complete description of any special activities or projects. Next, talk to your school librarian and ask whether you may send a student to do independent work as long as that student does not misbehave. If the librarian agrees, explain that you will give the student a pass each day and that the student is to ask the librarian to sign the pass and indicate the time that the student enters and leaves the library. (In schools with no library, find a counselor, coach, administrator, or teacher who can supervise the student and agree on a time period and location for this experiment. If no other location is available, place a desk outside your classroom door and have the student sit outside to complete schoolwork. If the student leaves the desk and wanders off, the student is now in violation of your school policy and then must be referred to the appropriate office.) Do not make any preface or provide any warning before you implement this plan. Simply call your student aside, hand the student the folder, and explain that the student will be working independently. Provide an instruction sheet that states your expectations about conduct in the library (or other applicable location), the procedure for getting passes signed, and the student's responsibility for returning the completed work to you at the end of the class period each day. Do not argue with the student. Hand over the folder, show the student to the door, shut the door, and teach the students who cooperate.

If your troublesome student decides to take a vacation, fill out the proper reports and let the discipline system handle it. If the student complies with your instructions, continue this policy for as long as necessary. Once I had to remove a student for an entire quarter, and I'd like to add that the day I reached the end of my patience and removed him from the class, several students privately thanked me for removing the troublemaker and making it possible for them to learn. As it turned out, he had threatened some of the boys and sexually harassed some of the girls, but they were all afraid to file formal complaints against him because he was a member of the prize-winning varsity football team.

Of course, there is a chance that your administrators (or, sadly, your fellow teachers) may object to your emergency independent-assignment procedure. If that happens, explain (and follow up with a letter summarizing your conversation to cover your back in case somebody decides to file a report at your district office) that you had exhausted every legal option and the student still made it impossible for you to teach and other students to learn. Provide dates and times when you asked administrators for support or assistance, copies of disciplinary referrals, minutes from any conferences, and dates and times of phone calls or meetings with parents.

IF YOU HAVE TO HAVE DETENTION, MAKE IT WORTHWHILE

Some schools insist on having a detention center, and many schools require that teachers take turns supervising detention. If that's the case in your school and you can't convince your administrators or fellow teachers to try a different approach, then do your best to make detention useful.

Instead of simply enforcing a no-talking rule or overseeing time-wasting activities such as word search puzzles (which seem to be popular detention room assignments for some strange reason), find some interesting articles—interesting to young people, not necessarily to adults. For example, my students have responded enthusiastically to critical reviews of popular movies; feature articles about sports stars or musicians; essays about controversial subjects such as UFOs, tattoos, and body piercing; pop psychology quizzes; and self-help articles on handwriting analysis, dating success, anger management, and ways to gain popularity.

Don't make your reading assignments mandatory if you have a room full of little rebels. Just pass out the papers and say, "Here's something interesting we could read." Then give them a few minutes to look it over. Read a little bit out loud. Some students will follow along, though they may pretend they are ignoring you. If anybody seems interested at all, ask for volunteers to read. If nobody volunteers, read the entire article aloud yourself. Encourage the students to discuss the article, but if they prefer to remain mute don't take it personally. Detention rooms may have some nasty bullies among the crowd, and many students prefer to keep a low profile. That doesn't mean they aren't interested, however. Hold your own discussion—with yourself. State your opinions. Collect the papers. Let the students go back to vegetating. Vegetating is boring, so some of them will think about what you just read. Some of them may even be inspired to think for several minutes in a row. That's a good start.

Beware: Your efforts to stimulate thought may backfire. One teacher reported that when she began using short psychology lessons and discussions about developing social skills during her assigned detentions, students often complained when the bell rang to signal the end of the period. After a few weeks, some students began asking to be sent to her detention because they enjoyed her lessons so much!

KEEP RECORDS

Regardless of what behavior policy you choose, create a folder for discipline problems. Keep track of your efforts to help students, with dates for each disciplinary action. You don't need to record quick chats and time-outs unless a student starts to show a pattern of serious misbehavior. If that does happen and you find yourself with a determined problem child, document everything—warnings, behavior cards, phone calls, notes to parents, office referrals. (Students can disappear en route to the office or forge signatures on passes.) Also document your conversations and requests for help from administrators and other teachers. This record will not only provide evidence in the unlikely event of a legal problem but will also show you whether you have a pattern of becoming too stressed and short-tempered at the end of a grading period or the beginning of a new unit.

CONSULT THE EXPERTS, TRUST YOUR INSTINCTS

Investigate resources and explore your options before you settle on a discipline program. Find a method that makes sense to you and that fits your own teaching style. Don't adopt somebody else's rules just because you think you should have rules. Children instinctively understand when adults are sincere, and heaven help you if they sense that you aren't. If you try to impose a behavior code that you don't really support, then nobody in your classroom—including you—will honor it.

After asking for advice from your professors and colleagues and conducting your own research, if you still find yourself at a loss for how to approach classroom discipline you might start with a modern translation of the Golden Rule: treat people the way you would like them to treat you. Don't merely post the rule in your classroom. Follow the rule yourself. Treat your students the way you would like them to treat you. They may be a little slow at first, and some of them may need a short vacation (or two or three) from your class, but if you sincerely respect them and maintain your own high standards of behavior, eventually they will come around. And eventually you will find an approach that works for both you and your students.

There are a number of popular programs such as Love and Logic, Positive Discipline, and Discipline with Dignity that many teachers recommend. My education students like to read the articles on the various Web sites and pick and choose their favorites. Some of them complain about the commercial aspects of the Web sites; one online student wrote, "I resisted reading the articles on those Web sites because I was so put off by all the ads urging me to buy this or that, but after reading the positive comments posted by some of the other students I took another look and found some really helpful advice. I guess teachers should be happy to take what they can get for free, considering."

Should you encounter a plethora of die-hard, incorrigible little stinkers in your classroom who steadfastly refuse to appreciate you, hang in there. And hang a calendar in your bathroom where each night as you brush your teeth you will have a visual reminder that you have survived one more day. Don't give up hope. Don't take the students' actions personally; they would torment another teacher just as they torment you. Do give up feeling guilty or unworthy. Most of us have had one of those years.

EMERGENCY MELTDOWN PLAN

Occasionally several factors combine to drive a teacher past the point of his or her tolerance. Even the best teachers can crack under certain conditions. When students sense that a teacher is near the breaking point, a handful of sympathetic souls may behave themselves, but most students will become relentless in their efforts to break the teacher. This can happen even with students who are not vicious or unfeeling. It is a result of specific ingredients and group dynamics that are beyond your control.

I remember a very professional young teacher with 7 years of experience successfully teaching advanced-level classes at a California high school. Her students adored her, and graduates often came back to offer their thanks. One day a student in her class stood up without warning and vocally criticized her teaching methods and curriculum. Caught by surprise, the teacher allowed the student to draw her into an argument, and before long the entire class of students polarized on the boy's side. A power struggle quickly turned into a shark feed. The teacher ended up running out of the room in tears, prepared to resign and give up teaching permanently. Fortunately, the principal refused to accept the teacher's resignation. He held a conference with the teacher, several students, and their parents. The parents supported the teacher and were able to apply enough pressure to force the students to stop attacking her. Within a few weeks, the students went back to adoring their teacher, but it took a long time before she regained her former confidence—and even then she admitted to having doubts.

When I observed that teacher's struggle, I felt sorry for her, but I didn't believe the same thing could ever happen to me. It didn't. Nobody ever stood up in my class, criticized my teaching, and stole my confidence. But just in case, I made an emergency meltdown plan and filed it away. A few years later, I took over a class from a long-term substitute who didn't want to be replaced and who worked hard to turn the students against me. She took another sub position at the same school and devoted her energy to sabotaging my class. I won't go into details, but I will say that those "regular" students were far more vicious and stubborn than any of the so-called at-risk, incorrigible, or behavior-disordered students I have ever taught, including delinquents who had spent time behind bars. When I realized that I was in the midst of my own shark feed, I pulled out my emergency disaster plan. Here's the plan, for what it's worth.

1. Be professional. Make sure your lesson plans (or a rough outline) are in order for the next few weeks. Check to see that your sub folder is in order.

2. Take a mental health break. This is an emergency. Don't feel compelled to provide specifics. Call in sick. If you have a spouse or friend who can call for you, even better. Pay at least one visit to a doctor, therapist, counselor, chiropractor, massage therapist, or other professional who can help you handle the stress, but don't make up a bogus excuse. Stress is a serious issue. It can kill you. Give yourself at least 2 days—a week is even better.

3. Do some serious self-reflection. Do you really truly want to teach school? Or did you think you would enjoy teaching, only to find that you hate going to work? Do you struggle with teaching, but find enough joy and satisfaction that you are willing to work on improving your classroom management

and leadership skills? Or do you have to admit that you just weren't cut out to teach?

You may conclude that you aren't the problem. Your school or district may be in a state of chaos. If so, consider applying at another school, working as a sub, or taking a sabbatical.

4. If you realize you don't want to teach, figure out how soon you can quit. Can you afford to quit right now? If you can't, create a plan for updating your résumé and doing a job search. Contact professional colleagues and ask them for general letters of recommendation. Don't whine about your job; just say you are thinking of making a career change in the future. Focus on creating the life you want instead of hating the life you have. Just changing your focus will make it easier for you to teach until you can afford to leave. Knowing you aren't stuck forever and that you have choices can make a big difference. You may even find that once you've decided to stop teaching, you relax and enjoy yourself so much that you decide to stay.

5. If you decide you do want to teach (or you must teach until you can afford to quit), make some serious changes in your classroom when you return. Change the look of your room—from the decor to the furniture arrangement, student seating, and even the rules and procedures. Also change your attitude, your approach, your posture, even your tone of voice. Cut your hair. Get new glasses. Buy a suit or some other clothing that shouts "Power!" Check your local library or bookstore for books on power dressing; a black suit with a white shirt is the ultimate power outfit. If possible, visit a military training camp or a police academy—or watch video clips of their instructors in action. Learn how to stand like drill instructors stand, feet planted a few feet apart, shoulders back, chin up, arms loose at your sides. When you talk, don't move. When you walk, march. When you want to speak, plant your feet again, wait a second, then begin talking. Use your serious voice. Practice your power speech for would-be interrupters: "Thank you for your input. Let's discuss that after school. Right now, we need to focus on my agenda."

It may sound frivolous, but check your footwear. You may have to give up comfort for a little while. Find a pair of leather-soled shoes (boots are even better) that make an authoritative clunk when you walk, as opposed to the dainty click of high heels or the squish of tennis shoes. When you enter, shut the door firmly behind you—not a slam but a nice, solid shut. The goal here is not to come across as mean or unapproachable but to make it clear who is in charge of your classroom.

And, most important of all, call your department chair or your principal and request a meeting prior to your return. Explain that you have been under too much stress in your classroom. Be honest. Ask for help with classroom management or whatever your particular problem is. Ask for somebody to be available to support you in person on the day you plan to return to work. Insist on a promise that if you call to request backup, a principal, counselor, or security guard will come immediately and support you. And explain that if you send a student to the office, you need administrators to hold the student out of your classroom.

6. Change the look of your room. Rearrange your desk and files. How you arrange it isn't as important as creating a new look. You want to feel that you're getting a fresh start and you want students to see that things are different. Put your desk in a different corner. Shuffle some file cabinets around. Hang a different calendar.

7. Rearrange student desks. If you've been using a U-shape or semicircle, move the chairs back into rows. If you've been using rows, find a different format. Place some student desks very close to your teacher desk—uncomfortably close.

8. Create a seating chart. Create a seating chart that separates the strongest students from each other. Put a major power player nearest to your home base. Put another near the door, where he or she will have less distance to travel when it's time to step outside. Place that handful of good, decent kids near each other in the center of the room so they can offer each other moral support.

9. Create a week's worth of lessons. Create extremely interesting and challenging lessons that require students to do the bulk of the work. Place the focus on them, not on you. Search online, and read magazines and journals for new ideas. www.teachers.net has a lot of good suggestions and links to other resources. Consider a lesson that makes use of differentiated instruction such as a menu where students select from among several possible assignments. Your goal is to engage students so thoroughly that they forget to misbehave.

10. Call your school on a Friday to confirm your return on Monday. Treat yourself to a movie or a special meal Friday afternoon. Try to relax because you will be working on the weekend (or Friday evening if you don't have weekend access—check with a secretary or custodian to make sure you can get into your room). Spend Friday evening or weekend rearranging your room and getting things in order. On Sunday night take a long walk or get some exercise to help you sleep better. If you can't sleep, don't worry. If you are tired, nervous energy will carry you through.

11. Wake up an hour earlier than usual on Monday. Do some calisthenics or yoga, meditate, or take a quick walk or jog—anything that will get your blood flowing and your heart thumping. You're in training for an important event, so eat breakfast with quality protein. Put on your power clothes, grab your lesson plans, and get to school ahead of the early birds. Post the instructions for your first assignment and station yourself in the doorway. Block the doorway so that only one student can enter at a time. When students begin to arrive, look each student in the eye, say, "Welcome to my new, improved classroom," and direct the student to his or her new seat. Don't discuss anything yet. If students ask questions, say, "We'll discuss our new plan later. Right now I'm busy and you need to get started on the assignment that is posted."

12. After everybody is seated, give a specific time to complete the assignment. Collect the assignments without chatting. Then stand still and look around until everybody is quiet. Do not speak until the room is absolutely silent. Tell the students you didn't like the dynamics of your classroom, so you have decided to make some changes. (If you have decided to stop teaching, don't tell them. It's not their business. If they want to know if you are leaving, just tell them that you are still considering different options for your future and that you have a lot of options because you are a college graduate.) From now on, you are going to conduct things differently. You choose the topic of conversation.

Remember to stand up straight, shoulders back, chin high, and plant your feet as you talk. This is one time you want to project your authority and power. If you don't know what to do with your hands, place your right hand over your left wrist and lightly grasp. Let your hands fall naturally in front of your body—or hold them behind you in the middle of your back, as though you were standing at military-style parade rest. This advice comes from a police academy instructor who teaches people to be calmly assertive when dealing with excitable people.

Don't shout, but use your most serious quiet voice. If anybody disrupts your conversation, don't hesitate. Tell them once that you want them to remain seated, be quiet, and listen. If they interrupt again, call your emergency backup. While you wait for your backup to arrive, don't talk; just fill out your referral paperwork. Then just stand and wait silently.

If it takes 5, 10, or 15 minutes for your support person to arrive, keep waiting silently. Students will feel uncomfortable, which is a good thing. They may mumble and whisper or talk out loud, but as long as they don't get out of their seats or start shouting obscenities at you, ignore them. Do not let them dictate your behavior. They have to get the message that you are in charge of your classroom and they will have to respond to your behavior. It's an important distinction.

When your support person arrives, ask him or her to escort your disruptive students to the office. (Any student who is out of his or her seat needs to go to the office along with the escort.) Before they leave, ask your class, "Does anybody else want to go?" Most likely they won't.

After 15 minutes, if nobody shows up to help you, alert the nearest teacher or staff member that you will be gone from your classroom for a few minutes. Then, turn to your disrupter and ask, "Would you like me to escort you to the office, or would you prefer to sit down and cooperate? It's up to you." If the student sits down, say, "Thank you. Good decision." And continue your conversation as though nothing had happened. If the disrupter ignores you or chooses to continue the rude behavior, escort him or her (or them) to the office yourself. Don't make small talk. Just say, "Let's go," and start walking. If a student balks, don't argue; keep walking. Deliver the student and/or the referral to the office. (If the student disappears along the way or lags behind, just deliver the paperwork and let the administration handle it.)

Inform whoever is present—the principal or the principal's secretary—that the student is interfering with your teaching and other students' learning and cannot return to your classroom until you have met with the principal and/or the student's parents. Then get back to your classroom. If your students are seated and reasonably cooperative, apologize for the delay and thank them for waiting. It not, insist that they sit and be quiet before you speak. Wait as long as necessary and look as serious as you can while you're waiting. Then finish your one-way conversation.

Tell your students that you have made some changes to help them be more effective students. Tell them everybody is starting with a clean slate but that *you expect them to conduct themselves with self-control and self-respect.* Give them a long, silent look after you say this. Make sure they get your message. Then start your first new, interesting, challenging lesson. There will definitely be some tension in your classroom, so if you can find an opportunity to inject some humor into that first lesson, so much the better. Humor, especially unexpected humor, is the number-one persuader and a great tension reliever.

There is an excellent chance your students will cooperate—because your unexpected behavior will catch their brains off-guard and the cognitive gears will slip a bit. This will allow you to persuade people to cooperate who might otherwise be difficult to persuade.

Of course, there is always the possibility that you have more than one ringleader in your room. Or several. If your entire class gangs up on you—which occasionally happens—and you end up sending the entire class to the office, one at a time, go ahead and send them. That will get the attention of your administration. (They shouldn't be surprised because you warned them in advance that you needed their help.) Something will happen. Either your administrators will support you or they won't. In the worst case, they may threaten to fire you. But if you have any record at all of asking for support prior to this meltdown and you can prove it, they will probably reconsider. Your union representative will ask why they didn't provide the support you requested. If you truly believe you are going to be fired, you might tender your resignation "for personal reasons" before they have time to complete their paperwork. Even if you do get fired from a teaching job, it doesn't mean you will never get another one. It may be harder to find a job, but not impossible, especially if you stay in the same area where future employers will be well aware of problems in other schools.

This is the plan I designed for my own emergency use. It may not be the perfect plan for you, but it may give you some ideas. Whatever you decide, good luck to you. Teaching can be darn difficult work, but if you make up your mind that you truly want to teach and you persist in trying to improve your skills, I believe your determination and sincerity will lead you in the right direction. It may take you a while. That's just fine. And it's perfectly normal. Even those super teachers at your school had to work at getting it right, although they may like to believe that they are natural-born teachers.

WHAT DO YOU THINK?

1. Articulate your own discipline philosophy in one or two sentences.

2. What classroom rules do you use (or plan to use)? Why these specific rules?

3. When and how should teachers present their classroom rules to students?

4. In small groups or in your journal, describe a time when you were disciplined in school as a child. How did this experience affect your attitude and behavior?

5. Working in small groups, create a good discipline plan for a specific grade level.

The Three Rs: Reading, Reading, Reading

Every teacher is a reading teacher, like it or not. To be successful in school, our students must be able to read well. All advanced academic classes require good reading comprehension; without it, students struggle to succeed. No matter how smart students are, if they can't understand the questions they can't provide the answers. So poor reading translates to poor test scores, regardless of students' intelligence. And although each generation uses more electronic media and less paper, reading isn't going away anytime soon. In fact, the Internet has exponentially increased both the amount of information available and the necessity of possessing good reading comprehension and critical thinking skills to understand, process, and assess the accuracy and credibility of all that new information.

At some future date, speech recognition software may advance to the stage where students will be able to listen more than read, but until that day arrives it is in the best interest of our students and our country to help young people develop their literacy skills to the highest possible degree.

WHAT'S THE PROBLEM?

Children are not born with a natural aversion to reading. When we introduce toddlers to books, they fall in love. They lug their favorites around and caress the pages with their stubby fingers. They gnaw on the edges of those beloved books as though they would like to eat them up. It isn't unusual for a child to request the same bedtime storybook fifty or a hundred times.

Why, then, is reading such a problem for so many elementary and secondary students and their teachers? What turns so many little book lovers into such adamant book haters? Instead of speculating, I went straight to the source—real-life reluctant readers.

My first teaching assignment, while I was still a graduate student, consisted of convincing a class of disenchanted high school sophomores to read and write. The following year, as a newly licensed teacher, I taught two different classes: one a group of limited-English freshmen and the other another group of disenchanted sophomores. The non–English speakers were eager to learn everything, but the sophomores, of mixed ethnic backgrounds but most of native English speakers, hated reading with a passion. And again—no big surprise—their reading skills were even worse than those of my students from the previous year.

How did these kids ever get to high school? I wondered. Didn't anybody notice they can barely read?

One day, I asked, "Who hates reading?" A sea of hands waved wildly, churning up the air with their negativity. We then spent the entire class discussing our feelings about books and reading. We talked about how we learned to read and how we came to love or hate reading. Many of those students admitted that during 9 years of school they had never read a single book.

As I got to know those students better, I found the answer to my original question: How did these kids ever get to high school? I realized how very talented they were at hiding their poor reading skills. Like blind people who develop more acute senses of smell or hearing, those poor readers had developed sharper skills in other areas to compensate. They were expert mimics. They convincingly parroted the comments and opinions of their literate classmates. They were excellent readers of body language, taking their cues from the slightest change in my facial expression or posture. And many of them had such well-developed memorization skills that they could repeat whole reading passages or long lists of definitions from our vocabulary lessons, word for word.

Those nonreaders had tap-danced their way through elementary school, struggled through middle school, and hit a wall at high school. They could no longer fake their way through math because the problems were now too complex and abstract. And even the best memorizers couldn't memorize an entire biology text or a 200-page novel. Suddenly they felt stupid. Even worse, they knew their teachers would think they were stupid. Worst of all, their classmates who did know how to read thought they were stupid and told them so. Understandably, many poor readers choose to nurture reputations as tough kids because there is a sort of negative glamour attached to outlaw behavior. But there's nothing glamorous about being considered too dumb to read.

I worked hard to convince those students that reading was a skill, not a natural-born talent, and that they were capable of learning. I offered the analogies of basketball and dancing, since many of them were NBA hopefuls and most of the girls spent their free time listening to music and practicing complicated dance steps in the back of the room.

"You can't sink a free throw if you never get on the court," I told them. "And you know even Michael Jackson had to practice moon-walking to get it down right." Because we had developed a solid rapport based on mutual respect and trust, those students agreed to give reading one more try. Together we created a new set of expectations and rules about reading. That group of sophomores, by the way, was part of the academy program, a school-within-a-school for underachieving teens where I had the opportunity to work with the same students for their final 3 years of high school. And I am delighted to report that every one of those students eventually passed the standardized reading and math exams required for graduation. Eight students in the first graduating class earned full scholarships to college, and the number of scholarships doubled for the second graduating class. But that's another story.

With each new class (even advanced placement and college classes, because many successful students still dislike reading), I asked the same question: Why do you hate reading? Later, when I began teaching college students, I asked: How did you learn to read? Did you ever enjoy reading? Why do you hate reading now? The same answers cropped up time and again. Following are the most common reasons those students offered to explain their aversion to reading:

1. Reading gives them a headache or makes their eyes hurt.
2. They fear they'll be forced to read aloud and others will laugh.
3. They can't read so fast as their peers and they get left behind.
4. They always get put into the slow group.
5. They are too far behind to ever catch up.
6. They believe they have to finish every reading selection, no matter how long or difficult.
7. They expect to be tested on what they read—and to fail.
8. They have zero interest in the required reading material.
9. They get lost and can't remember what they have just read.
10. If asked for their opinion of a book, they will be wrong.
11. They resent being told what to do all day every day.

WHAT'S THE SOLUTION?

I hope several possible solutions came to mind as you read the list of complaints and fears from those reluctant readers. The following suggestions are simply that—suggestions. Ideally, they will serve as springboards for your own ideas, using feedback from your own students. After all, reading is an individual activity, even if we learn it in groups. So individualizing our methods of reading instruction makes sense.

Reading Causes Headache or Eye Pain

Students who claim that reading makes their heads hurt may have light sensitivity, vision convergence deficiency (double vision), astigmatism, a lazy eye, or some other physical or perceptual problem that makes reading difficult, uncomfortable, or even painful. Here is one specific case in point.

In 2007, the *New York Times* published an article, "Not Autistic or Hyperactive. Just Seeing Double at Times," about a 9-year-old girl with 20/20 vision who refused to read or write. She was tested and retested and prescribed three different drugs for attention-deficit disorder (ADD) and depression. The drugs didn't work, but fortunately a reading specialist suggested an additional eye exam. Bingo!—the optometrist discovered that although the girl had 20/20 vision, she also had convergence insufficiency, which is a fancy way of saying double vision. Her eyes simply couldn't work together at close range. That's an important point: typical eye exams simply test visual acuity (how close you are to 20/20 vision). But when reading is a problem, often there is nothing wrong with a student's visual acuity; it's something else.

The article also stated that experts estimate 5 percent of school-age children have convergence insufficiency, which can cause them to suffer headaches, dizziness, and nausea when they try to read. These symptoms can inhibit their ability to concentrate, which can lead to false diagnoses of ADD or attention-deficit/hyperactivity disorder (ADHD). Dr. David Granet, professor of ophthalmology at the University of California, reported that 10 percent of his young patients with double vision also had been diagnosed with ADHD. However, when he examined the hospital records of 1,700 children, he found that 16 percent of those diagnosed with ADHD also had vision convergence insufficiency.

This story has a happy ending. After several months of wearing special eyeglasses with prisms and undergoing vision therapy, the girl entered fourth grade with the ability to read at grade level. You can read her full story on the *New York Times* Web site (www.nytimes.com/2007/09/11/health/11visi.html).

If you have reluctant readers in your classroom, talk to your students about issues that may make reading difficult. Discuss lazy eyes, amblyopia, astigmatism, and other eye conditions. (Young children often enjoy learning big, scientific words and concepts.) Let them know they are not unique; many people struggle with reading, including adults. Make sure your students understand that reading is a skill, not a measure of their intelligence. Even highly intelligent people may find reading difficult for any number of reasons. The following steps may help you identify those reasons:

- Be alert for visual or perceptual problems. Don't assume the student's defiance or laziness is at fault. And remember that a standard eye test for visual acuity is not enough. Students can have 20/20 vision and still have eye problems.

- Ask students to share their feelings and early experiences with reading. Ask questions to try to determine when their reading problems started. Sometimes, it will be obvious that the issue is psychological—being forced to read before the child was ready to learn, for example, or fear that learning to read alone will mean no more nightly bedtime stories read by a beloved parent. Other times, a student will report fuzzy vision, words moving around, or other physical problems.

- Talk to parents of struggling readers, and suggest a visit to an eye doctor to check for any conditions that may affect reading.

- Take note of any students who squint, rub their eyes, hunch over their books, or complain of headaches or stomachaches when reading. These are signs of light sensitivity.

- Provide at least one area where students can read under natural daylight or regular incandescent lighting. If your classroom has no natural daylight, find a sheltered outdoor area, a library with large windows, or an indoor atrium where students can read.

- Allow students to experiment with transparent colored overlays that may help students who lose their place frequently or who find reading uncomfortable.

- Find out if your school has a counselor trained to detect scotopic sensitivity syndrome. (See Chapter 8 for more detailed information on this topic.) If so, ask the counselor to explain light sensitivity to your students. Find out your school's procedure for requesting that students be tested.

- Talk to other teachers and classroom aides. Sometimes students have dyslexia and light sensitivity, for example. In that case, the interventions for dyslexia may not work until the light sensitivity is addressed.

- Ask your school custodians to provide full-spectrum fluorescent lighting for your classroom—or for at least one section.

- Be alert for new research on what is being termed *vision therapy* or developmental optometry. An August 2004 news release from the College of Optometrists in Vision Development (www.covd.org) reported that "because symptoms may be quite similar, visual disorders caused by faulty skill patterns may be misdiagnosed as learning disability or ADHD." The article goes on to say that students who fail to respond to ADHD medication can sometimes experience dramatic improvement with vision therapy. To read more about vision therapy for problem readers, visit www.vision3d.com.

They Fear They'll Be Forced to Read Aloud and Others Will Laugh

When teachers require students to take turns reading aloud in class, good readers don't mind. But most students begin counting paragraphs, trying to figure out what and when they will have to read. Cognitive function decreases when anxiety increases. Learning stops. The whole point of the reading assignment is now lost.

My suggestion? Make reading aloud purely voluntary. Give students the option of reading to you silently so you can assess their skills and progress. Allowing students to opt out of reading aloud will improve attendance, punctuality, and morale in your classroom. When students volunteer to read, don't allow other kids to laugh at mistakes. Beware the sneaky snickers. If you ask students to read aloud in your classroom, you owe it to them to make sure nobody shames or humiliates them for trying. If you have shy or timid students who never volunteer, work with them individually until they develop the confidence to read aloud. (Some kids will never volunteer, but that doesn't mean they aren't learning—and at least you won't have made them dread reading.)

If you call on students to read aloud as a way of keeping them awake, you could call on a willing volunteer who is seated next to your drowsy or daydreaming student. When his classmate begins to read, the daydreamer will tune back in without feeling embarrassed or hostile.

And, finally, if you require students to read out loud simply because your own teachers required you to read out loud, I urge you to find some of your classmates who hated reading and ask how they felt. Most teachers enjoy reading. We don't know how it feels to hate reading so much that we are willing to jeopardize our grades or cut classes to avoid reading out loud. We need to have more empathy if we truly want to help our struggling readers.

They Can't Read as Fast as Their Peers

Because the imprint of the first experience with reading makes such an impact for so many years, I encourage elementary school teachers and reading instructors to allow students to read at their own pace, even if it means that slower students don't cover as much ground as quicker classmates. Parents repeatedly ask me to tutor young children whose teachers claim that a learning disability prevents the children from learning to read. Invariably, the real problem turns out to be speed. Those children simply can't read at the fast rate their classmates do. But when they are allowed to read at their own individual pace, they do learn to read. Here are just one example among many from my own experience.

A precocious 8-year-old boy with an impressive vocabulary sat down across the table from me on our first session and announced, "I'm the second dumbest kid in my class." When I asked him how he knew this, he said that the teacher posted their grades on the wall. I said I didn't believe the teacher would post their grades and names. He said, "She didn't put the names. They're in alphabetical order, and I figured out which one was me. I'm the second dumbest."

His solution to the problem was to demonstrate his intelligence by reading faster than everybody else in class. Unfortunately, in his haste he skipped so many words that he had zero reading comprehension. After I convinced him to slow down, which took several weeks because he was determined to be the fastest instead of the dumbest, his reading skills improved quickly, and within a few months his grades improved to the point where he no longer needed tutoring.

Tennessee reading teacher Vicki Cline graciously agreed to critique this chapter. She filled me in on the speed problem that plagues so many young readers. Cline says that some children become confused after taking the DIBELS reading test, in which they are instructed to read as quickly as possible and still maintain 90 percent comprehension. That makes perfect sense because even now, working with teens, students assure me they understand the criteria for a specific assignment—but later on, I realize they didn't fully understand. So it makes sense that young children would remember just the fast part of the instructions and form the impression that they were to read as fast as possible all of the time.

Since reading really is the cornerstone of academic success, we have to take special care to pinpoint the cause of reading problems, and the responsibility doesn't rest with reading teachers. We need to work together when we see a student struggling. Otherwise, some of those students will completely lose confidence or become behavior problems. And some poor little people will become victims of psychosomatic illnesses that literally make them sick when they have to face another day in the classroom. My youngest brother is a good example. He often vomited in the mornings before school because reading was such a traumatic experience for him. Nobody in the family realized he couldn't read because the rest of us were all voracious readers. We just thought he preferred to play outdoors. When my older sister and I finally identified his problem and worked together to help him learn to read, his illnesses gradually disappeared as his grades rose from failing to above average.

They Always Get Put into the Slow Group

I have a theory based not on research and statistics but on thousands of conversations with students and teachers across the country. Since those conversations, I have come to believe that our first experience with reading influences our perceptions of our intelligence even as adults. Here's why. If you ask adults, "Do you consider yourself above average, about average, or below average?" most of them have a clear picture of where they fall on the intelligence spectrum. But what I find most interesting is that when I ask those same adults how old they were when they formed their opinions of their own intelligence, nearly all agree that they decided how smart they were during the first few years of school, when they were learning to read. Call them bluebirds and sparrows, stars and stripes, bears and bobcats, children always know who are the fast readers (translate smart kids) and who are the slow readers (translate dumb kids). They know exactly where they fall on the reading-speed spectrum, and they believe this correlates to intelligence. Most of them will believe for the rest of their lives that they are smart or dumb or average depending on how quickly and well they learned to read.

If teachers can find a way to group students that doesn't depend on their reading ability at least some of the time, I think they may avoid the situation where students correlate their intelligence to their reading group. Better yet, teachers can create classroom environments where students sincerely want to help each other and don't tease or torment the slower students. Sometimes students who process information slowly turn out to have much higher IQs than fast processors. Finding ways for slow readers to shine in other areas can help all students understand that there are multiple forms of intelligence.

Two years ago, in one of my courses for future teachers, I asked students to write about their memories of learning to read. Emily's journal entry almost made me cry:

> My teacher separated the class into three reading groups by skill level. Although the groups were given nonjudgmental bird names, it was quite clear that my group, the robins, were the lowest … My group of robins were forced to read a series of unimaginative low-level books. All of these books were stored in an old, dusty box and had to be read in order. They all had yellow covers, and the illustrations were no more than simple black-and-white figures. The high-level cardinals, however, were allowed to choose any book in the room to read, including

the beautiful storybooks on the shelves in the back of the room. I saw these as the "smart kid" books and wanted desperately to read them. One book in particular caught my eye—a book of poetry with colorful pictures of fairies and forests. One day while the teacher was busy with another group, I snuck to the back of the room and pulled this book from the shelf. I was so engrossed in reading I didn't notice the teacher coming up behind me. I was punished for reading the wrong kind of book; she embarrassed me in front of the class and created an even more negative reading experience. I have been angry with Mrs. R. for years for making me hate reading so much, but looking back on the experience now from a teacher's perspective she did have her hands full with a large class. I was later diagnosed with dyslexia and moved to a private school where a special program taught me the skills I needed to excel in reading and in other subjects.

Surely this teacher was the exception and not the rule. I have met hundreds of reading teachers, and they are a compassionate lot. I shared this student journal with you not because I believe most reading teachers punish students for reading the wrong books but because it shows how clearly students remember their first experiences as readers, down to the color of the books and the dust on the covers. We owe it to our students to introduce them to books and reading in the gentlest, most encouraging manner. And we must never forget that we are creating future memories in our classrooms every day.

They Are Too Far Behind to Ever Catch Up

When students read below grade level, they don't understand that increasing their skills to the next level won't take a full calendar year. A ninth grader whose test score places him at fourth-grade level, for example, often thinks he will run out of time before he can catch up with his peers. So first we must explain that a grade level in reading doesn't correspond to a calendar year. It is just a measure of how well a student reads a specific level of complexity in vocabulary and sentence structure. Encourage students to learn how to derive the meaning of unfamiliar words from the context of a sentence and to practice reading every day to improve their reading rate.

One method I have used successfully is to photocopy a one-to-two-page-long generic magazine article or selection from a textbook. I distribute copies of the pages and ask students not to begin reading until my signal. When I say, "Begin," everybody starts reading. They read for 1 minute until I say, "Stop." They circle the last word they read. Then I teach them how to count the words on a page without counting every single word. Count the number of words in four individual lines, and then add the numbers and divide by four to get the average number of words per line. Then the students count how many lines they read, multiply that by the average, and get a word count for 1 minute. They write that number down in the margin, and I collect the papers. We put the reading-rate papers away for a month.

At the end of the month, we read the same reading-rate selection again and see how many words we have read. Students will nearly always improve if they have been making an effort in class. This shows them that practice doesn't make perfect, but it certainly makes improvement. We file those papers away, and after another month we try again with a new selection. We use a selection two or three times and then change it when it starts to sound familiar.

They Believe They Have to Finish Everything

One of the quickest ways to discourage poor readers from becoming good readers is to make them finish reading things they hate. Have you ever brought home a stack of books from the library and then opted not to finish one or two because they just weren't as good as you thought they would be? Or did you ever put down a book halfway through and never go back to it because it just wasn't compelling enough to compete with the other activities in your life? I'm betting you occasionally fail to finish something you start. That's why I suggest letting reluctant readers stop reading things they hate. Not forever. Just until they become good enough readers that reading isn't a dreaded chore. A challenge is good, but an impossible task is not. Forcing people who don't read well to finish reading materials that are too far above their ability level or that have no relevance for them turns reading into a chore instead of a means of gaining information or being entertained.

Once students become good readers, they are more willing to read assigned materials. Good readers will tackle anything because they know that although sometimes reading requires real effort, they will be rewarded by gaining a new perspective, acquiring new knowledge, encountering an exciting but unfamiliar idea, experiencing a brain tickle, entering a completely new world, or simply enjoying the satisfaction of having conquered a difficult mental challenge. Poor readers don't experience those rewards, so you cannot convince them that reading is enjoyable until they learn to read well enough to forget that they are reading.

This suggestion may go against your teacherly grain, but I urge you to consider it: promise your students that you will expect them to read half of any article, novel, nonfiction book, essay, story, or dramatic play that you give to them. At the halfway point, you will take a vote by show of hands to see whether the majority of your class wants to finish the given selection. If more than half of the students vote against the reading material, put it away. Allow students to finish it on their own if they choose, but do not pursue the reading as a class. Ask students to write a critique of the selection, to figure out why they didn't like it—so they don't think all they have to do is vote no and the reading will go away. To the contrary, if we stop reading one thing, we immediately begin reading something else.

I still use the same policy now, teaching advanced placement high school students. Of course, when I announce the read-half policy, students always grin and warn me that we aren't ever going to finish anything because they are going to vote it down. "Especially Shakespeare," they say. But I have never had a class, regardless of how much they hate reading, who voted to discontinue reading *The Taming of the Shrew, Othello,* or *The Merchant of Venice.* (I will discuss my approach to teaching Shakespeare later in this chapter.)

Once in a while, a group will vote down everything, just to be obnoxious. In that case I assign a really long and difficult reading assignment so that by the time they reach the halfway mark they are more than willing to read any short selection I offer.

They Expect to Be Tested—and to Fail

I know, I know, testing is important, especially today. So give the standardized tests when you have to. But if you have the choice between testing students about their reading or giving them an opportunity to honestly respond to their reading, go for the honest response. There will be plenty of time for testing once your students improve their reading skills and their self-confidence as readers.

Even at the college level, there are always a few reluctant readers in any group. They sometimes skip important reading assignments if they believe they won't be tested or required to write about or discuss the reading. Some teachers design quizzes to "catch" those students. That method works, but it doesn't motivate reluctant readers; it makes them even less inclined to read because their prediction has come true. They read something; they take a test. We can motivate many more students to read—at any age level—if we change our approach. We can still create assignments and activities that students won't be able to complete if they don't read, but we can design them differently so that they engage students in the reading instead of testing them.

In my opinion, the best way to overcome the read-and-test cycle is to break it completely. Read a few short things as a class. After each one, open the floor to comments. Ask, "So, what do you think about that?" Accept every comment as valuable. If nobody comments, say, "Well, let's let that one percolate for a while." And move on to the next activity. Let your students see that reading isn't a chore, a competition, or a test. It's a lifelong skill that we use to gain information, find a new perspective, and tickle our brains or our funny bones. As one of my former students wisely pointed out, "You don't have to discuss the crap out of everything you read. Some things you just read. That's it."

I'm not suggesting abandoning tests or assessments, just changing the format. For example, when reading as a whole group, we can stop and ask students to jot down their response to a single question about the reading assignment—Which of the characters is the most honest? Why in the world did he do what he did? What would you have done in that situation?—and give them credit based on the amount of thought and effort devoted to the answer instead of whether the answer is correct. Following this up with a quick discussion will give all of the students an opportunity to hear what other people think about the reading without putting them on the spot. This teaches them how to analyze a text without realizing they are learning. It will feel to them like you are just talking about the book.

Another option is to divide students into small groups and give them a set of questions to discuss about the reading assignment. Those students who didn't read won't be able to participate. Circulate the room and listen in on the group discussions. A few minutes into the activity, you might interrupt and announce, "It seems that some people didn't get a chance to do the reading. That will make it hard for you to contribute to the discussion. So everybody who didn't do the reading, please join me over here and we'll do a quick skim and discuss." Students who didn't complete the reading will now have to sit with the teacher and read, definitely more work than discussing your opinions with your peers. But then again, some students may welcome the opportunity to engage in some guided reading and discussion with the teacher because that will give them a chance to discover the right answers. Either way, you have a very different classroom dynamic from one in which you test and fail the students who struggle with reading.

They Have Zero Interest in Required Reading

Scholars can be enticed to read anything to analyze and evaluate it; poor readers, struggling readers, and students who are still in the process of developing good critical thinking skills are harder to convince. But struggling readers will blossom if you give them material that is so interesting they can't resist reading it. That's the trick: finding something so compelling that students forget they are reading.

You may have to abandon textbooks for a bit, even if they do contain interesting stories. Textbooks by definition are not interesting. (I sometimes make copies of a story or poem from the textbook and distribute it to students who enjoy it and are surprised to learn after the fact that it was in their textbook all along.)

Find some compelling magazine articles about people the same age as your students. Check anthologies for essays on controversial subjects such as gun control or immigration. Look online for true crime and sports stories and articles on topics of interest to young people—how to be popular, find a friend, get into college, or choose a pet, for example.

As you search for materials, keep in mind that boys often hate fiction. Many grown men prefer nonfiction as well. Check out the bookstore aisles. You'll find more men in the biography, science, military history, and do-it-yourself sections than in the literature stacks. Perhaps they simply cannot or will not suspend their disbelief long enough to become engaged in something that isn't real (unless it is science fiction). But boys will read nonfiction—about bugs, dinosaurs, race cars, sports, spaceships, and dragons. If you allow children who dislike fiction to read nonfiction until they become good readers, they will be better able and more inclined to read fiction when you ask them to. Once they can read more easily, you will have done far more than help them improve their reading skills. You will have taught them that books can be enjoyable.

One activity that I've used with good success is the book exchange. I get a number of books from the public or school library on a wide array of topics, from spaceships to teen romance novels to horror stories. Then I place an index card and a book on each student's desk before class begins. Students read the books on their desks for 3 minutes, give the book a rating of one to ten on the index card, and pass their book to another student. They read for another 3 minutes and then rate the books. They repeat this until they have read at least five books. If they like a particular book, they can keep it. Students who don't like any of the books continue to exchange until they find something they like. Some students may have to spend a class period (or two) in the library before they locate something irresistible.

If stubborn students refuse to find something simply to avoid reading, you'll be able to tell. In that case, provide a book and insist that they read it for one session. Tell them that if they can't find something, you'll continue to provide different books for them. When they realize that they are going to have to read sooner or later, they will find a book. They may still dislike reading, but if they choose the book there is a better chance they may enjoy reading once their skills improve.

They Get Lost and Can't Remember What They Have Just Read

Unfortunately, many students can read quite well without understanding what they are reading. They somehow missed the important idea that when we read we must create some kind of mental reference. Without that reference, words are just words. One boy described his experience this way: "It's like I'm reading one of those signs in front of the bank where the letters move. As soon as I read the words, they disappear."

You don't have to be a reading teacher to give students some basic pointers on reading comprehension. First, explain that when we read we create a mental picture of what we are reading. As we add details, the picture becomes sharper or changes to adjust to new information. If you lose the picture when you are reading, you are starting to lose your comprehension. Back up until you can see the picture again, and continue reading. You can demonstrate this with a story or article. Read a paragraph, ask students what they see, and discuss their different visions. This will help students who still don't get it. Read the next paragraph and stop again to ask students to describe their mental pictures. When I do this with a class, some students become very excited because they finally (some for the first time) understand what all the fuss is about and why some people enjoy reading. This exercise works far better than simply asking questions to check their comprehension after they have read a selection.

If you have Internet access in your class, consider showing a short animated video from RSA.org (Royal Society for Advancement of the Arts). Its videos, called blogs, show an artist sketching as the narrator explains a particular topic. The drawing takes place in fast-forward so it keeps up with the narrative. It's an excellent way to show students what you mean by creating a mental picture as you read.

If you detect serious comprehension problems, or if a student asks for more help, find out if your school has a reading specialist on the staff or as a regular visitor. Also, look for good Web sites devoted to reading. Do an Internet search for "free online reading instruction." You will find a plethora of books, articles, exercises, games, and instructional materials.

If Asked for Their Opinion, It Will Be Wrong

So many students—most with tears in their eyes—have told me about the same experience: a teacher asked them to write their opinion about a book or story. The students worked hard on their essays and expected high marks for effort and content. Their teachers assigned either a D or F with no explanation or wrote some insulting comment such as "Wrong!" or "This is ridiculous!" in red ink across the top of the paper. In other words, their opinions are worthless.

If you ask for an opinion, accept what you get and grade the writing on composition and content—not on whether the student agrees with your opinion. Sometimes young people simply aren't able to appreciate things we think they should appreciate. Instead of belittling them or lowering their grades when they don't, reward their honest effort and encourage them to develop their ideas logically and completely. If you allow your students to maintain their dignity and self-respect, they will continue to progress. With advancing maturity and practice, their reading and writing skills will improve and they will be better able to appreciate literature that demands a more sophisticated mentality.

Once they have a bit more confidence, you can teach your students the difference between a personal opinion (*I don't like stories where animals get killed*) and an academic critique (*The characters in this story are unbelievable*). First, teach them how to analyze the reading selections and articulate their personal opinions about what they are reading. Even little children will have an opinion about whether a story is interesting, informative, or exciting; whether characters are good or bad; whether descriptions paint vivid pictures; and whether the ending satisfies the reader. Prompt your students with questions: Why do they dislike certain stories and books? Is the vocabulary too hard? Can they give some examples of difficult vocabulary words? Are the sentences too long and complex or too short and choppy? Are the characters unlikable or unrealistic? Where does the plot become unbelievable? Is the pace of the story too slow or fast? Is it hard to tell who is talking?

When students can intelligently articulate their opinions, they are ready to learn how to analyze a story on its literary merits. Now students must use specific references to the material to make their point, using specific vocabulary and terms that you have taught them. It may be helpful to teach these two different critical approaches as the personal versus the professional response to a book or story. You can personally like a book that you know isn't really written very well (characters are one-dimensional and the plot is predictable) just as you can dislike a book that you know meets all the criteria for a well-written book (symbolism, great plot, and so on). The key to success—in school, at least—is to learn the criteria the experts use to evaluate books.

And one last thing that I think is very important to teach students who struggle to write acceptable literary critiques in school: once you get out of school, you can think whatever you like about any book, and nobody can give you a grade on your opinions. People can disagree with you all they like, but there's no report card in real life. You'll get to be the judge and the jury for all the books you read—or don't read.

They Resent Being Told What to Do

This is a personal issue, not a reading issue, but it often spills over into reading, so teachers can waste a lot of time and energy trying to win the battle of wills. Sometimes it can be difficult for people who enjoy reading (most teachers are book lovers) to empathize with people who don't. And many teachers worry about lowering academic standards. I'm suggesting not that we lower standards but that we focus first on why our students don't want to read instead of on ways to convince or force them to read. In some cases, nonreaders simply need to assert their independence. They will resist our efforts to make them do anything, especially reading. In other cases, people have been taught through experience to hate reading. I liken people's attitudes about books to their attitudes about such things as dogs, horses, broccoli, or sex. If the first experience was enjoyable, people tend to look forward to future encounters. But if that first experience was traumatic, painful, or shameful, many people find it hard to forget. And if that painful first experience was followed by an equally uncomfortable third or fourth encounter, people understandably develop deep-seated aversions to specific activities.

If you work to establish good relationships with your reluctant readers before you ask them to read, you'll find them much more willing to work at things they don't enjoy. If you are thinking, "I don't have time for such nonsense," consider the amount of time you waste on arguing with students or on discipline issues that arise from them not wanting to work. The time you spend creating a classroom environment where students feel motivated to cooperate will come back to you tenfold.

ONE TEACHER'S EXPERIENCE

I'd like to share an excerpt from a post on the discussion board of an online course I taught at Santa Fe Community College. All the students in the course were college graduates pursuing their teaching credentials. One assignment asked the future teachers to share their own early experiences of learning to read. This student does an excellent job of articulating her feelings as a child, and her testimony reinforces the truth that many school memories stay with us forever. Sadly, this woman is one of many students who reported similar experiences. My hope is that by sharing her thoughts, you will be inspired to find ways to make reading enjoyable for all your students.

> When I took a look at the discussion post required for this class, I decided to skip it. I felt nervous and wanted no part of this idea—it just made me feel like that kid who couldn't read again. I remember my own experience of learning to read. It was awful and reading was difficult for me. When I would read out loud in class I was made fun of when I mispronounced a word. I remember dripping sweat, my heart racing, and just wanting to run out the door. This took place in elementary and middle school and part of high school. I had to attend a reading class when I was younger. I never felt like the reading class helped me, but we had fun. That teacher just passed me. I felt so stupid at the time that I began to believe I was dumb like the other kids would tell me. This still hits me hard because no person should go through that kind of treatment.
>
> Whenever a teacher would make us read out loud, I would ask to go to the bathroom. I would go for 10 or 15 minutes and complain of a stomachache. I started to find all the tricks to get out of class. My freshman year in high school in my religion class the teacher wanted us to read out loud every time. I can remember freezing a lot when I read out loud. I never asked my parents for help. I still don't know why—my mother was a teacher. I just wanted my reading problem to go away.
>
> When I got to St. Francis College (NY) I decided to challenge myself and take psychology as my major because I knew I had to read a lot of textbooks and write papers. I pushed every day to show myself I was

a smart person. How bad is that? I'm in college and I have to prove to myself I'm an intelligent student? That's how I felt.

I became an avid reader about the age of 25; I began reading a lot of good books. I still can't pronounce some words but look at the dictionary for help. Honestly I wish a never had this problem. Now that I have started teaching, I have not had the chance to motivate reluctant readers. I just work with ESL students. I don't like the idea of having kids read out loud—not unless the student reading wants to read to classmates and has a nice, clear and loud voice. When you force students to read you can tell by the way they sound that they want no part of class.

USE MUSIC TO INTRODUCE POETRY

Because so many students are prejudiced against poetry for one reason or another, I like to sneak in the back door with a little rhythm and rhyme. I feel compelled to share with teachers that the producers of the movie *Dangerous Minds* took some liberties when they portrayed my poetry-reading approach. Yes, I did use song lyrics, but not Bob Dylan's "Tambourine Man." Instead, I typed out the words to the Public Enemy rap song "911 Is a Joke," Smokey Robinson's "Tears of a Clown," a translation of the Hispanic folk song "Guantanamera," and the Garth Brooks hit "We Shall Be Free." When my students walked into class, I distributed the lyrics without saying anything.

"What's this?" they asked.

"Something I think is interesting," I said. After a few minutes, one of the kids said, "Hey, I know this song." Several private conversations sprang up around the room. Finally, somebody said, "Hey, Miss J, how come you gave us these songs?"

"I wanted to know if you think they are poetry," I said. (I love it when the kids play right along with my script.)

"Poetry?" a few kids mumbled. They shrugged and looked at each other. "Is this poetry?"

"You tell me," I insisted. "You know what a poem is, don't you?"

"Yeah," they said. "Poems rhyme."

"They got rhythm too," somebody else interjected.

"Right. Poems have rhythm or rhyme and sometimes both," I said. I held up the lyrics sheet. "So is this poetry?"

"You're the teacher," one girl said. "You tell us if it's poetry."

"You're the student," I said. "You tell me. Take your time. Think about it. Feel free to discuss it among yourselves. I'll wait." And I sat down with a very patient look on my face.

After a few minutes, one of the boys ventured a tentative "I think they're poems. They all have music, and music has rhythm. And most of them rhyme."

"I agree," I said. "I think many song lyrics are poetic, and the best songs are very good poetry. And I'm going to give you the opportunity to bring in your favorite song lyrics to share with the class. But there is one condition. You will need to explain to the class why you admire your particular song choice as good poetry."

"That's it?" a boy asked. "We just have to say why it's a good poem?"

"Yes," I said. "Of course, you'll have to learn to talk about poetry." A few kids frowned, but before they could voice the suspicion that they had been had once again, I launched into my introductory lesson on onomatopoeia. Slam! Bam! Pow! Ping! Before they knew what had hit them, those students were reading poetry.

I'd like to share with you the results of that poetry experiment with those antireading students. Everybody in that class, including me, expressed very distinct preferences for music. Before we started that project, I dismissed the idea that any student could find a poetic heavy metal song, but somebody did. And students who claimed they hated rap or country found themselves responding to the lyrics of songs when we read them without hearing the music. We discovered that it was often the beat we disliked, not the song itself. Students from very disparate backgrounds realized that they shared common emotions and dreams. Also we learned that filthy, disgusting, racist, sexist, or violence-promoting songs can't be passed off as good poetry. One young man (an angry young man who usually sat with his arms crossed and his mouth clamped shut) brought in a rap song filled with profanity and obscenities. Instead of dismissing his song choice, I asked him to tell me what he admired about that particular song as poetry.

"I like the beat," he said.

"We aren't looking just for good beats," I said. "We're looking for really fine words in this project. Which words in this song do you really admire as good poetry? Can you show me some internal rhyme or a metaphor? Maybe some alliteration?"

He frowned at the lyrics he had scribbled on a sheet of notebook paper. "Well, I don't really like the words that much," he admitted. "But it has a really good beat."

"Then you need to find another song with words that you do admire," I said. The following day he brought another song. It wasn't exactly the kind of song parents would appreciate, but it wasn't vulgar and obscene—and he actually participated in the project.

Two amazing things occurred after we completed that poetry project. First, my students didn't protest when I announced that we would be moving on to our textbooks to analyze and discuss classic poetry, including Shakespearean sonnets. Clearly, because they had analyzed and evaluated so many songs and original poems, they felt confident of their ability to tackle any poetry they might meet.

The second amazing thing was that my belligerent, pugnacious, disenchanted students unanimously elected "We Shall Be Free" as the best poetry of all the songs we read, which made me realize that instead of being amoral, apathetic young rebels, they were idealistic and hopeful children desperately in need of good adult leadership. For those who are unfamiliar with the song, here are the phrases that my students voted as best poetry:

When the last child cries for a crust of bread
When the last man dies for just words that he said
When the last thing we notice is the color of skin
and the first thing we look for is the beauty within ...
... then we shall be free.

SHAKESPEARE FOR EVERYONE

Before we begin reading Shakespeare, I always ask, "What do you know about Bill?" Students laugh—until I say his last name. Then the groans and moans begin.

"It's boring" and "It's too hard" are the most frequent comments. So I promise my students that they won't be bored and that if they will open their minds they will find out that reading Shakespeare isn't so hard. It's like learning Pig Latin or any other code. I also promise that after we have read exactly half of the first play, we will take a class vote. If the majority of the students want to stop, we will close the books and move on to something else—without any penalty—although I will ask for their reasons for not wanting to continue and we will not watch the movie version. (Before they begin, they always vow to quit reading halfway through, but I have never had a class that actually opted to quit; students always want to know the ending because William tells a good tale.)

Why should they have to read plays by another "boring, dead, White guy" from the boring old literary canon? Because aside from the fact that he was a White guy and he is dead, he was an intensely talented and prolific writer. Quotations from Shakespeare appear in so many aspects of world culture that being unfamiliar with his works puts students at a disadvantage in society. (Fickle men are often referred to as Romeos, for example; and speech makers often begin by saying, "Friends, Romans, countrymen, lend me your ears.") In addition, every college student in the United States and Europe is expected to have read at least a few plays and sonnets at some time during high school if they expect to be considered well educated.

After I first mention Shakespeare to the class, I wait a week or so. Then one day I write several backward-style sentences on the board: "Where goest thou after class? He thinks to woo the fair maiden. 'Twere better, methinks, to run than to tarry." I ask my students to figure out the sentences and to try to write more of their own to get them used to interpreting an entire phrase rather than word by word. Then I make a short glossary of words from the upcoming play, such as *marry, tarry, prithee, hence, 'tis,* and *whence*. (Students always raise a delighted ruckus when we get to the word *ho*.) We make a poster of the glossary and keep it on the wall for reference.

The Art Part

Next comes the art part, to pull in the visual learners. On the board or on a large piece of paper I sketch a scene like the one in Figure 7.1 to represent the play and the main characters. If we are reading *The Taming of the Shrew*, I draw the two sisters, one smiling and one frowning, and the suitors standing in the street. Petruchio is about to enter town on horseback from one direction, while Lucentio and Tranio enter from the opposite direction.

Note to the artistically challenged: As you can see, I never learned how to draw in perspective. Bad art is actually good in the classroom because students love to improve on my drawings. Sometimes students discover new talents as they try to teach me to draw a horse or a castle.

The Ground Rules

Before we begin reading, I post the Rules for Reading Shakespeare:

1. Nobody is required to read out loud.
2. Nobody has to participate in discussions.

3. Points will not be deducted for quiet listening. Points will be deducted for sleeping, laughing at people who volunteer to read, or disrupting the class during reading or discussions.

4. To earn a passing grade for the unit, students must remain seated upright, awake, with books open to the page that we are currently reading. They must pay attention and ask questions if they become lost. And they must listen quietly, even if they choose not to take notes.

The Opening Curtain

We begin slowly. I explain the basic setup of the play. Then I read the first few lines and stop to paraphrase them. I read a scene, trying to add drama by using different voices for the characters. After a short while, I stop and ask students to help me out by reading a part. If nobody volunteers, I continue to read, stopping frequently to sum up the action. Occasionally I read an entire act by myself before students feel confident enough to try reading aloud.

In the beginning we do not spend the entire class period reading Shakespeare. We read one or two scenes, discuss them briefly, then go on to something different.

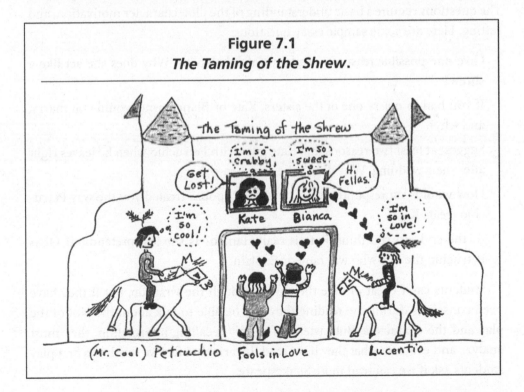

Figure 7.1
The Taming of the Shrew.

After we finish reading one act, we make a set of class notes. I ask students to state in one or two phrases the most important things that occurred in each scene. When we have finished reading the play, they have a complete outline of the plot, and I allow them to use their plot outlines during the post-reading questions. (Those students who opt not to take notes are not permitted to copy other people's notes at the last minute. I don't force them to take notes, but I remind them that if they don't take notes they won't have notes on hand when the questions begin. By the time we have read the second act, the holdouts have usually joined the note takers.)

If students seem to be really trying, I sometimes show a brief segment of the movie, just the first scene of Act I, to give them a preview of coming attractions. This is especially helpful for motivating visual learners, and it helps everybody "see" what the play is about.

The Final Curtain

When we finish the play, we watch the movie version if one is available. Then each student writes an essay response to the play. (I call them journals because some students think *essay* is a dirty word.) They choose two of five questions I provide. The questions require a basic understanding of the plot, character motivation, and setting. Here are some sample essay questions:

Give one possible reason to explain Kate's behavior. Why does she act like a shrew?

If you had to marry one of the sisters, Kate or Bianca, who would you marry, and why?

Suggest at least two reasons that Kate goes with Petruchio when he leaves right after their wedding. Why didn't she refuse to go?

How would you respond if your newlywed spouse treated you the way Petruchio treats Kate?

At the end, do you think Kate is really tamed? Is she just pretending? Or is Petruchio the one who was tamed? Explain.

Students can't cheat or fake their way through the wrap-up, but if they have been conscious during the reading they will be able to talk about the plot of the play and the characters. But instead of simply recalling information, they must analyze and evaluate what they have read. Invariably, after we finish the first play students ask if we can read more Shakespeare.

Reading Shakespeare this way takes more time, at least the first few times, but the payoff is huge. Students learn that Shakespeare is accessible and that the quality of his writing makes the effort worthwhile; most important of all, students who lack confidence in their reading skills learn that they are not stupid and can indeed read what the smart kids read. It's not unusual after reading the first play to hear students trying to use old Shakespeare talk in their conversations. "Check out Tyrone—he be wooing the fair Tyeisha." Because my postreading assignments focus on understanding the characters and their motivation along with student evaluation and analysis, students finish each play feeling that they have reviewed the play rather than being tested on it; methinks that difference be a huge one.

WHAT ABOUT EAGER READERS?

Much of my advice is based on working with reluctant readers because most teachers struggle with at least one or two students who hate reading. But good readers can also be a challenge in their own way. Advanced placement and gifted students often have strong feelings about reading and how it should be done in school. For example, some students love to read aloud in class only if they are the one doing the reading. They can't tolerate hearing another person's voice competing with the one in their head, or having to read at somebody else's pace that is faster or slower than their own. They may resent being rushed—or expected to slow down and wait for slower processors.

My standard practice for any class is to provide a short survey sometime during the first days of school. Questions include: Do you like to read aloud? Do you like to listen to others read aloud? Do you prefer to have the teacher read difficult passages aloud, or do you like the challenge of reading them on your own? After each question, I give the options of checking yes, no, sometimes, or no preference. If I find that I have students who can't stand listening to other people read, I give them the option of doing their reading in the corner, in the library, or wearing a headset to play music that drowns out the other voices in the room. Sometimes I assign students to work in pairs or small groups to read and analyze a particular story, a scene from a play, a novel chapter, or a nonfiction article. After a given time period, we gather as a group to discuss our findings and opinions.

One popular activity I have used with high school students from freshman to senior is the short story project. I select four or five grade-appropriate short stories of varying degrees of difficulty and complexity. Usually, I include some stories from our literature textbook and some handouts from recent literary journals. Students have the option of working in pairs or groups of three. (If there is a Lone Ranger in the class, he or she can opt to work alone.) For one recent group of advanced placement seniors, I chose five stories by Tobias Wolff ("Smokers," "Powder," "Say Yes," "Hunters in the Snow," and "Bullet in the Brain"). The feedback from that class was unanimously positive.

Before we begin the project, I provide a written assignment sheet that outlines the individual and group tasks. Students must read each story and keep a journal where they jot down their personal responses and ideas about each story—to be used later when they will write a two- to three-page analysis of one of the stories. Each team must discuss all the stories, sharing their personal notes, and determine which story they think is the best. They must develop their own criteria for judging the stories, identifying at least three key elements of a good short story. They apply their own criteria to choose the winning story. Then, they must create a visual representation of their evaluation (a rubric, poster, pie chart, graph, or slide show) to explain how they picked their winner. One or more people from the group must present their findings to the class. Following the presentations, students write their critical analysis. Then, they complete a feedback sheet on which they rate their own performance and contribution to the team project, summarize what they learned from the project, and what changes they would make if they could go back and correct any errors they made or procedures that didn't work as well as they had planned.

Recently, a class of twenty-six sophomores completed the story project. Some of the end results were disappointing to the students. They had trouble putting their ideas on paper. But we made learning from our mistakes part of the project. In the end, every student in that class could discuss each one of the stories intelligently and articulately. We judged the project an overall success.

AND NOW FOR SOMETHING COMPLETELY DIFFERENT

One elementary school teacher told me about a boy in her class who cooperated with all her instructions but still couldn't seem to read. After vision tests and hearing tests and all kinds of interventions, she and the counselors were still stumped.

Upside-Down Did the Trick

"One day I decided to turn his book upside down," the teacher said. "I don't know why. It just occurred to me. And—bingo—he started reading. He had some kind of visual processing disorder or something. I never did quite understand, but he learned to read upside down. And later on, he turned the book around and started reading right-side up."

Reading upside down is a good example of a teacher using one of the most readily available and important resources any teacher can tap into—your own brain. Don't be afraid to try something just because it seems silly. When you run into a problem that seems unsolvable, brainstorm every conceivable idea you can come up with. (The hardest part about brainstorming, as you know, is resisting the natural temptation to judge.) Brainstorm with another teacher—or with students. You never know when you're going to hit on an idea that works. And even if it works for just one student, that's still a huge contribution to that student's life and education and tends to have a ripple effect. If you teach a student something that changes his or her life for the better, that positive change will affect the student's family.

The Read Right Approach

At an education conference I met a teacher who was very excited about a new method she had recently tried based on Dr. Dee Tadlock's book *Read Right! Coaching Your Child to Excellence in Reading* (McGraw-Hill, 2005). Tadlock was a reading specialist and the mother of a very bright young boy who couldn't read. When the teachers and reading specialists failed, Tadlock wasn't worried. After all, she was a reading specialist; she'd teach her son herself. When she failed and her son gave up hope of ever learning, she gave up her job and went back to school to study the brain and how it learns. She developed her own approach to reading instruction, taught her son, and then wrote about her experience in the hope that her method might help others.

The teacher at the conference gave me a copy of *Read Right!* which I read on my return flight. Although the book is intended for working with beginning readers, I decided to try some of the suggestions for my own high school students—and they worked! The basic idea, as I understand it, is that our brains need to have an internal model of excellence to follow if we want to learn to perform a new skill with a high degree of excellence. Poor readers don't have that internal model. They hear other people read well, but they don't know how it feels to read well themselves.

Excellent reading feels comfortable, sounds like normal conversation, and makes sense. Most of my remedial high school readers read in monotone voices, without inflection, or they read with inflection but without acknowledging punctuation or other indicators. They clearly don't understand what they were reading half the time. Even when they read as well as they can, they are nowhere near excellent.

So I followed the book's advice about giving feedback. I explained what I was trying to do so that my students wouldn't become frustrated or embarrassed. I would read a sentence from our literature book and ask a volunteer to read it out loud in the same manner that I did. (Some students opted to do this privately, but most were willing to do it as a group since they weren't required to volunteer.) Students had to read the sentences, not just mimic them or repeat what I had said without reading. Instead of praising them and saying, "Good, thank you," I would say, "That was not excellent. Try it again." The student would read the sentence again. If the second reading was better, I would say, "Better, but still not excellent." Then I would model excellent reading again. The student would try again. If they read excellently, I would say, "That was excellent." Now their brains knew what they were striving for. They had an internal standard of excellence and could make adjustments to achieve it.

As more and more students took the chance and read out loud, others became braver. They wanted to know what excellent reading feels like, too. This experiment has helped a good number of my remedial readers move up to the next level. It isn't my only tool, but it is a great addition to my teacher's toolbox. Obviously, I can't do justice to *Read Right!* or this reading approach in a few short paragraphs, but I mention it because it has worked well for some students and it is based on common sense. Even if it doesn't work for your students, it might spark an idea or lead you to another alternative approach. If we don't look for solutions, we'll never find them.

WHAT DO YOU THINK?

1. Describe your own early experiences with reading: how did you learn to read?
2. Which of the techniques you have used to motivate reluctant readers has worked the best?
3. What is your opinion of requiring students to read out loud in front of peers?
4. How can we use music and art to enhance reading for students?
5. What is your opinion on the use of sustained silent reading in school?

Light and Learning

As I reviewed the research for this third edition of *Teaching Outside the Box*, I found dozens of scientific studies and research experiments involving the connection between light and learning. In school, we tend to consider light from one perspective—how well our students can see to do their work. We sometimes forget that light influences every aspect of our lives: sleep, mood, vision, blood pressure, respiration, hormone production, emotions, and cognition. All of those factors affect the behavior and achievement of our students. To quote researcher R. J. Wurtman, "Light is the most important environmental input, after food and water, in controlling bodily functions."

Based on the effect they have on our bodies and health, here is a quick list of options for lighting a classroom, from best to worst: natural daylight via windows or skylights, full-spectrum incandescent lights, regular incandescent lights, full-spectrum fluorescents with electronic ballasts (to reduce flicker), fluorescents with a colored overlay to correct the color spectrum, plain fluorescents.

Unfortunately, most schools use regular fluorescent lighting because it is the cheapest, but the savings may end up costing us dearly in the way of disruptive behavior, underachieving student readers, lower test scores, and expensive remedial reading programs. According to ergonomics experts, there are two basic problems with fluorescent lights. One is that they do not provide the full spectrum of light that we get from the sun. Insufficient exposure to full-spectrum light interferes with our circadian rhythm, resulting in sleep problems, eyestrain, migraines, and hormone disruption, among other things. The second problem is that fluorescent lights flicker because they are lit by gas that glows when electricity passes through it. Since the electricity is not constant, the lights tend to pulse. Most people's brains accommodate the flicker and essentially tune it out, but when an individual's brain perceives the flicker, it results in stress, anxiety, eyestrain, headaches, and even seizures.

Sometimes humming is a problem with overhead fluorescents. If the lights in your classroom hum, it may be that the ballast where the bulb meets the base is loose. Ask your building custodian to check the bulbs to make sure they are properly situated and defective in design.

So what can one teacher do? Buy a table or floor lamp with an incandescent bulb and place it in a corner of your classroom to provide lighting for students who are sensitive to fluorescent lights. (Don't be surprised if all your students huddle near that natural light.) Take your classes on reading field trips to the library or a sheltered outdoor space—outdoors in direct sunlight is not a good option because it's too bright. Sometimes gymnasiums have large windows that create a perfect reading environment because the natural light tends to counteract the effects of the fluorescents. And try to convince our school districts to invest in better lighting.

We may not be able to convince our administrators to spend the money required to provide natural daylight or full-spectrum incandescent lighting, but we may be able to convince them to try full-spectrum fluorescents, which are now widely available and affordable. If they need published data to support your request, the following studies will provide the necessary facts and statistics.

LIGHT AND READING LINKED

Several researchers collaborated on a paper titled "Illuminating the Effects of Dynamic Lighting on Student Learning," which was published May 6, 2012 (http://sgo.sagepub.com/content/2/2/2158244012445585). According to the article abstract, improved classroom lighting resulted in a 36 percent increase in oral reading fluency of third graders. The study involved students in four different classrooms over the course of a full calendar year. The results: students in the improved lighting group initially scored slightly lower than their counterparts in the control group, but by mid-semester students in the lighting group increased their reading fluency at a rate almost double the rate of the control group.

The results and discussion portion of the study concludes with this statement: "Such a finding, in light of previous research on lighting effects for well-being (concentration, focus, motivation and cognition), reading speed and reading performance, behooves educational researchers to examine lighting effects on reading comprehension as well as other academic content learning in authentic classroom settings."

More than 40 scientific studies are referenced in this one paper, spanning more than 30 years of research on the ways that light affects learners. Most are highlighted and hyperlinked so you can quickly access the original research online.

BETTER GRADES—AND FEWER CAVITIES!

Physicians, teachers, social workers, nutritionists, and dentists in Alberta, Canada, led by W. E. Hathaway, collaborated on a 2-year study funded by Alberta Education involving elementary school students and four different kinds of lights: "A Study into the Effects of Light on Children of Elementary School Age: A Case of Daylight Robbery." The results, reported in 1992, showed that students in classrooms with full-spectrum light learned faster, tested higher, grew faster, and had one-third fewer absences due to illness. Interestingly, they also had fewer cavities than expected (http://www.healthyschools.org/downloads/daylighting.pdf).

According to the executive summary, the study was funded by the Policy and Planning Branch of Alberta Education in Edmonton and took place between 1987 and 1989 to replicate an earlier study that also showed positive results of full-spectrum lighting in schools. You can view the executive summary report for the Alberta study and find links to other studies online at http://www.netnewsdesk .com/lfh/index.cfm

SUNNIER CLASSES = HIGHER TEST SCORES

In 2003, the Mahone Group, a consulting group based in California, used architectural studies, photos, and in-person visits to rate the amount of daylight available in more than 2,000 classrooms in California, Washington, and Colorado. The school districts in the study had similar building designs and climates, and the 21,000 students in the study had similar backgrounds. The results? Students in the sunniest classrooms advanced between 18 and 26 percent faster in reading and between 7 and 20 percent faster in math over a 1-year period (http://www.h-m-g.com/projects/daylighting/summaries%20on%20daylighting.htm).

Of particular interest are three studies. The first, under the link "Daylighting in Schools: PG&E 1999," was funded by Pacific Gas and Electric and involved school districts in Seattle, Fort Collins, and San Juan Capistrano. This study found that students in Colorado and Washington classrooms with the most daylight had 7 to 18 percent higher test scores. In California, students in rooms with the most daylight progressed 20 percent faster on math tests and 26 percent faster on reading tests in 1 year than students in the classrooms with the least daylight. The second study, "Daylighting in Schools: Additional Analysis," funded by the California Energy Commission in 2001, continued the San Juan Capistrano study and identified a central tendency of 21 percent improvement in student learning rates between classrooms with the least and most daylight.

The third study detailed research involving over 8,000 students in Grades 3–6 located in 500 classrooms in 36 different schools in Fresno, California. Researchers made on-site visits to measure the light in every classroom during this study. They found that glare negatively affects student learning, especially in math classrooms, where instruction is often visually demonstrated. When teachers do not have control of their windows and lighting, student performance is negatively affected. Physical characteristics of classrooms, most notably windows, were as significant and of equal or greater magnitude than teacher characteristics, number of computers, or attendance rates in predicting student performance.

A ROOM WITH A VIEW IMPROVES GRADES

Another interesting study led by C. Kenneth Tanner, head of the School of Design and Planning Laboratory at the University of Georgia, analyzed the impact of the features outside a classroom on the grades of the children inside. After studying more than 10,000 fifth-grade students in seventy-one Georgia elementary schools, Tanner and his associates found that students who studied in classrooms that offered unrestricted views of gardens, mountains, and other natural scenery for at least 50 feet outside the classroom windows had higher test scores in language arts, science, and math than students whose classrooms offered views of parking lots and roads. The report, "Effects of School Design on Student Outcomes," was published in 2009 in the *Journal of Educational Administration* (http://sdpl.coe.uga.edu/research/TannerResearchAward.pdf).

THE VIEW FROM MY ROOM

You may notice students who hunch over their desks and wrap their arms around their books and papers. Or you may have students who behave beautifully until you ask them to read independently—then they wiggle and squirm and disrupt everybody around them. You may have students who squint and frown, who rub their eyes or press their noses into their books, who blink rapidly or lose their place when they read on their own. All of these behaviors can point to the same problem: light sensitivity. The students who hunch over their books, for example, may not be trying to hide anything; they may be trying to create a shadow over the page to reduce the glare. And the others are all trying to cope with a problem they aren't even aware that they have.

I wasn't aware of the existence of light sensitivity until my second year as a teacher when I met Alex Gonzales. (He asked me to use his real name when I share his story because he is very proud of his accomplishments, given the obstacles he had to overcome as a student.) I was part of a four-teacher team for the Computer Academy, a program for at-risk teens at a high school south of San Francisco. "I hate school," Alex told me when he applied for entrance into the program. "I'd rather go to prison than college, but my parents want me to at least graduate so I need to get into the academy."

Alex didn't seem like an at-risk student—at first. He was intelligent, polite, witty, and popular. He participated in discussions, wrote articulate compositions, and listened attentively to other students when we read aloud. Then I assigned independent reading, and Alex became the at-risk underachiever who had failed his entire freshman year of high school. Instead of reading, he drummed on his desktop, hurled paper projectiles, "accidentally" dropped his textbook on the floor, picked fights with other students, and defiantly invited me to send him to the office—anything to avoid reading on his own for more than a few minutes.

As an academy student, Alex had signed a contract promising to stay off drugs, away from gangs, and in school. He maintained that he wanted to improve his study skills and habits. He claimed he was willing to do anything to improve his chances of graduating—anything except read.

"I just hate reading," Alex insisted. "I've always hated it."

Poor reading comprehension wasn't the problem, nor was vocabulary, phonics, or any other testable aspect of reading. Alex earned above-average grades on every achievement test. I began to wonder whether his previous teachers were right when they said Alex's problem was power, that he had chosen reading as the one area where he refused to give up control. They believed that because he could read well when he wanted to, he simply didn't want to.

One morning I cajoled Alex's class into independently reading a scene from *Othello*—a difficult task for any group, but especially challenging for disenchanted, academically impoverished teens. Two minutes into the silent-reading period, Alex began his usual disruptive behavior. Out of patience I shouted, "Alex, would you just sit down and read your dang book?"

Alex slammed his book open and bent over it. Ten minutes later he walked to my desk and said, "This is why I hate to read." He motioned toward his eyes, which were red-rimmed and bloodshot. Tears streamed down his cheeks. I was astounded. "Reading makes my eyes hurt," he said.

That evening I called Alex's parents to make sure they had health insurance. I asked them to schedule an appointment with an eye doctor to have his eyes examined. I accompanied him and his mother to the appointment because I was so curious about his problem and I wanted to make sure the doctor took him seriously. After a complete exam, the doctor shook his head.

"He has a slight astigmatism," he said, "but there is nothing wrong with his vision, no medical reason for the bloodshot, watery eyes."

Back at school the following day, I asked my coworkers whether they had ever encountered a situation like Alex's. Some had, but none had an explanation or suggestion. After school I called Diane Herrera Shepard, a colleague from Albuquerque who worked as a tutor for learning disabled college students. She arrived at my classroom the following day toting a briefcase packed with 8-by-10-inch transparencies in an array of colors—shades of rose, peach, yellow, gray, purple, green, and blue. She held out a paper on which a series of black Xs formed the shape of a pumpkin and asked Alex if he could count the number of Xs in the middle row of the pumpkin without using his finger as a guide.

"No," said Alex. "The Xs are moving."

My students crowded around Diane. Some quickly counted the Xs. Others agreed with Alex that the Xs were "wiggly." One student said the Xs looked like they were burning off the page. Diane placed a purple filter over the page and asked Alex if he could count the Xs. Without hesitating, Alex correctly counted the Xs.

"Cool!" he exclaimed. "How did you do that?"

Diane explained that people with scotopic sensitivity syndrome (also known as Irlen syndrome) may find reading difficult, painful, or impossible under fluorescent lights, especially when reading black letters on a white page, which creates a very high contrast. By placing a colored overlay on the page or wearing specially created colored lenses, many people who suffer from scotopic sensitivity can read without eyestrain or headaches—even some who have a long history of problems with reading. Diane distributed transparent overlays, and the students placed them over their textbooks, comparing the different colors. Placing a blue transparency over my own book made it much easier for me to read.

"Light sensitivity is a controversial subject," Diane warned me. "I offer this to students as a possibility. If it helps them, then I'm happy to provide whatever information is available."

SCOOP ON SCOTOPIC SENSITIVITY

At the time, in the early 1990s, very little information was available on scotopic sensitivity syndrome (SSS) aside from the fact that a psychologist named Helen Irlen had discovered a recurring visual perceptual problem during her work with adult students who had trouble reading. The patented filters were not available to the public. When I tried to research the topic, I found a wide disparity of opinions, ranging from the claim that scotopic sensitivity affects one out of two learning-disabled students to complete denial that light sensitivity even exists.

Four years later, after I moved from California to New Mexico, I encountered another student who convinced me that scotopic sensitivity exists. Valerie, an outgoing girl in my freshman remedial reading class, displayed behavior very similar to Alex's. She complained of headaches during every independent-reading assignment and became defiant and obnoxious if I demanded that she read silently for more than a few minutes. When I realized I might be working with another light-sensitive student, I was delighted to learn that one of our school counselors had been trained at an Irlen center. The following week, I invited the counselor to test my students. One-half of them responded favorably to the use of colored transparencies for reading.

Valerie responded exactly as Alex had. The moment she received a reading overlay (hers was such a dark purple that I could not read the print through it), she became the official reader for the class. She often read aloud for 20 or 30 minutes without complaining of any discomfort. Her grades shot up to As in every subject.

"I'm so glad I found this out," Valerie told me, "but now I'm really mad. For 10 years I've been telling people that reading hurt and all that time they've been calling me crazy, lazy, stubborn, and stupid. I used to think maybe I was crazy or something, because I would say reading made my eyes hurt, and teachers would say that couldn't be true. They said I was lying. They thought I was just trying to get out of work, and so did my parents. So everybody was mad at me all the time. I was starting to think I really might be stupid and crazy."

I can imagine how frustrating it must be for children to be told their heads don't ache and their eyes don't hurt, to be accused of being lazy and stubborn. One of the most disheartening aspects of this situation is that when people who suffer from light sensitivity concentrate harder on reading, their symptoms become worse. No wonder so many remedial readers also have behavior problems! Sadly, many students who struggle with light sensitivity or vision convergence insufficiency (double vision) may be placed in special education classes or programs for behavior-disordered children because they refuse to read or they misbehave in order to avoid having to read.

After my experience with the remedial readers who responded so positively to using the patented transparencies, I started buying colored transparent report covers at the office supply store because at the time you couldn't buy the overlays unless you were certified as a counselor trained to diagnose light sensitivity. (Today, the filters are readily available for purchase online at Irlen.com, NRSI.com, and other sites devoted to reading improvement.) I distributed the report covers to all my classes during the first weeks of school and briefly described light sensitivity. Something very interesting happened in many of my remedial classes. Students who were in the tenth or eleventh grade and reading at a fourth- or fifth-grade level but who showed no signs of having light sensitivity would often grab a transparency and place it over the page and then invite me to teach them to read. One

17-year-old boy who had previously resisted any help suddenly decided he was ready to learn to read. Using the overlays allowed him to save face and accept reading instruction—something he had previously insisted was for "little kids" and "dummies."

"I'm not stupid, you know," he said. "I have a condition. That's how come I couldn't read before."

SIGNS OF LIGHT SENSITIVITY

Light-sensitive students commonly exhibit the following behaviors:

- Red or bloodshot eyes after reading
- Rubbing eyes or repeatedly touching face while reading
- Fidgeting and squirming during reading or close work
- Refusing to read or reading for very brief periods
- Squinting or holding book in awkward position
- Arching body over book or desk to create shadows
- Holding book beneath the desk or in lap while reading
- Complaining of headache or eye pain while reading
- Reporting that letters look "squiggly"
- Skipping words or lines while reading
- Frequently losing their place, even when pointing
- Reporting that words seem to be moving around

Note: Many light-sensitive students are mistakenly identified as dyslexic. Some students have light sensitivity along with dyslexia. In my experience, when students have both conditions, interventions for dyslexia are likely to be ineffective until the student's light sensitivity is addressed.

FEEDBACK FROM FUTURE TEACHERS

In 2010, while teaching the online course Teaching and Learning Theory for teacher candidates at Santa Fe Community College, I gave an optional assignment of experimenting with transparent colored reading overlays and reporting the results. I expected only a few students to choose the assignment, but after the first few reported their results other students were motivated to see for themselves. Here are just a couple of excerpts from the dozens of postings on the chat board:

Student A wrote:

> I had the opportunity to use one of the transparencies earlier in the week in class on campus. I noticed a total difference. It was interesting that my initial repulsion to reading the article the instructor passed out was not clear to me. I didn't know WHY I did not want to read it. I looked at the words but understood none of them. It was as if I could not "find" them although I could see them. But once I put the transparency over the article it was way more inviting and it had a feel of a children's book with big print and clear communication. Again, I was surprised that I did not initially sense the difficulty seeing the print. It felt more like an unconscious dislike. When I visited the Web sites, it felt like they were "selling" something and if I had not used the transparency in class, I would likely not believe how much the transparency improved my reading comfort.

Student B wrote:

> I ended up getting two different colors, blue and yellow. I do not like the yellow as much as the blue. The yellow reminds me of ski goggles. I don't like sunglasses. Having said that, I did read a bit of my textbook today using the two different overlays. I immediately preferred looking at the page through the blue one. I ended up using the blue overlay to cover my laptop screen. I like it.

Student B logged back into the chat room later on to share another experience:

> I am exhausted. It's been a very busy week for me and on top of that I came down with a head cold. As I sat here to write my posts, my eyes started to really hurt and I felt drowsy. I pulled the blue overlay off my PC screen and felt a sharp pain in BOTH of my eyes! I knew it was from the bright white document here on my screen that I'm currently typing in. Wow. I'm going to keep on using the blue sheet.

I taught that same class online four times, and each time my graduate education students reported similar experiences using colored overlays for reading. Their response was overwhelmingly positive.

PASS THE WORD

In the two decades since the day I first met Alex Gonzalez, I have presented keynote speeches to over 100 organizations, and I have shared his experience with every audience. After every speech, multiple individuals have shared their own stories of students who struggled with light sensitivity and how much the colored overlays helped them.

In Austin, Texas, after I addressed the annual conference of the Association of Texas Professional Educators, one teacher ran up and hugged me. "Bless you for telling that boy's story," she said. "You never know who it will help. My daughter is in fourth grade, and we just got her some tinted lenses to wear while she is reading. It has changed her life. Before that, nobody knew what to do with her. She's been in every special education program at the school, but nothing worked. Now she can read."

Principal Courtney Madden at Piedmont Community Charter School in Gastonia, North Carolina, told me he first used colored overlays when he was principal of a public school. He used to gather groups of errant boys in his office every afternoon and have them read to him while using the overlays. "I was just piddling around, didn't really know what I was doing at the time," says Madden. "I had read about the overlays and got some samples, and they worked with those young fellows. So when we had thirty-six kids last year here at Piedmont who hadn't been able to make any progress in reading, I decided to try scotopic screening as one of many pieces to the puzzle. After using the overlays, all but two of those students passed the EOG [end-of-grade] exam."

In addition to providing overlays for use in school and at home, Piedmont Community Charter School provides a variety of colored papers for teachers to use in making assignments and worksheets for students who use overlays. Children's names are posted above the appropriate colors in the workroom. And because North Carolina has approved overlays for use during end-of-grade testing, students can use the overlays during the testing itself.

"I know a lot of people are skeptical about the overlays," says Madden. "They want something real challenging and difficult as a solution to reading problems.

And had I not experimented years ago, I would have thought, 'This cannot be.' But those overlays have really helped some students who used to earn 30s and 40s and are now making 90s and 100s on their work. In one year our school went from 75 percent of our students passing the state test to 89.4 percent passing."

SCIENTIFIC SUPPORT

Today an Internet search on "scotopic sensitivity syndrome" or "colored overlays for reading" brings up dozens of sites in a variety of languages, including colleges and universities that have conducted research, people relating their own stories and successes, and agencies that conduct testing and training for scotopic sensitivity. Colleges now routinely offer continuing education units for teachers and psychology professionals who want to learn how to screen students to determine whether they are good candidates for colored overlays or tinted eyeglass lenses. And for the skeptics, scientific studies confirm the validity of using colored overlays as a tool for helping readers whose difficulties do not stem from visual acuity.

Paul Whiting, a professor of education at the University of Sydney, is one of the primary researchers in the field of scotopic sensitivity syndrome. He has written several papers, including one published in 1993 in the *Australian Journal of Remedial Education* titled "Irlen Coloured Filters for Reading: A Six-Year Follow-Up" (http://www.dyxleciaservices.com.au/Six-Year_Follow-Up.htm). Whiting reports on a number of other published research involving Irlen patented filters, other filters, and commercial colored overlays. He concludes that the majority of people involved in the filter-use studies reported improved visual perception of print, greater ease of reading, and improved written language skills.

Among the studies Whiting summarizes are the following:

- A study in Louisiana where over 90 percent of participants who used filters reported improved reading, with 49 percent reporting fewer headaches.

- An Australian study where 91 percent of participants reported improvement in overall ease of reading, 86 percent reported less eyestrain, and 85 percent experienced improved reading fluency.

- A 3-year study conducted in four Western states where 86 percent of participants indicated that filters had been helpful.

Another researcher, Dr. Daniel Amen, of the University of California–Irvine School of Medicine, has screened patients for more than 10 years. He performs

3-D image scans of patients before and after wearing Irlen lenses to see if reading with them makes a difference. Some of the brain imaging studies can be accessed directly by selecting the "Light at the Brain" link at http://www .dyslexiaservices.com.au/BrainRes.htm.

Other research has been conducted at the U.S. Naval Education and Training Center, the University of Utah School of Medicine, and the University of New Mexico.

Based on the research reports I have read, my own observations of students, and the anecdotal evidence supplied by hundreds of teachers across the country, I believe schools should routinely test students for light sensitivity, just as we routinely check their vision and hearing. It seems almost criminal to do otherwise. Light sensitivity testing is quick and easy, but it can make the difference between a student who struggles and suffers for years and eventually gives up on school and a student who experiences the joy of learning and goes on to develop his or her educational potential.

WHAT DO YOU THINK?

1. Share any experience you have using transparencies or other reading aids designed to address lighting issues.

2. Experiment by different colors of tinted transparencies over the page of a textbook, and share your results. Do you think light students should be tested for light sensitivity?

3. What areas of your school might provide good lighting conditions for readers?

4. What other factors might we overlook (other than lighting) that could have a significant effect on student achievement and test scores?

Motivation and Persuasion

Enthusiasm is contagious—usually. But all veteran teachers have had days when we walk into the classroom bursting with enthusiasm and armed with a great lesson plan—only to be met with yawns and apathy. Sadly, some of us also face a sea of blank faces class after class and day after day, even if we exude confidence, demonstrate good leadership skills, create brilliant lesson plans, and plan interesting activities. Sometimes, no matter what we do, we struggle to keep our students motivated and engaged.

Generally speaking, reluctant learners fall into two broad categories: (1) students who care about education but who sometimes require external motivation to get started or to keep working; and (2) students who don't care about school or are resistant to authority or unwilling to follow instructions.

GROUP 1: A LITTLE BASIC MOTO

Let's talk about the first group first. Usually, basic psychology and motivational techniques will get them back on track because the human brain is wired for learning, and the brain's emotional control center is keenly alert for the new and unusual—particularly during adolescence. So sometimes all we need to do is change things up a bit to engage our students' brains. Instead of giving a quiz, for example, we can assign students to create a good quiz. That idea is not truly out of the box, but if you haven't done an activity before—or haven't done it for a while—it may be enough to generate some enthusiasm. Once students are engaged in an activity, they also tend to stay engaged as long as the tasks and skills involved fall into their zone of proximal development. (This refers to Vygotsky's sensible theory that students need to be challenged enough to keep them interested but not so much that they feel overwhelmed and incapable of succeeding.) Hopefully the ideas in this section will inspire more of your own.

Be Your Own Guinea Pigs

One of the most effective methods I have ever tried to motivate students—including adult graduate students—is to use our class as guinea pigs to test various theories or research. One class of future teachers was discussing an article from a psychology magazine that summarized research on the value of making mistakes. According to the article, people retain information better if they make mistakes while they are learning. We decided to test the theory. Our method was very rudimentary and would not meet scientific standards, but that wasn't the purpose of our exercise. My goal was to get those students to consider the value of making mistakes and think of ways to incorporate mistake making into their own classrooms.

The guinea pigs were good students. They arrived on time, read the assignments, and willingly participated in discussions. But occasionally I'd notice someone checking the clock or gazing out the window, disengaged from the current activity. During our mistake-making exercise, every student was fully engaged for the entire class. They were so enthusiastic that they bubbled, although they were frustrated at not being able to do the lesson perfectly. I gave them two lists of difficult words (e.g., *jacamar, baggala, inchoate, icteric*). For the first list, they had to write definitions for each word, making them up if they didn't know them. Then I gave them the correct definitions to compare with their versions. For the second list of words, I provided the correct definitions for them to copy. Then we put the two word lists away until the end of the class, almost 2 hours later. We did a small-group exercise based on the previous week's reading assignment. Then we looked at the two word lists again and they wrote down as many definitions as they could remember. Our results upheld the research—we all remembered many more of the words from the first list, where we had corrected our mistakes.

Nobody wanted to leave the room that day. They wanted to discuss ways to teach their students how to make mistakes and learn from them.

My high school students have been just as receptive to being guinea pigs as the future teachers were. Spelling tests are not popular, but when I suggested to one group that we try various strategies and record our results in our journals, everybody became interested and excited about taking the different tests. First, we pretended we were in kindergarten. We chanted the words slowly aloud. We did this Monday through Thursday and took our test on Friday. We recorded the results. The following week, we tried air-writing with our fingers as we chanted them. Overall, we tested six different methods. During those weeks, nobody complained about having to study spelling words. They were so interested in seeing which methods worked best that they forgot they were supposed to hate spelling.

In the same class, I built some lessons around articles on metacognition— thinking about thinking. We took all kinds of self-help quizzes. Some of them were simplistic or silly, but if a student found a quiz that had anything to do with learning, we took the quiz. We took sample SAT exams, IQ tests, and quizzes meant to categorize our personalities. My students began to see themselves as learners, as active participants in their education, instead of as passive recipients of unwanted knowledge.

Request Frequent Feedback

Students are far more likely to cooperate when they have the opportunity to provide feedback about the level of difficulty, required assignments, and so on. Of course, it's important to remind students that you, the teacher, make the decisions about what and how you teach. And some students may need a reminder that constructive criticism offers a thoughtful suggestion for improving something and not just complaints. I usually make names optional. (Some students do include their names because they want me to know they gave a thoughtful response.)

Whether you allow students to comment on your teaching methods is up to you. Some teachers prefer to stick to questions on lesson content and format.

AP ENG III Student Survey   Name: (optional) _____

Already Read It		Let's Read It	No, Thanks	No Opinion
____ *Hamlet*		____	____	____
____ *Merchant of Venice*		____	____	____
____ *The Scarlet Letter*		____	____	____
____ *The Crucible*		____	____	____
____ *A Separate Peace*..........		____	____	____
____ *Of Mice and Men*		____	____	____
____ *The Great Gatsby*		____	____	____

Do you plan to go to college? ___Yes ___No ___Maybe, I'm not sure

Do you feel prepared to do college-level reading and writing? ___Yes ___No ___ I'm a little worried

Do you know how to write a thesis and a critical literary essay? ___Yes ___I need practice ___No

What is your attitude toward homework? ___Always do it ___Never do it ___Sometimes I copy it

Do you like to read poetry? ___Yes ___No ___It depends

Do you write poetry? __ Never ___Only in school ___ Sometimes at home ___I'd like to learn

Which do you like to read? __Fiction __Nonfiction __Essays __Poetry __Plays __Everything

Do you like to read aloud in class? ___Never ___Not my favorite thing, but I'll take my turn ___Yes

Do you like to listen to others read? ___I hate it ___If the person is a good reader ___Yes

Do you like doing projects? ___Yes ___No ___I don't mind

Do you like to design projects yourself or do you like guidelines? ___Myself ___With Guidelines

How do you prefer to do assignments? ___As a class ___With a partner/team ___On my own

Would you rather work with one partner or in a team of 3–4 students? ____partner ____team

What would you like to learn in this class?

_____

What activities would you like to do?

_____

So far, this class is: ____Too easy ____ Too hard ____Okay for me ____Too noisy ____Too slow

Feel free to add any comments on the back. Thank you for your input. I appreciate it.

If you ask open-ended questions, be sure to allow ample space. Students tend to write very brief answers when spaces are small.

Here is a sample survey I recently used for a section of advanced placement juniors who were falling behind my other classes. Immediately after I distributed the surveys, I noticed a change in the attitudes of several students. One of the more motivated students, who frequently sighed and rolled her eyes at me when her unmotivated classmates disrupted the class, smiled for the first time in weeks, clearly delighted to be able to express her opinions. And several disruptive students settled down—they all had checked the phrase "I'm a little bit worried" about college-level reading and writing. Seeing that statement in writing seemed to get through to them in a way that my comments had not.

After reviewing all the surveys, I made some changes to the curriculum. The work isn't easier, but it does involve more student interaction and peer feedback. Attendance, behavior, and motivation, along with the quality of student work, have all improved.

Use Project-Based Learning

Projects are like computers: they're wonderful when they work and frustrating when they don't. The first few times I tried to use projects in my classes, I gave up because the students just couldn't seem to handle the independence. They lacked the self-motivation, self-control, time management, and conflict-resolution skills that successful projects require. Fortunately, I'm stubborn. I don't give up easily. And even more fortunately, I had some excellent mentors when I began teaching, including Dr. Marilyn Raby. She laughed when I told her how disappointed I was with my first attempt at getting students to work in groups.

"Of course, your students can't do group work," Marilyn said. "They don't know how. They have to practice things before they get good at them. And before they get good, they're going to be bad. But don't give up on them. Teach them to self-reflect after every activity. Ask them what they could have done better. Then give them a chance to do better, and let them know when they do." I took her advice. Once again, I realized it was a case of Fix the Teacher, Not the Students. If I wanted students to behave in a certain way, I needed to be very explicit in my instructions. Instead of telling them I expected them to cooperate with their partners, I needed to explain what cooperation meant in my dictionary—not in theirs.

There are hundreds, if not thousands, of good Project-Based Learning lesson plans online, and it's impossible to create one plan that would work for elementary through high school students. However, I believe we can create a basic blueprint for creating successful group workers.

Where to Begin?

My approach is to work backward—from goal to start. First, I sketch out the activity or project I want to use. Then, I go back and fill in the blanks to make sure I'm covering the required curriculum and incorporating the necessary benchmarks and standards into the lessons. Next, I consider several key questions:

What do I want students to learn from this activity?

What do I want them to be able to do when they finish?

What standards and benchmarks have I used?

How will I assess this new learning?

How will I give students the opportunity to reflect on their successes and failures?

How can I assess participation and final outcomes without penalizing them for making mistakes?

How long will they need to complete the project?

What holidays, test days, or other distractions are likely to occur during the span of this project or lesson?

How will I handle student absences during the project?

How can I avoid personality conflicts while assigning teams?

What materials will students need? How can I pay for supplies?

What practice have they had working in teams?

Getting Good at Group Work

For the sake of discussion, let's divide students into four basic groups based on their experience and skill as team learners. Level I students lack maturity, experience, self-discipline, and social skills. They need practice with short, simple group tasks before they tackle longer projects. They require constant supervision and encouragement. Level II students have some experience working in groups but lack self-control. They tend to wander off task or let one person do all the work. They need structure and guidance. Level III students know how to work in groups. They get the job done with light supervision and minimal structure.

Level IV students are teamwork experts. They require no supervision, create their own structure and benchmarks, and often hope to surprise the teacher with the quality and creativity of their work instead of being monitored.

Level I students need to learn basic collaboration skills. Divide them into pairs. Demonstrate the signal you will use to start and end the activity. Then assign an appropriate quick task: complete a few math problems; look up some words in the dictionary; draw a diagram of something; define two subject-specific terms. Give the start signal and circulate, offering praise and encouragement to those who are on task. Guide the ones who seem lost. After you give the stop signal, thank everybody for cooperating. Ask them to evaluate their own participation and success. Did they accomplish the task? Did they give their best effort? Did everybody participate? What could they improve? Repeat this exercise several times, gradually moving from pairs to groups of three or four until you have functional teams.

Level II students need practice. They have the basic idea, but they need reminders to stay on task and occasional time checks. Design longer projects (15–30 minutes) that require more than one step: Define five subject-specific terms and draw a diagram showing how they relate to each other; watch a short video and write down three important things they learned from the video; circulate and provide guidance. Remind them when every 5 minutes has passed, giving them a countdown. Grade each group on participation, effort, and the final product. Some groups may work hard but not accomplish the goal perfectly. Give them as much praise and credit as more able students who completed the task easily. Remember that your goal is to teach them how to work independently as teams—not to complete the assignment perfectly.

Level III students are ready for longer projects. Begin with a 2- or 3-day project where you spend the first day preparing as a whole class: Read a short play; learn a new math formula or a new sports game. Choose something interesting and fun. At the start of the second day, provide an assignment sheet outlining the requirements students will need to complete on their own during the next day or two. Sample projects might include: Write a scene from a play; create your own game using a ball and be prepared to teach us how to play it; create a quiz using the math formula you learned. Explain your grading criteria—participation, cooperation, finished product. A rubric is helpful. After you have discussed the assignment, assign the teams. (If you assign teams first, some of them will begin socializing—even from across the room—and they won't listen to the instructions.) Make sure everybody understands the instructions and requirements.

Let them go. Try to be a silent observer as much as possible. Provide guidance only when necessary.

Level IV students remind us of the joy of teaching. We can design complex projects and watch them learn and demonstrate their creativity, passion, artistic talents, time-management skills, and intellectual achievements. Hand them a challenging project and set a due date. If they need clarification, they will let you know. Otherwise, let them get to work. Students at this level enjoy grading their own projects, providing peer feedback to classmates, and completing self-critiques.

A Few Sample Assignments

Working backward from your goals and assessments, break your project down into individual tasks and activities. Until you have some practice designing projects, it may be difficult to decide exactly how much time each step will take. Don't stress about it. Block out the amount you think students will need, but be prepared for some students to work much faster or slower than expected. Have an independent assignment on hand for the early birds, and decide whether to reduce the requirements or extend the deadline for students who aren't going to be able to finish with the rest of the class. Give yourself permission to be imperfect. Like our students, we improve with practice.

There are endless variations for projects, but my basic design remains the same: overall objective or end product, individual tasks, group tasks, specific grading criteria, where to seek help, status report date, due date and signature, feedback. Begin with simple projects and increase the complexity as students develop better skills. A quick note on the difference between complexity and difficulty: adding more of the same to an assignment increases the difficulty but not the complexity. Instead, ask student to use different skills, think a little deeper, and move to the next level. For example, giving a student twenty math problems instead of ten increases the difficulty, but it's more of the same. If we give students ten of one problem and ask them to create five similar problems on their own, we have dramatically increased the complexity of the task and the learning opportunities. When designing projects, go for complexity over difficulty.

Amateur Level

Elementary students.

Assign pairs. Each pair receives a clipboard and a list of names of students in the class. Within a given time, pairs must circulate and get the signature of each classmate next to his or her name. Teams are instructed to choose a role: one person is responsible for asking classmates to sign, thanking them and shaking their hands; the other person is responsible for carrying the clipboard and placing a check mark in front of each name that has a signature. The goals are to learn and practice listening and speaking, cursive writing, and time-management skills.

Verbal feedback: What did you think about this assignment? How did you choose your roles? Would you like to switch roles next time? What grade would you give yourself and why?

Intermediate Assignment

Middle school students.

Create teams of three or four. Allow 15–20 minutes total.

Materials: newspaper, tin foil, string, masking tape, Popsicle sticks.

Goal: build the tallest possible structure that can stand without support using only the materials provided.

Team tasks: Brainstorm possible structures; choose one; build it. Individual tasks: contribute at least two ideas to the brainstorm list; participate in project design and construction.

Brief written feedback (for teacher's eyes only): Which ideas did you contribute? How did you contribute to design and construction? How would you rate your own effort? How would you rate the efforts of each teammate?

Optional writing component: Students write a brief summary of their experience.

Expert Project

One-week duration.

Create teams of three or four. Provide written assignment sheet outlining individual assignments, team tasks, grading criteria and due date.

Materials provided: five short stories, poster paper, markers, string, tape, construction paper, tablet computers (if available). Students may bring their own laptops or tablets to use during project.

Team tasks: read each story aloud or silently as a group and discuss it afterward. Collectively, identify three key elements of a good short story: What must it have to be considered good, in your opinion? Using your three key elements as criteria, create a rubric to analyze and compare the four stories and choose the winning story that meets your criteria. Design some kind of visual representation—poster, chart, graph, video clip, PowerPoint, pie chart, infographic, or art project that includes your criteria, a brief summary of your analysis, and your winning story.

Individual tasks: keep a journal and jot down notes about each story—what you liked and disliked and your general opinion. Write a two-page critical analysis of one of the stories (student choice). Sample critical analyses are available in the literature textbook. Students all sign their assignment sheets. Teams work independently to complete their projects.

Timeline: Monday through Friday and presentations the following Monday.

Note: The first time I give this project to a class, I allow them to present just to me instead of to the class. This eliminates the fear of public speaking and allows students to focus on their collaboration skills.

Advanced Challenge

Two- or three-week project depending on class size.

Getting stuck with all the work is a huge concern for some students whenever teachers assign pairs or teamwork—a legitimate concern, unfortunately, because every class has its share of skaters who are along for the ride while the rest of the students do the work. I address this concern by making sure I include some form of student feedback in any activity that involves working together. The amount and detail of feedback depends on the age and ability level of students as well as the complexity of the task. For a quick pair share, I might ask for verbal feedback: Did you both participate? How would you grade your own effort, on a scale of 1 to 10? Most students will answer honestly, but even when they don't their body language and facial expressions will give you the details they omit. For very young students, I might ask who did the most work on this and why? I want students to think about whether the students who didn't participate as eagerly were being lazy—or feeling overshadowed by a stronger personality or a partner with a much higher academic skill level. The goal is to get students to figure out how to include those students who are shy or less confident.

Note: students tend to fit their comments to the space provided. Allow enough space on your form to encourage deeper thinking.

SELF-CRITIQUE FORM

Self-reflection is necessary for excellence in any field of endeavor—so please be thoughtful and honest. Information on this form will be kept confidential—between you and the instructor.

Your Name: _____ Date: _____ Class Period: _____

Name of partner (if applicable): _____

Project Description: _____

Rate *your* overall participation & input to project on a scale of 1 (lowest) to 5 (highest):

1   2   3   4   5   *(circle one)*

Rate the overall participation of your partner on a scale of 1 (lowest) to 5 (highest):

1   2   3   4   5   *(circle one)*

What, specifically, was *your* major role and/or contribution to this project:

_____

_____

_____

Briefly state what you learned from this activity:

_____

_____

_____

_____

What could you have done to improve your project?

_____

_____

_____

What grade do you believe you (individually) deserve on this project? _____ **Explain:**

_____

_____

_____

What grade do you believe your team (if applicable) deserves?

_____

_____

_____

I designed the Learning Brain project and the Gender Gap project as complex projects for my high school Advanced Placement language arts classes. Although they were originally designed for advanced older students, they can be adapted for elementary students by simplifying the project requirements. For example, with younger students, I might eliminate some tasks or reduce the amount of reading or writing. Or I might replace the reading and writing tasks with something visual such as watching a video clip or PowerPoint slide show or viewing and responding to a series of colorful posters.

The Learning Brain project evolved after my seniors had read and discussed several articles about our brains and learning. Interest was high, and I wanted to do something more engaging than just asking them to write an essay or critique. When I first suggested the project, the students stared at me as though I had asked them to perform brain surgery. They were used to quizzes and timed writing responses. In other words, they expected the teacher to do more work than they did. But the person who does the work does the learning.

I showed them a chart of Bloom's Taxonomy of Cognitive Domains to establish the credibility of what I was asking them to do. Then I gave them an entire class period to decide whether they wanted to do the project or have me create quizzes and worksheets for them based on the reading we had already done and the video clips we had viewed together. I left the room so they could talk freely. When I returned, students said they wanted to do the projects but didn't know where to start, so I gave them another class period for thinking. I roamed around and chatted with students, encouraging them to use their imaginations and to stop worrying about whether they were going to get it right. I started to wonder whether the whole idea had been a mistake. Then one student announced that she was going to design an experiment to test the memories of students and teachers, keeping track of everybody's ages, to see whether old people had better memories than young ones. Her idea sparked a lot of discussion. A few minutes later, the room was buzzing, as one student after another thought of projects they might do. One boy whose mother had recently suffered a stroke decided to research exactly what was happening inside her brain and how he could help her recover. And like that, we were off.

The Gender Gap project was inspired by a discussion in one of my classes about the so-called boring novels that are assigned reading in high school. One of the boys complained that there were too many girl books and plays on the curriculum and not enough manly reading. Shortly after that conversation, I came

ASSIGNMENT SHEET:
THE LEARNING BRAIN PROJECT

We watched the sophisticated RSA Animate Video "The Divided Brain," took a quiz to determine our right- or left-brain hemisphere dominance, solved some brain puzzles and right-brain games, and took a short IQ quiz. We also read five magazine articles from *Scientific American Mind*: "The Bilingual Advantage," "The Big Similarities & Quirky Differences Between Left and Right Brains," "The Split Brain Revisited," and "Smart Jocks." We also read my compilation of information on brain research as it relates to learning and memory ("Use Your Noodle"). Each article had a different audience and purpose, as we discussed in class.

You may work alone or with one partner. Your assignment is to reflect on the video, quizzes, articles, classroom activities, and discussions and to create your own Learning Brain Project to demonstrate your understanding and analysis of some aspect of the relationship between our brains and how we learn. You may choose to create a computer infographic, a trifold brochure, a magazine article, a quiz of your own design, a research project, a short video or other technology-based presentation (10 minutes maximum), or some other design of your choosing. The following criteria will apply for grading purposes:

Created for a specific audience

Demonstrates a clear purpose

Synthesis of info from more than one source. (All sources *must* be credited.)

Concise yet comprehensive coverage of information

Individual design—not just parroting or paraphrasing original sources

Visually appealing (if applicable)

Proper grammar & spelling (if applicable)

Appropriate complexity for an AP student at your grade level

Completed on time—points deducted for late work

Individual Critique (separate handout)—your input will be considered during grading

Fill in the blanks below. Briefly describe your project, identify your audience and state your purpose. Your signature indicates that you understand your project must be turned in on time, even if you or your partner is absent on the due date. All extensions must be preapproved.

Your Name: _____ Partner: (optional) _____

My project is: _____

My audience is: _____

My purpose is: _____

Signature: _____

Due date: _____

THE GENDER GAP PROJECT

We will work on this assignment for one week, Monday through Friday. You may work in the classroom, on the patio, or in the library. Working alone, or with one partner, complete the following:

Monday

1. Read the short article "The Gender Gap at School" by David Brooks.
2. From the five questions following the article, answer questions 1, 2, and 4 on notebook paper. If working with a partner, submit one paper with both names on it.
3. Prepare a short verbal answer to this question: Since boys and girls learn differently and prefer different books, how should language arts classes be designed to motivate both boys and girls to read? For example, what kinds of lessons should we have? How should we select books?

Tuesday

4. Using a smartphone or library computer, look up the book *Why Gender Matters* by Dr. Leonard Sax. Search for reader reviews, summaries, and critical reviews of the book. Decide whether you think the book is credible based on your research.
5. Write a brief summary of your research on the book *Why Gender Matters* and the information you found. Explain why you believe the book is credible or not. (If working with a partner, submit one paper with both your names on it.)

Wednesday

6. Read the collection of short quotations about education (separate handout). Choose one quote, and write your response to the author's ideas about education. (If you are working with a partner, you may discuss the quotations, but you each need to write your own response.)

Thursday

All written assignments are due at the BEGINNING of class. Partial credit will be given for late work. (If you have an excused absence this week, you must check with me to get an extension.)

We will have round-robin small-group discussion based on the topics included in this assignment. Questions will be provided as guidelines, but the discussion format will be up to you.

Friday

We will have whole-class discussion, feedback, and self-critiques. Volunteers will share their responses to the quotes about education. We will discuss some topics from this assignment and evaluate the project.

across an op-ed article in the *New York Times* about gender and reading choices ("The Gender Gap at School" by David Brooks, http://www.nytimes.com/2006/06/11/opinion/11brooks.html?_r=0). The project evolved from there.

Get Positive with Parents

Parents and guardians are used to receiving phone calls from school staff and teachers complaining about unexcused absences, tardiness, missed assignments, bad attitudes, and disrespectful behavior. Often they become defensive because they believe teachers are blaming them for their children's misdeeds. Parents are equally responsible when their children behave respectfully and decently, so we need to call and let them know we appreciate their effective parenting.

When a student in your class behaves especially well, call the parent or guardian to say, "I just wanted to thank you for doing such a good job of raising your daughter/son. I know kids don't behave well by accident—children learn good manners at home. I wish all my students were as well behaved as yours. Thank you for making my job easier." You will earn the gratitude and support of those parents just by telling the truth.

Better yet, write a note instead of calling. Positive notes from teachers are often displayed proudly on the refrigerator in the student's home and may result in special privileges for the student—which may come back to you in the form of increased cooperation and undying loyalty from that student.

In addition to creating a good relationship with parents and improving student performance, good-news phone calls let students know that you and their parents are working together. And if you should ever need to call those same parents or guardians because of a behavior problem, you will find them much more receptive than they might have been otherwise.

I've found phone calls so helpful that whenever I have a new group of students, I take home my roll sheets and call four or five parents each night. I write notes to those I can't contact. I introduce myself, provide my phone number and e-mail address, and ask them to let me know if they need any help from me during the year. I also find something good to say about their child, even if it takes some serious effort to find that good thing. When parents respond positively to my overture, it's very likely that their children will respond positively as well. And all it takes is a few individuals to get the good-behavior ball rolling in your classroom.

Another very effective strategy is to send notes home to the parents and guardians of your worst-performing students (yep, those little stinkers who make you want to quit). They expect bad news, and so do their parents. So if you write a positive note (it must be true, so you'll have to work to catch them doing something good before you write), you are bound to get everybody's attention. One mother called me in tears and said, "I have two children in your school, and in 10 years I have never heard a good word about either one of them." I had both her children—they were twins—in my class, and I could see very clearly why nobody had ever praised those rambunctious, ill-mannered children. However, I didn't tell her that. I said, "Well, they certainly have a lot of energy, and they are basically good kids." It was true. They weren't murderers or child molesters or drug dealers or bullies; they were just ordinary, obnoxious teens, struggling to cope with family problems. Those positive notes made a huge change in their behavior: they didn't become scholars overnight, but they did tone down their behavior in my class because they wanted the rewards and love that they received at home in response to my positive progress reports.

GROUP 2: POWERFUL PERSUASION REQUIRED

Now, let's talk about your second group—the truly unmotivated, defiant, or stubborn students. This group requires powerful persuasion along with some psychological manipulation. Once these students are receptive you can use basic psychology and motivational techniques, but first you need to lay the foundation. Except for cases where students have genuine physical disabilities, most underachievers struggle with emotional or mental issues that keep them from developing their natural talents and abilities. Fear and anger are the predominant emotions among students who refuse to even try to learn. What are they afraid of? Teachers, parents, principals, bullies, bad report cards, critical peers, physical changes in their bodies, sex, drug dealers, drive-by shootings, and so on. Why are they angry? They feel powerless and hopeless. They know they deserve more than they are getting out of school, but they don't believe they are capable of success and thus choose not to try. "If I don't try, I can't fail" makes sense to them.

These students are stuck in survival mode. When human brains perceive danger—whether it's physical, emotional, or mental—we switch to survival mode to protect ourselves. We run or fight or do whatever else we need to do to make ourselves less vulnerable. Getting kicked out of a classroom where the teacher is going to make you read aloud in front of your peers removes the threat that people will laugh at you or call you stupid. You may have to deal with disciplinary issues, but we know the principal isn't allowed to kill us. We will survive the trip to the office. On the other hand, we believe we may not survive being laughed at in the classroom. We might die from embarrassment—or wish we were dead. Here's another scenario. If there is abuse or neglect at home and we can't escape physically, we can withdraw emotionally and try to become invisible—and so on.

Teachers are not officially psychological counselors, but a good understanding of basic human psychology and the stages of emotional and mental development can make your job much easier and more enjoyable and can help you learn how to teach your unteachable students. Many of the techniques in this section come directly from my experience in teaching at-risk, supposedly unreachable teens, many who were active or former gang members. By trial and error, I developed activities and strategies that helped me reach them and teach them. Those same basic techniques work just as well with more skilled and motivated students because human brains all operate the same way, regardless of people's age, income, culture, or IQ.

My hope is that these same strategies, or your own variations, will help you reach and teach the frightened, angry students hiding behind the bad attitudes and pseudo disinterest of the students in your classroom.

Develop Your Persuasive Powers

If you took psychology classes in college, you already know that people have reasons for everything they do—even if they are unaware of the reasons. Here are just a few examples of things students my own students have done. In every case, the behavior happened and I found out much later why it had occurred. The reasons would never have occurred to me: a boy jumped up and turned over his desk because a girl across the room had been flashing him while he was trying to read; a boy wrote the word "nigger" on his tennis shoe because he was deeply depressed and hoped that another student would kill him; a girl hit a boy over the head because she wanted to be suspended from school so she could go to the hospital and visit her dying grandmother.

The first thing we need to do when working with difficult students is to remember that we don't know what their lives hold. We don't know why they do what they do—and they may not know themselves. By making that simple change in our thinking, we can avoid doling out punishments we later regret. And we have a much better chance of creating a connection.

My second suggestion is to do a bit of research on the topic of persuasion. There are a number of helpful articles and videos on the Internet. I won't provide a list because social psychology is a fast-growing field and new information is made available every day, but I will suggest two video clips on YouTube. "RSA Shorts—The ABCs of Persuasion" is a 3-minute look at basic persuasion. (RSA Animates also has a longer video titled "Choice" that is worth viewing.) The second clip, titled "The Science of Persuasion," is narrated by Dr. Robert Cialdini and his colleague, Steve Martin.

To Bribe … or Not to Bribe?

Praising students for cooperating seems like such a simple idea, but it is far from simple. Using praise as a bribe can backfire. I tend to agree with psychologist Carol Dweck's assertion in "The Perils and Promises of Praise (http://www .ascd.org/publications/educational-leadership/oct07/vol65/num02/the-Perils- and-Promises-of-praise.aspx) that praise used correctly can motivate students to learn, but used wrongly it can create self-defeating behavior. This is one area where I think it's crucial to read the research and listen to the experts because we can unintentionally inhibit our students' motivation and learning if we get it wrong. Here's one of the key ideas in the article: Praising students for being intelligent results in short-term good behavior and long-term bad behavior; praising them for their efforts results in self-confidence and increased effort.

Recently, I watched several documentaries about the teenage brain. Apparently, teens differ from younger and older students in that teen brains are primed for immediate satisfaction and significant rewards. They don't want the little things that please elementary students—a sticker on their homework or an extra minute at recess. Instead, they want a pizza or 10 minutes of free time to text their friends. So, when dealing with teens, I tend to offer incentives, but on the whole I prefer intangible rewards for student cooperation—handshakes, praise, applause, and acknowledgment. Rumors persist that I hurl candy bars at kids in my classroom. That rumor probably began with an anecdote from *My Posse Don't Do Homework,* where I described my desperate efforts to persuade a group of remedial readers to tackle Shakespeare. They were convinced they were too dumb to read *The Taming of the Shrew*, yet I maintained that they were highly intelligent in spite of their poor reading skills. I insisted that somebody had to be willing to take a shot at interpreting the first few lines of the play. Nobody volunteered. I refused to give up. I stood and waited—for quite a long time—until a very shy student raised his hand and offered an idea. He wasn't right. He wasn't even close. But I had my hand in my pocket, where I found a stray dollar bill. I pulled out that dollar and handed it to the boy who had volunteered to think. This wasn't planned. It just happened. His eyes widened.

"Am I right?" he asked. "No," I said. "That dollar is just for thinking, because you will never get the answer right if you are afraid to be wrong." Immediately, another student volunteered to think. His answer was much better than the previous one.

"Am I right?" he demanded. When I said, "You're getting warmer," he held out his hand and said, "Where's my dollar?" I told him I couldn't afford to give out a dollar for every answer.

"Ain't that just like school," he muttered and shook his head. "He gets a dollar for a wrong answer, and I don't get nothing for a righter answer." I realized I was going to lose all my volunteers if I didn't find some kind of tangible reward. I happened to have some candy bars on hand that were left over from a spelling contest. (For a few months when I first started teaching, I did give out candy, but when I realized it was not healthy for my students' brains or bodies, I stopped.)

I grabbed a candy bar and tossed it to the boy with the half-correct answer. More hands shot up into the air. Within 30 minutes, I had given away my lunch, my rubber-covered paper clips, pens and pencils, and everything else I could find in my desk and backpack. The students were proud to win prizes for thinking about Shakespeare. The following day hands waved as soon as I asked for volunteers, and they continued to wave throughout that school year, although I had made it very clear after the first day that there would be no more tangible rewards—just recognition and occasional applause for really courageous thinking.

That said, I do sometimes offer tangible rewards such as a homework lottery or stickers on papers or award certificates to motivate reluctant readers and unmotivated students (including adult students), but I do this only when necessary to convince students to try. Once they make a sincere effort and realize how good it feels to learn and to overcome challenges, they no longer need external motivators.

According to nearly all of the articles and books I have read about brain-based learning, the long-term use of external rewards can actually be counterproductive. (Eric Jensen is my favorite author on this topic.) The arguments against tangible rewards are convincing, and I believe the scientists who claim that we don't need them because our brains create endorphins (those feel-good chemicals) when we learn something new. I believe that explains why some students like school immediately and continue liking it. If their first days at school are happy and successful ones, their brains get hooked on learning—literally. But other students, for myriad reasons, don't have those positive experiences. Those are the students who may need temporary external motivators.

For some students, one bribe is enough to get them started. Others need a few positive experiences—or a few years' worth of positive experiences—before they learn to love learning. But once that internal motivation machine kicks on, it keeps right on running.

Adjust the Attitudes
The Power of Choice

You might ask your unmotivated students how they feel about school. Some of them will be eager to tell you, especially if they are younger, but many older students opt to observe instead of participate in class discussions; they don't want to talk about school. They don't want to write essays or paragraphs about it, either. Most of them will be willing to give you a few comments if you absolutely insist, though. Go ahead and insist because you want maximum input from them on this topic.

In step 1, distribute index cards and ask your students to write down their thoughts about school in general and your subjects in particular. Tell your students they will earn a grade for cooperating and everybody who fills out a card will earn the maximum grade. Make sure they understand that names are optional, so they can freely state their opinions without fear of offending you or feeling vulnerable. (If you walk down the rows and collect the cards in order, putting each one on the bottom of the stack, making a point of not looking at the cards, you will still be able to figure out which students said what just in case you find any extreme comments that need your attention.)

Some groups will go to town on this project, but others will require a little prompting. Visual learners will respond better if you post what you want them to tell you on the board. You might choose to write your own answers to the questions you ask your students. Even if your students decide they are more interested in reading your answers than writing their own, you will probably be able to engage them in a conversation about school, which is your goal.

Step 2 is optional. If your students are reasonably well behaved and paying attention, you might consider reading a few comments from the cards after you have collected enough that students won't be able to identify the author. Read comments you think might elicit a response from others: "I hate writing because

I always run out of stuff to say," for example, may prompt a discussion and alert you to the need for a lesson on prewriting.

Whether you discuss the cards or not, thank your students for taking the time to share their opinions. Take the cards home and read them carefully. Look at spelling, sentence structure, vocabulary, and handwriting for clues to student personalities and areas of difficulty. Look for areas of common concern and specific problems that you can address in the future.

In step 3, teach your students the power of choice. (Don't use a handout with written instructions for this exercise because some people read an entire worksheet before they begin writing. If students know you are going to ask them to change some of their words, the exercise won't be as powerful or useful—or it may not work at all.) Give everybody a new blank index card. Explain that the activity is ungraded and that they don't have to share their answers with anybody. They can tear up their cards and throw them away as soon as you finish the activity. On the board, print in large letters:

I HAVE TO …

I CAN'T …

Ask students to copy the two phrases from the board and finish the sentences with whatever comes to mind: *I have to __* and *I can't ___*.

Next, tell them to draw an X through the word *have* and write *choose* above it. Ask them to read their new sentences to themselves and see if they are not more accurate than the original sentences. About 99 percent of the new sentences will be true because there are very few things in this world that we truly have to do. In fact, there are five. Share this knowledge with your students. On the board, write these two statements:

> There are only five things humans HAVE to do to stay alive: eat, sleep, breathe, drink water, and go to the bathroom.
>
> Everything else is optional.

Ask for volunteers to share their *I have to* sentences. Somebody will argue that he or she has to go to school or do homework or babysit or take out the trash. Not true, you will counter. They *choose* to do those things because they don't like the alternatives. They don't want to be grounded or punished or flunked or expelled or whatever is held over their heads to convince them to cooperate. But if they truly didn't want to do the things in their sentences, they could choose *not* to do them and accept the consequences.

Be prepared: some students will find this exercise very distressing, and for some it will take time. Eventually, a few students will get it and will relentlessly insist that other students stop fighting the truth and admit that they choose to go to school, no matter how much they may claim to hate the place.

Next, ask students to draw an X through the word *can't* from their second sentence and replace it with *don't want*. Students will surely argue that they do want to pass algebra or lose weight or get along with their stepfather or wear their pants sagging around their ankles at school—but those things simply can't be done. They will reject your suggestion that they don't want to do those things. So you may have to add the words *badly enough to do what it would take to make it happen*. For example, if somebody really truly wants to pass math class, he or she could stay after school for tutoring, hire a private tutor, spend 5 hours every night on homework, and so on. But if somebody is not willing to do those things, he or she must tell the truth—he or she doesn't want to pass math (badly enough to do what they would need to do to make it happen).

Students may argue about their *can't* sentences, and in some cases they may be right. If they give examples of goals that have legitimate limitations or physical impossibilities (a girl with severe astigmatism probably cannot become a brain surgeon, and a boy cannot have a baby, at least not yet), accept and acknowledge any valid answers. But the majority of *have to* and *can't* sentences will not hold up to honest inspection.

Once your students understand and accept the truth of this lesson, they realize how much power they have over their own lives. They have to accept responsibility for who they are and for everything they do. They have to admit that when they misbehave or fail in your class, it is because they choose to misbehave or fail. They don't have to let somebody copy their homework. They don't have to respond to another student's insult by launching an insult in return. They don't have to come to your class if they don't want to learn—they may choose to come because they don't like the alternative. And if they have trouble learning required material, they can ask you for help or arrange for a tutor or spend more time on homework. Unless they have a true mental disability, students have no valid reason for failing your class, graduating from school, finding a decent occupation, learning to make friends, developing useful skills, and being successful people.

Check Your Own Attitude

After you have adjusted your students' attitudes, it's time to adjust your own. You may think your attitude is just fine, but if you are having any problems with discipline or participation you may be part of the problem. Perhaps you aren't prepared when class begins, so students follow your disorganized example. Maybe you believe you treat your students with respect but you have a hidden agenda to save them from themselves—and they have detected your patronizing attitude. Instead of focusing on how to fix your students, find ways to fix yourself. For example, if students constantly shout out answers instead of raising their hands before speaking, perhaps you have created the problem or contributed to it in some way. For example, at one point early in my teaching career I realized that if I wanted to stop those students who couldn't seem to stop themselves from blurting out whatever was on their minds, I would have to pretend I didn't hear them. Acknowledgment only encouraged them, even if I reminded them to raise their hands. It took some practice on my part to become selectively hard of hearing, but eventually it worked. Students started raising their hands to get my attention when they couldn't get it by shouting.

Teaching requires constant self-reflection. We must ask questions. How much do you listen—really listen—to your students? And how do you respond to their comments? Do you always have the last word? Do you correct their grammar when they are talking passionately about something? Do you imply that your values and standards and lifestyle are superior to theirs? Do you belittle their ideas or brush off their concerns as trivial? Do you use a dismissive or singsong tone of voice? Even if you think you are always courteous and respectful, try setting up a tape recorder near your desk and taping your class for 30 minutes. You may be surprised to hear the way you speak differently to different students.

One more tweak to your attitude may be in order. If you earned consistently high grades in school or if you haven't been to school for a while, try taking a very difficult class, one that you will have to struggle to pass. If you are creative, for example, enroll in statistics or advanced mathematics. If you are scientifically minded, try an art class. Your goal is not to earn an A but to remember (or find out for the first time) how it feels to be intelligent yet unable to easily grasp a new concept. Some teachers find that an academic adjustment enables them to better empathize with their students.

Alter Student Self-Perceptions

After you have adjusted the attitudes, in your classroom, students may be receptive to a perception shift as well. We can't make students care about getting an education, but if we can convince them to care about themselves they will begin to care about school. The tricky part is figuring out how to shift their self-perceptions. If only we could say, "I think you are an intelligent, capable person" and have the student say, "Oh, you're right. I guess I am intelligent. So I think I'll start taking my education seriously and make some plans for my future." Ho ho ho. We have to be a bit subtler and a lot more patient.

Subtlety and patience don't come naturally to me. I have to work at them. When I first started teaching, I thought I could muscle students into accepting my point of view. In a passing conversation, I once asked a high school junior what he planned to do after graduation.

"I'll probably go to prison," Julio said.

Surprised, I asked him if he was in trouble with the law.

"No," he said.

"Then why would you go to prison?"

"Because that's where all the men in my family go."

"Well, you don't have to go to prison. You're going to graduate, and you already have a job waiting for you."

"You don't understand," he said. "The men in my family always end up in prison."

"You don't understand," I said. "You don't have to go to prison."

Neither of us understood. Of course, I was upset by this conversation and was determined to change Julio's mind. I never could. And he did eventually go to prison after graduation. But a couple of years later, one of his friends called me and said, "Julio is out on parole, and he has a good job. He just wanted you to know he's doing all right."

That phone conversation was my wake-up call. I realized that Julio had been listening to me but that I hadn't listened to him. I heard his words, but I didn't realize what he was telling me: that he felt hopeless to change what he believed was his destiny. I needed to change my approach. Instead of trying to bulldoze students into accepting my perception of their talents and potential, I needed to find a way to help them change their perceptions of themselves as hopeless losers or powerless pawns—a subtle but powerful difference. First, I had to figure out how my students perceived themselves. I began by asking the group general questions when I felt they were in a comfortable and talkative mood.

"How many people plan to go to college?" (Some hands waved.)

"How many would like to go, but you don't think you can do it?" (More hands.)

"How many people here think they will end up on welfare someday?" (A lot more hands.)

"How many people think they will travel all over the world?"

"How many people see themselves having pretty good jobs?"

"How many think they will probably go to prison?"

"How many people think they will be married and have a family in 10 years?"

Eventually, all the hands were waving. I didn't respond individually to students during these quick surveys, but I did make notes of the students who raised their hands in response to the negative questions. Then, during the normal course of a school day I created opportunities to tell those students how I saw them and the possibilities for their future. For example, I might say, "Do you know how much artistic talent you have? I could see you as an architect or a graphic artist someday." To kids who are especially interested in computers, I might say, "You have such a good imagination, I bet you'd make a great video game designer. I could also see you working as a systems analyst, helping people figure out what kind of computer system they need for their business."

I persisted in telling students how I saw them every chance I got. It took weeks or months—a year in some cases—but eventually they began to see themselves as people with talents and skills. Sometimes I'd ask them to humor me and try a visualization experiment. I'd ask them to close their eyes and imagine themselves getting up in the morning, getting dressed, grabbing their briefcase and a cup of coffee, and driving to work in a spiffy car. Then they enter the reception area of a big company, greet the receptionist, and head for their office, where they turn on the computer and check their e-mail. "Can you see it?" I'd ask. Most couldn't, but one or two could.

Another day I might ask them to imagine themselves getting up very early, eating a hearty breakfast, and grabbing their toolboxes. They jump into their pickup trucks and head off to a construction site where they install kitchen cabinets in a new housing development. A few more could see.

These scenarios were very helpful, I think, because most students have no real idea of what occupations actually involve, other than the most familiar ones—doctor, lawyer, or teacher. They may hear about other jobs from the counselors and see people portraying different occupational roles in movies, but they don't know what those people actually do on the job. I try to give them details so they can imagine what it might be like to work as an x-ray technician, a hotel manager, a bartender, a restaurant owner, a construction supervisor, an engineer, a dental assistant, a veterinarian, a sports promoter, a tailor, a shoemaker, or a security guard. I encourage them to think of themselves in a variety of situations until they find one that feels right for them.

This may seem like New Age foo-foo hocus-pocus, as my father likes to say, but it isn't. When you tell a student, "I see you as an intelligent, talented person," that student can no longer think of himself as a stupid or untalented mess. Even if he rejects your idea, it's now in his thought repertoire. He won't change his perception immediately, but we do know that once you introduce a new idea to a brain it can't go back to its former state. The seed of that new idea will grow, even if it isn't watered.

Catch Kids Being Good

Children crave attention. If they can't get it by behaving well, they will misbehave because they know we won't ignore bad behavior. And we know we should focus on the positive, but we still tend to accentuate the negative in school. It seems to be the default setting of adults. We spend much more time trying to stop bad behavior than we do rewarding good behavior. We remember having to ask a student to sit down or be quiet, but we forget how many times that same student cooperated quietly. With practice and persistence, we can change our default settings. We can learn to notice when children behave. There are many more opportunities to catch them being good than there are to catch them being bad. If we want children to be kind, considerate, compassionate, and honest we need to notice and thank them when they do act in those ways. We don't have to give them candy or points, but we do need to give them acknowledgment.

If you'd like some suggestions for ways to start catching your students being good, visit Dr. Mac's behavior advisor Web site (www.behavioradvisor.com/Catch Good.html), where you'll find fifteen descriptions written by teachers about working with real students and keeping an eye out for good behavior.

One way I remind myself to catch students being wonderful is to take three blank index cards to class every day with the names of three students written on them. During that day I make sure I notice when those students do something kind or admirable—lending somebody a pen, offering to collect papers, picking up litter from the floor and placing it in the trash, erasing the board without my asking, helping another student complete an assignment. The specific act isn't important as long as it is honestly spontaneous. I take a minute to write notes that I hand to students at the end of class. The notes aren't long:

> "Thanks for helping to keep our classroom clean today. I appreciate you."

> "I applaud your generosity in sharing your supplies with classmates."

> "Thank you for being kind and tolerant. It sends a good example for other kids who don't have good role models at home."

Don't be surprised if a student confides that yours was the first positive note any teacher ever wrote to him or her. It's enough to make a grown teacher cry.

Help Students Believe in Success

Brains, like engines, don't operate at peak efficiency when they are low on fuel, clogged by dirty oil, or missing small but critical parts. If your students are fed well, adequately parented, emotionally well adjusted, and well educated prior to entering your classroom, you probably won't face any serious problems when you try to motivate them to learn. But it's much more likely that some of our students will come to school hungry, tired, high, emotionally distressed, abused or neglected, and ambivalent about education. Don't despair. What you bring to your students is just as important as what your students bring to your classroom.

We have all heard the statistics, and we have learned from our own experiences that the teacher's attitude toward students is a key factor in student success. When we believe students can succeed, they can. However, our belief is only half the solution to the problem of poor performance; we must also convince our students that success is possible. If students themselves don't believe in their ability to learn, it doesn't matter how intelligent they are or how easy we make the material—they will not succeed. The sincere belief that success is possible is the key that unlocks the door to learning.

How do we convince students that success is possible? Some people recommend giving an easy exercise or activity that guarantees success for every student. I disagree with that approach. Easy lessons and activities defeat their own purpose. Instead of convincing students that they are capable of achieving, easy assignments and esteem-boosting activities may send a message that students aren't capable of handling truly difficult challenges. Students are savvy. Once, I gave a class of at-risk students an easy assignment, hoping to build their confidence. After everybody had completed it successfully, one student shoved the graded assignment off his desk. When I asked him what was wrong, but he shrugged and said, "Nothing." I persisted until he finally told me, "You gave us that baby work because you think we're too dumb to do hard stuff." Another lesson learned.

So, instead of creating easy lessons for my low achievers, I started designing much more difficult assignments—and helping my students complete them. At first, some resisted, but when I explained that I believed they were much smarter and more capable than their grades and test scores indicated, they agreed to try. I'll never forget the day I convinced my sophomores, most of whom read at a third- or fourth-grade level, to tackle an essay from a college textbook. I didn't tell them where I got the essay. I just distributed copies and cajoled them into reading the first paragraph. They were hooked immediately because the essay questioned whether marijuana should be legalized. One boy read a sentence aloud and then leaned over to punch the boy sitting beside him. "They be talking about you, dog."

After we finished reading, I asked everybody to write a short response to the article in their journals. Then we shared our opinions about the essay. Finally, I held up the book where I found the original essay. "This is a college textbook. It says so inside the front cover, if you want to check for yourself. And the essay you just read came from this book. You just read a college assignment. What do you think of that?"

"Let me see that." One of the girls held out her hand. I gave her the book. She flipped through the pages and handed it to another student. After the book made the rounds, I could see my students trying to reconcile the idea of them being able to read college-level work. Nobody in that class expected to go to college. They didn't think they were smart enough. I could see them considering the possibility—literally. Brows furrowed, eyes narrowed, lips pursed. Several of them did eventually go to college, but that's another story.

Right now, the story is about you and your students. Raise the bar. Believe in them until they believe in themselves. When you introduce a difficult task, explain that you understand it is difficult and that you don't expect anybody to do it perfectly the first time. Tell them you are going to tackle this project because you believe they are intelligent and you know they can learn because you see evidence of many things they have already learned: they know how to care for animals or babies, they know dozens of addresses and phone numbers, they can fix meals, they can play musical instruments and a hundred different games, they know the words to a lot of songs, and they know how to operate machines and power tools and computers and electronic gadgets.

Even if you must teach a prescribed curriculum, you can still add challenging lessons of your own. Where do you find them? One good place to look is at your own school. If you teach second grade, for example, ask a fifth-grade teacher for a sample vocabulary lesson. Tell your students they are going to do an assignment that kids three whole grades ahead of them are doing, just to see what those kids are up to. If you teach middle school or high school, find a college textbook related to your subject. Begin by giving full credit to everybody who tackles the tough assignments. Show them you don't expect perfection—just a little cooperation. Eventually, they will become hooked on learning. Then you can start adding grades based on accuracy and completeness.

Go Right-Brain

Brain hemisphere dominance is a topic that goes in and out of favor, depending on the latest research (and perhaps who funds it). The idea first gained popularity in the late 1950s when doctors learned they could help prevent severe seizures in epileptics by severing the corpus callosum that connects the two brain hemispheres. This discovery sparked decades of research. Based on my own research and experience as a teacher, I believe the basic concept is sound: the right- and left-brain hemispheres have different specializations.

The left is analytical. It performs arithmetic computations, monitors speech, understands the literal interpretation of words, and recognizes words and numbers. Arousing the brain's attention to deal with outside stimuli is a left-brain specialty. The right gathers information from images, looks for patterns, and interprets language through context—body language, emotional context, tone of voice—rather than through literal meanings. It specializes in spatial perceptions, recognizes places, faces, objects, and relational and mathematical operations such as geometry and trigonometry.

People tend to be right- or left-brain dominant, just as they are right- or left-handed. However, logic is not confined to the left hemisphere, just as creativity is not restricted to the right. Both hemispheres are engaged in logical thought and creativity. Because the two hemispheres do not function independently, it is impossible to educate only one hemisphere. It is possible, however, to design activities that encourage right- or left-brain brain activity. Turning a drawing upside-down, for example, and trying to copy it will engage the right hemisphere rather than the left.

Research into brain dominance most likely inspired the creation of the brain gym exercises, which have been instrumental in helping some preschool children develop early literacy. Toddlers who can't crawl or who have poor eye–hand coordination may have trouble learning to read. The exercises are simple, but they involve moving the arms and legs so they cross the median of the body. This strategy is also used often by physical therapists. When people's coordination improves (tapping the right knee with the left hand, for example, and vice versa) other positive changes occur. Children who learn how to crawl more gracefully are more likely to be able to learn to read.

Although making generalizations can be dangerous, I believe it would be safe to suggest that the majority of teachers are left-brain dominant (detail-oriented) thinkers. Left-brainers like school because their natural preference coincides with the left-brain paradigm of most traditional school systems. Unfortunately, the majority of students may not be left-brain dominant. For the sake of argument, let's assume that half the students in a given class are right-brain (big-picture) dominant thinkers. They think differently from their left-brain teachers, and they often become discouraged or uninterested in school because they are made to feel unintelligent by virtue of the way their brains operate.

If you are unfamiliar with the subject of brain dominance, you can find an excellent introduction to the topic in David Sousa's book *How the Brain Learns* (Corwin Press, 2006). Chapter Five of that book, on brain specialization and learning, provides an overview of hemisphere dominance, along with notes about interesting research on gender, language acquisition, and learning to read. And Daniel H. Pink's bestseller *A Whole New Mind: Why Right-Brainers Will Rule the Future* (Riverhead, 2006) presents an interesting case for the importance of cultivating the brain's right hemisphere, inside and outside the classroom. And you can watch an excellent video on *TED Talks* by psychiatrist Iain McGilchrist titled "The Divided Brain" (http://www.ted.com/talks/iain_mcgilchrist_the_divided_brain).

Take a Brain Dominance Quiz
Teachers can take a brain dominance quiz that offers tips for teaching at www2.scholastic.com/browse/article.jsp?id=3629.

Students can take a similar test designed specifically for them at homework-tips.about.com/ … /brainquiz/bl_leftrightbrain_quiz.htm.

Add Some Right-Brain Activities

You can change the dynamics in your classroom by adding some right-brain activities and educational games. If you do an Internet search for "wacky wordies" and "right-brain games," you will find many resources.

To get you started, here are two brief examples. Exhibits 9.1 and 9.2 contain some word puzzles that I like to use to identify my right-brain students. Don't read the answers immediately. Instead, read the directions and try to solve each puzzle. If you are a left-brainer, this may be very frustrating for you.

If you do this exercise with your students, you may find that the students who enjoy it most are those who do not have the highest grades in your class. The left-brain dominant scholars sometimes become very upset because they are used to being smarter and faster than their classmates. Your right-brain dominant students will enjoy being the smart kids for a change. (Be prepared: sometimes students may figure out alternative answers that aren't on the answer list but are equally correct.)

Exhibit 9.1.
Wacky Wordies.

Directions: The words in each box represent a popular phrase. The placement, size, and shape of letters inside the box give clues. For example, the word "pigs" when printed three times in small letters inside the box would represent the phrase "three little pigs."

| five | cof
fee | **SHOT** | ever
ever
ever
ever |

Answers:
high five, coffee break, big shot, forever.

Exhibit 9.2.
Right-Brain Word Puzzles.

Directions: Each group of words shares a common trait (but not common definitions). Only one answer shares that same trait. Figure out the common trait and select the correct answer.

1	2	3	4	5
sexes	golden	tea	modem	youth
level	tallow	eye	willow	usher
redder	clamp	sea	domed	item
a. dined	a. trace	a. wee	a. clash	a. water
b. mom	b. crawl	b. ate	b. winter	b. there
c. start	c. oven	c. you	c. tablet	c. hero

Answers:

1. mom: the word spells the same forward and backward
2. trace: remove the first letter to form a new word
3. you: sounds like a letter when you say it (tea, eye)
4. tablet: the word begins and ends with the same letter
5. hero: the word begins with a pronoun

Copyright © 2015 by LouAnne Johnson

Look at Learning Preferences

After you do your right-brain activity, tell your students you would like to help them identify their own learning preferences (and be sure to write the three primary preferences on the board for your visual learners): auditory (listeners), visual (lookers), and kinesthetic (movers). Then ask your students to think about how they approach a new game. Do they like to have somebody explain the game and the rules and give them verbal instructions? Do they like to watch other people play for a while and then jump in themselves? Or would they prefer to just get into the game and learn as they go along?

Another example that helps students identify their learning preferences is to give them directions. For example, tell them to imagine that they have asked you how to get to the post office. First, say, "You exit the school and turn right. Go two blocks and take the next left turn. Go up the hill and around a curve and then take the second right. After the second stop sign, turn left and then make an immediate right into the parking lot." Ask how many students feel confident that they can get to the post office after listening to your instructions. Those who raise their hands are your auditory learners (probably a small percentage of students).

Next, draw a map on the board or distribute copies of a map you have drawn. Use the same instructions that you gave verbally. Next, ask how many students feel confident that they can get to the post office. Probably more than half your class will raise their hands; these are your visual learners.

Watch for students who are frowning at the map or turning it sideways. Perhaps they are tilting their heads. Ask, "If I drove you to the post office right now, how many of you would be able to retrace that same route, even if we drove it only once?" Those frowning students (your kinesthetic learners) will shoot their hands into the air, relieved to learn that there is a third alternative.

I would also suggest, if you have time, teaching your students how to ask for help from teachers, tutors, or parents. Students often say, "I don't get it." And we repeat what we have said, either more loudly or more slowly. But that response will help only auditory learners. Auditory learners do need to say, "Could you please repeat that?" or "Could you please explain that to me again, a little more slowly?" Visual learners need to say, "I can't quite picture that. If I could see a drawing or a graph or video or something, I think I could understand it better. Maybe an example would help me." And your kinesthetic learners need to say, "I learn by doing things. Could you walk me through a couple of examples step-by-step so that I can practice doing them and get the hang of it?"

Of course, teachers need to remember that different students learn in different ways, so we need to vary our methods of instruction to incorporate visuals and movement as well as listening activities. When you discuss a new concept, for example, be sure to provide some kind of visual to accompany your verbal introduction. And make sure you walk students through several examples. Kinesthetic learners need to do the examples themselves, however. Copying your work from the board isn't enough.

Experts suggest that we should encourage students to strengthen their weak areas. A visual learner, for example, may need to work on developing better listening skills. Likewise, an auditory learner might benefit from working on kinesthetic skills such as eye–hand coordination. However, it is helpful to know a student's preference so that when problems arise during instruction you can use examples that favor the student's strengths and help them move forward.

Make Mistakes Mandatory

Have some fun making mistakes. We often tell children that mistakes are OK because everybody makes them but we then turn around and punish students academically for being less than perfect. Imagine that your supervisor expected you to perform eight out of every ten tasks perfectly. Few salespeople can boast a 70 percent success rate; most would be happy with 50 percent or even lower. Baseball players are considered top-notch if they can hit more than 30 percent of the pitches thrown at them. Yet we expect children to perform with 70 percent accuracy when they are working with unfamiliar material and learning new skills. How unreasonable can we get?

Of course, we have to have tests and other measures to assess how well students are learning, but if we want children to be interested in learning we must allow them to make mistakes without embarrassing or penalizing them. For example, instead of grading a regular classroom assignment as soon as students finish it, why not let them keep their papers while you go over each item and discuss the correct answers, possible answers, and common mistakes? Let students redo the assignment before they turn it in. Their comprehension will improve, and they will be much more likely to remember the information if you correct any misconceptions immediately than if they have to wait a day or two (or six) to see how well they did. In the meantime, that misinformation percolates in their brains and may work its way into their long-term memories.

In subjects such as math, this is especially important. If you simply present the lesson and then instruct students to complete an assignment, some students will get about half the answers right and it may appear that they understand. But those correct answers may be accidental or the result of faulty logic. Correcting faulty logic is important for long-term student success. My 8-year-old nephew, for example, looked as though he understood the concept of carrying numbers to another column when adding three-digit numbers. He got about 60 percent of his math problems correct. Because he got that many problems right, his teacher and his parents thought Anthony was simply being lazy or trying to work too fast. When he did his math homework at my house one night, I asked him to explain each step he made. When he carried a number, it was often incorrect, because, as he explained, "If the number is 10 or higher, you write a number up here and keep going." When I asked him how he knew which number to write up there, he said it didn't matter. You just put a number. When I showed Anthony how to correctly carry a number, he was thrilled, and his math grades immediately began to improve. I could see how his teacher might have missed Anthony's faulty logic because it certainly looked like he knew what he was doing, and if you asked him he would assure you that he did.

Celebrate mistakes, even yours. When you make a mistake, ask the students to give you a round of applause for demonstrating that although you are an educated and undoubtedly intelligent teacher you are also a human being. Don't worry that students will lose respect for you when they learn that you aren't perfect. On the contrary, they will respect you more for admitting your mistakes and helping them learn from theirs.

During class discussions, when a student offers an incorrect answer or idea, instead of simply saying, "Wrong," or asking another student, try saying, "That's an interesting idea. I hadn't thought of that. Could you explain your thinking?" Not only does this teach students that mistakes are acceptable, but also you may identify misinformation before it solidifies in a student's mind. For example, if a student identifies 0 as an improper fraction, that student may not understand the basic principles of fractions. If you ask how she arrived at that answer, you may be able to adjust her thinking and set her back on the right track.

Never, ever let other students laugh if somebody makes a mistake. Sometimes students will insist that they are only teasing or that the student who is the object of the laughter is their best friend. It doesn't matter. Nobody likes to be made to feel like a fool. It isn't funny. If people laugh at themselves, that's a different matter, but still I don't encourage others to join in the laughter. It's one thing to laugh at yourself; it's an entirely different thing to be laughed at.

Connect Through Private Journals

If you use journals but your students aren't writing very much, there is a reason. I could suggest a few possibilities based on my own students' comments about journal writing: you don't read the journals; you grade entries on spelling and grammar, which inhibits expression; you don't allow enough time, so they feel rushed and unable to think; you allow too much time, so they procrastinate and lack focus; your prompts are not inspiring.

Inspiring prompts are a must if you expect journal writing to produce results. Prompts such as "Write a letter to Abraham Lincoln" or "Write your own obituary" may sound interesting to adults and may appeal to more scholarly students, but they won't work for students who aren't excited about school or are frightened by death. If you want students to write a letter to somebody, choose a person (or let them choose a person) they would actually consider talking to in the first place. Most children wouldn't be inclined to talk to a dead president or a historical figure. They would, however, talk to their parents, relatives, teachers, principals, and friends. If you use letter writing as a prompt, assure your students that you will not send their letters off and that students can destroy them as soon as you have recorded their grade for completing the writing assignment.

Letter writing can be very cathartic for students who are distracted by emotional stress or too keyed up to focus on school. Writing down our feelings, especially when we are angry, helps dissipate pent-up energy and may help us calm down.

For teachers who haven't used journals or haven't used them successfully, my students created the following list of dos and don'ts:

- Read the journals. If you aren't going to read them, don't ask us to write in them.
- Make at least one comment on every page.
- Give us choices of what to write or let us make up our own.
- Show us some good journal entries that other kids have written.
- Let us know when we write something especially good.
- Let us use our journals as rough drafts for essays.
- Make journal writing a regular activity, at least once a week.
- Let us use curse words sometimes, when we are really mad.

Recently a teacher e-mailed me to say that she had decided to use journal writing as the starter activity for the first 10 minutes of every class but that her students balked at the assignment. I advised her to continue with the journals so that her students wouldn't think that they could make her give up any activity they didn't feel like doing. I also suggested that she require journals for 2 or 3 weeks and then stop for a few days. A few weeks later, she sent me an e-mail that said, "I did it. Now my students are complaining that they never get to write in their journals. They liked having that quiet activity to help them calm down and focus."

When working with reluctant writers, it may be helpful if you make the journals anonymous to everybody but you. Create a code, using letters or numbers to identify journals by class, but don't label them in alphabetical order. Randomly code them so that if they are lost nobody will know whose journal they are reading.

I also offer students the option of writing the required number of pages in their journals, showing them to me for credit, and then destroying them if it makes them feel too vulnerable to have those words in print. For seriously reluctant writers, I give them the option of writing what they have to say and then folding the page in half so that what they have written is not visible. I then check to see that they have written a page or two or whatever the assignment was, but I don't read what they have written. I give them credit for doing the assignment and respect their request for privacy. Only once did I break my promise not to look. I had a student who made it clear that he didn't like teachers, including me, from the moment he entered my classroom. I worked hard to connect with him, but he wasn't having it. He rarely wrote more than a sentence. One day, he wrote and wrote and wrote. I was so excited. I couldn't wait to read what he had written. But when I got home and took out the bin of journals to grade, I saw that he had turned down the page in his journal, indicating that I was not to read it. I couldn't resist. I opened the page. He had torn out the pages of writing and on the page that remained, he had written, "I knew I couldn't trust you, you f**king liar." He was right. He couldn't trust me. I had to work hard to regain his trust—it took 2 years. Fortunately, I had the same students for 3 years, so I had that time. He taught me a very valuable lesson: Don't make promises to students unless you know you can keep them.

Introduce Ethics

Children have an innate sense of justice, but they also tend to view themselves as the center of the universe, which can cause problems because they are unaware of the effects that their actions have on other people. By introducing students to sociology and psychology, you can help them see the bigger picture and realize that they each play a small but important role in a large society. Our goal as teachers is not to impose our own values and ethics but to encourage students to explore, form, and articulate their own.

I first introduced an ethics exercise to a class in which negative peer pressure was causing a lot of stress and behavior problems. I wanted my students to realize that each person has an individual code of ethics, even if he or she isn't aware of it. I thought that if they could articulate their values and morals, they would be less likely to succumb to negative pressures. For the first experiment, I used something relatively impersonal but universal—money. I asked students to select their best answers to the questions shown in Exhibit 9.3 in their journals.

Exhibit 9.3.
Ethics Exercise.

Ethics Exercise: Too Much Money

In your journal, answer the following questions.

1. If a sales clerk or a waiter gave you back too much change, would you return the money or keep it?

   a. Yes, I would definitely keep the money.

   b. No, I would never keep the money.

   c. Maybe I would keep the money. It would depend.

2. If you answered a or b above, please explain.
3. If you answered c in question 1, what would affect your decision—the amount of money, whether anybody else would know, or something else?
4. If your answer to question 3 depends on the amount of money, where would you draw the line? What amount would it take before you felt it necessary to return the money?

After students wrote their answers, I took a quick survey and tallied their responses to question 1 on the board for each category: yes, no, and maybe. Then we had a quick class discussion about the topic. Next, students formed groups of three to five people and discussed the questions for another 10 minutes, trying to see if they could reach a group consensus. After their small-group discussions, students returned to their desks and wrote down their thoughts about the discussions, particularly if they had changed their minds. I asked those who had changed their minds to write the reasons. Finally, we took another quick vote to see if people had changed their views. Many more students had joined the no group: those who would return the money. Students enjoyed seeing where they fell along the ethics spectrum, and many of them expressed admiration for the students who originally said that no, they would never keep the money. Those students were steadfast in their refusal to compromise their ethics. Apparently, it is easier to convince people to be more ethical than it is to make them abandon their ethics.

You can slant ethics exercises to fit your subject. In a social studies class, for example, after conducting the exercise about whether to keep money that doesn't belong to you, then you could assign the project of researching crime statistics for 10, 20, and 30 years ago and have students chart the trends. Math students could figure the percentage of people who would keep or return the money and the percentage of people whose votes changed after the discussions. Computer classes could generate charts or tables to display voting results. Art students could make drawings or posters expressing their feelings about money and greed. English composition students could write essays about their thoughts on ethics in general or stealing in particular.

With a bit of practice, you will be able to design ethics and sociology activities that are appropriate and effective for your students. I suggest beginning with a journal write so students can think about their own ideas first before being influenced by others.

Relinquish Responsibility

It is difficult for some teachers (it was for me for many years) to let go and stop taking responsibility for student behavior. Assigning detention, giving demerits, requiring student behavior contracts, making office referrals, deducting points from grades, and calling parents all involve taking responsibility for student behavior. I resisted accepting that truth for a long time, but finally I became desperate and exhausted enough to put the responsibility for student behavior back where it truly belongs—in their own hands. This wasn't a gentle process for me. I was teaching a summer school class at a high school in California where students came from a number of school districts. I didn't know them and they didn't know me, so I couldn't count on the rapport I had established at my own school. These student were tough, especially a girl named Araceli. One day, after I distributed an assignment and everybody else was working, Araceli stabbed the paper with the tip of her pencil and said, "I ain't doing this stupid shit." Of course, everybody else stopped working.

Normally, I would have explained the objective of the assignment, but that day I was tired. For weeks, I had been explaining and reminding and threatening and pleading and worrying about the futures of these difficult students.

"Fine," I snapped. "Turn it over and write on the back, 'I ain't doing this stupid shit,' and sign your name. I'll save it in case you or your parents wonder why you have the grade you have."

"What?" Araceli sneered. "I ain't signing nothing."

"Okay, then throw it away. There's the trash." Araceli hesitated. I held out my hand. "Here. Give it to me. I'll throw it away for you."

"I ain't throwing it away," Araceli said.

"Then you can leave the room."

"Oh, you're kicking me out?" Now we were on familiar territory for her. She loved fighting with teachers. Or so it seemed.

"No," I said. "I'm giving you choices. Do it. Sign it. Throw it away. Or leave the room. Everybody here has the same four options. I'll give you a fifth—you can sit and quietly vegetate if that trips your trigger. But you do not have the option of wasting my time and disrupting people who are trying to earn their diplomas."

Araceli crossed her arms and scowled at me for the remainder of the class period, but she didn't say anything else and didn't disrupt the others who went back to their work when they realized there wasn't going to be an argument for their entertainment. After class, she asked me if she could take the assignment home and bring it back the next day. I had to force myself not to laugh—or scream.

"What would you do if you were the teacher and you had a student who acted the way you do?" I asked. Araceli shrugged and struggled to hold back a smile.

"I'd give her one chance," she said. "Everybody deserves one."

She brought the assignment the next day.

The next fall, when classes resumed, I stopped trying to make people behave. I started giving them options and letting them choose what to do. "Is this really what you want to do right now?" I ask and walk away so they can decide without having to save face. Most students opt to stop traveling down the road to self-destruction. I still use my emergency folder to send students to the library or elsewhere on campus to work on their own if they choose to continue their disruptive behavior, but I no longer make myself responsible for correcting their behavior. They know how to behave. It's all about choice. If they choose to behave, they stay in my classroom. If they choose not to behave, they remove themselves—to the hallway outside my room to think, to the library to work, to the computer lab, the counselor's office, the gym, a favorite coach's office, to take a walk with a campus security guard—wherever they need to go. When they return, I smile and welcome them back. Then I call their parents and report their good behavior. It's not what they expect. I think that's one reason that it works. Two more reasons: first, students realize they are not powerless and can choose their own behavior minute by minute; second, it's hard work being obnoxious all day long.

WHAT DO YOU THINK?

1. How can we discover student self-perceptions if they are reluctant to talk to teachers?

2. What are some ways we can catch students being good?

3. Create your own wacky wordy puzzles.

4. Take a brain dominance quiz. How might your preference influence the way you teach?

5. Do the Too Much Money ethics exercise with a group of teachers. Share your thoughts about how to design and present such activities for students at your school.

Foods for Thought

Americans have finally gotten the message: we can't ignore the fact that nutrition plays a huge role in learning. Therefore, if we want our children to do better in school we must give them the freshest, most nutritious food available. In this chapter, I'll be exploring some topics in-depth, but first I'd like to start with a few bite-size summaries to give you something to chew on. (Forgive me. I just couldn't resist the pun. It's a genetic weakness—probably caused by eating too many tuna casseroles as a child.)

A FEW APPETIZERS

Central Alternative

If you watched the 2004 documentary *Supersize Me* by independent filmmaker Morgan Spurlock, you may remember Central Alternative High in Appleton, Wisconsin. The school was highlighted because administrators were making the switch to fresh, local food. Intrigued by the idea, I followed the school's success online and was delighted to learn that making the switch didn't break the school's budget—and it paid off in both academic achievement and better behavior. Their success encouraged other schools to challenge the biggest argument against changing the way we feed schoolchildren: it would cost too much to make the necessary changes. School after school has proved that claim to be false. In fact, switching saves money in the long run. In fact, Central Alternative's principal reported a few years after making the switch to healthy foods that her school was saving money because truancy, drop-outs, expulsions, weapons, and suicide attempts had all but disappeared from their campus.

Feingold Diet

Need an accessible article with statistics to convince school boards of the importance of school lunches? You can find a short article on the Feingold Web site (www.feingold.org). It's titled "A Different Kind of School Lunch." The site offers a link to a short documentary from the Natural Press's "Roadmap to Healthy Foods in School." Dr. Benjamin Franklin Feingold is an important name for any teacher who teaches students where attention-deficit disorder/attention-deficit/hyperactivity disorder (ADD/ADHD) and other behavioral problems interfere with student learning. Dr. Feingold designed a diet to eliminate what he believed (and research supported) were primary causes of disruptive behavior in children: food dyes, artificial flavors, and preservatives. The success of the Feingold diet was dramatic and inspired ongoing research that continues to be reported in peer-reviewed professional journals. You can read the success stories of twenty children whose lives dramatically improved when chemicals and preservatives were removed from their daily diets. You can also read about a simple science experiments involving mice and yellow or yellow food dyes that clearly show the connection between the dyes and dysfunctional behavior. (See Science Fair Projects link on the Feingold site.)

Jamie Oliver

Chef and food activist Jamie Oliver is another champion of nutrition. His television series, school visits, and programs for training young chefs have made him a worldwide celebrity, but his message is a simple one: If we continue to let our children eat junk food, their life expectancy will be 10 years shorter than ours. Oliver's 22-minute presentation "Teach Every Child About Food" can be seen online at TEDTalks. It's well worth viewing—for both adults and children.

Healthy Vending

Vending machines are one of the most controversial topics on school campuses. There are big bucks involved in this issue, and many school are tied up with contracts that bring in needed money at the expense of students' health. But it's only a matter of time before vending machines are hit by the nutrition revolution. FarmersFridge.com has done for businesses in Chicago what the rest of the country needs to do for our schools. It has created a vending machine system built around fresh, healthy foods: salads, proteins, snacks—everything comes in a jar to prevent spoilage Its menu is appealing: yogurt and berries, fried rice, sliced apples or veggies, salads, hummus, salmon salad, tofu, lemon pepper chicken. FarmersFridge proved that we can offer healthy alternatives from a machine. The first time I saw one of its ads, I thought: Why can't we do that at schools? We have the machines. We just need somebody local to buy the food and fill the machines. Maybe we should stop trying to do all the work. Maybe we should involve the students. I have no doubt that with our support students could come up with creative and economical ways to bring healthy food to vending machines on campus.

Farm to School

In the late 1990s, a handful of schools were involved in the farm to school movement to bring local foods to local schools. In 2007, Occidental College joined forced with over thirty organizations to launch the National Farm to School Network. In just 5 years, the organization grew to include over 40,000 schools in all fifty states. The organization's Web site offers information for communities who want to establish farm to school programs along with success stories from schools that have switched to fresh local foods, webinars, and information about government grants to help fund local programs. Many states also offer toolkits, conferences, guidance, and advice.

THE BIG, FAT PROBLEM

Americans are too fat. We know that. We also know that childhood obesity and diabetes are running rampant in our schools, along with asthma, allergies, attention deficit, and a host of other learning problems. Fat and failure in school may be linked, according to recent research. I had read some bits here and there about the effects of nutrition on learning and behavior, and I was intrigued. However, after attending the 2003 European Council of International Schools conference in Hamburg, Germany, I became convinced that nutrition and neuroscience were going to change the way Americans view the connection between eating and learning. In fact, since then I have read considerable new research about the effects of nutrition on brain function and behavior. It seems that we chubby Americans may finally be getting the message that it isn't how much we eat but what we eat that makes all the difference.

In Hamburg I had the good fortune of hearing Dr. Madeleine Portwood, an educational psychologist from the United Kingdom, present the preliminary findings from the Durham trial, a research experiment involving elementary school students whose behavior and academic achievement improved as a result of essential fatty acid supplementation. Before Dr. Portwood began speaking, I had been feeling a bit sorry for myself for having to spend the Thanksgiving vacation week away from my family. After hearing her lecture, though, I was thankful to be thousands of miles from home, sitting on a hard, plastic chair in a chilly auditorium. And I was in a hurry to go home—not just to hug my family but also to share what I learned.

First, a brief disclaimer. I am not a scientist, a chemist, or a trained nutritionist. I have read extensively about diet and nutrition. Since I have no formal background in nutrition or neuroscience, however, I hope that the scientists and chemists among you will forgive me if I simplify enough to make a complicated subject more understandable to those of us who don't routinely ponder molecular structure and neurophysiological properties. I took copious notes while I was listening, and I have done my best to transcribe them accurately.

Fat is a dirty word in most Americans' vocabulary, and that is a big part of our problem. We need certain fats. Essential fatty acids (EFAs) are necessary for proper brain function and health. Omega-6 fatty acids and omega-3 fatty acids are both EFAs—essential in that the body requires them but cannot manufacture them itself. Of the EFAs, the omega-3s are probably the most important because they suppress inflammation, which is the cause of many degenerative diseases. Very briefly, here's the difference:

Omega-3s (alpha-linoleic acid or ALA) can be found in foods such as wild-caught salmon, mackerel, walnuts, flaxseed, and green, leafy vegetables. Omega-3s are metabolized by the body into two beneficial fatty acids, eicosapentaenoic acid (EPA) and docosahexaenoic acid (DHA). Many nutritional labels now tout the inclusion of EPA and DHA.

Omega-6s (linoleic acid) come from plants and can be found abundantly in common cooking oils such as corn, sunflower, safflower, and soybean oil (but not olive oil). Omega-6 fatty acids stimulate hair growth and maintain bone health and reproduction. Most Americans have an abundance of omega-6 EFAs in their diet. Too much omega-6 causes inflammation, the root cause of many illnesses.

Omega-9 fatty acids are sometimes included in the mix, but they are not considered essential because our bodies can make them from unsaturated fats. Regardless of how they are labeled, omega-9s are required for proper brain function and health. Omega-9s are found in animal fats and olive oil, and the oil manufactured by human skin glands is the same fatty acid (oleic acid) that is found in olive oil.

The Omega Ratio: The Key to the Puzzle

Many nutritional supplements boast that they provide omega-3s or 6s, but most do not warn consumers that the ratio of omega-6 to omega-3 EFAs is the most important piece of the fat picture. The optimum ratio of omega-6 to omega-3 is two to one (2:1). Our brains can cope with a higher ratio—until it surpasses 20:1. Then we have trouble because of the molecular structure and behavior of the EFAs. When omega-6s are present in much more abundance than omega-3s, the omega-6s will actually block the gaps between the molecules of omega-3s, interrupting or even canceling the transmission of electrical impulses in the brain, which directly relates to the ability to think, focus, and concentrate. In unscientific terms, eating too much of the wrong kind of fat makes us stupid.

Foods with Omega-6-to-Omega-3 Ratios Below 20:1

Cream, butter, and canola oil	2:1
Soft margarine (not polyunsaturated)	4:1
Yogurt	6:1
Soybean oil	7:1
Olive oil	11:1

So far, so good. We are still under the 20:1 cutoff point. But the typical American diet contains ratios of omega-6 to omega-3 EFAs that far surpass the optimum 2:1 ratio that nurtures our brains. Corn oil, perhaps the most widely used vegetable oil in the country, has an omega-6-to-omega-3 ratio of 56:1. That is more than double the maximum ratio that the brain can handle without dysfunction. It gets worse—much worse, as the following list demonstrates.

Foods with Omega-6-to-Omega-3 Ratios Higher Than 20:1

Sesame oil	144:1
Polyunsaturated margarine	370:1
Diet spreads (70 percent polyunsaturated)	370:1
Sunflower or safflower oil	632:1

During her presentation, Dr. Portwood said, "Give a child a bag of chips fried in sunflower oil for lunch, and that child will be unable to learn in the afternoon." Sadly, many fast-food companies, in response to consumer demand that they stop using corn oil, switched to sunflower or safflower oil. And nearly every bag of chips in this country, even organic chips on the shelves of health food stores, list the oils used in their preparation as sunflower or safflower oil.

Americans Lead the Poor Nutrition Parade

Dr. Portwood said her research team was especially interested in the American diet because the United States tends to lead the rest of the world in diseases and problems such as attention deficit and other learning issues. She said that studies indicate 50 percent of children in the United Kingdom at age 3 now show signs of developing behavior and learning problems. Because the surge in attention and focus difficulties has been so sharp in the United States, in the United Kingdom researchers now do not believe the cause is likely to be organic (within the children). When a disease trend arises this quickly, scientists look to the environment for the cause of the problems. Nutrition is one of the key environmental factors that scientists study. Dr. Portwood said that 20 to 25 percent of neurobiological disorders are metabolically based, which means that they have something to do with the food we eat and the way our bodies respond to that food.

Corn appears to be a major culprit in the United States, not just because of the abundance of omega-6 EFAs in corn oil but also because of the high-fructose corn syrup that is so widespread in our diet. It is hard to find a cookie, cracker, or juice in the supermarket today that doesn't contain high-fructose corn syrup (HFCS; more on HFCS later in this chapter).

Dr. Portwood didn't spend a great deal of time discussing HFCS because the focus of her research and presentation was EFAs, but she did say that the body can't break down high-fructose corn syrup and that its consumption may lead to weight gain and other health problems. The irony is that many American foods use HFCS instead of sugar and that many Americans have virtually eliminated fats from their diets in the belief that fats and sugars will make us fat. It may very well be the fat and sugar substitutes we eat that are doing the damage!

MOTHER'S MILK VERSUS FORMULA

Dr. Portwood began her presentation about the Durham trial by summarizing the results of previous studies conducted to evaluate the effect of different formulas on infants' brain activity and IQ. These babies were not the victims of callous scientists; they were premature infants who had to be fed formula for their survival. The first studies compared two different kinds of formula, one with a superior nutritional content that resulted in significant differences in the infants' mental activity. Then scientists pitted their superior formula against mother's milk, believing that the formula would emerge as the winner. Not only were they wrong, but also babies who drank breast milk (from their own mothers or donors) showed significantly higher brain activity and IQs than formula-fed infants. These results led to more studies to find out what ingredients in mother's milk made such a drastic difference. The answer: mother's milk contains two kinds of omega-3 fatty acids: arachidonic acid (AA) and docosahexaenoic acid (DHA). DHA is the primary structural fatty acid in the gray matter of the brain and the retina of the eye, and it is important for the transmission of signals in the brain, eyes, and nervous system. Low levels of DHA have been linked to depression, memory loss, and visual problems. The infant formulas contained more linoleic acid and more alpha-linoleic acid than they did DHA and AA.

Dr. Portwood's team designed the Durham trial to test the effect of EFAs on the behavior of 200 children; nearly all had problems with physical coordination. Eighty-two had been clinically diagnosed as having attention deficit hyperactivity disorder (ADHD), and forty had reading problems such as dyslexia. Instead of taking a blood test, which would have involved needles and caused fear, the scientists devised a breath test to monitor the children. Each child was given six capsules per day of a supplement containing a ratio of 20 percent omega-6 EFAs and 80 percent omega-3 EFAs. No other change was made to the children's diets. The supplements were administered during the school day by school staff in a blind study, which means that nobody, including the researchers, knew which children were receiving the supplement and which were receiving placebos. Two months into the study, results began to impress the parents, and eventually they impressed the scientists as well. The researchers found a dramatic drop in excitability and improved concentration among the students taking the EFA supplements.

When I returned from the Hamburg conference, I visited the Web site that discussed the research of Dr. Portwood's team (http://www.durhamtrial.org), and did further research to learn more about EFAs. After reading a number of studies and journal articles, I have come to believe that many of the health problems that plague Americans—ADHD, obesity, depression, and Alzheimer's—are directly linked to an overabundance of some fats and a deficiency of others.

DOCTOR'S ORDERS

If you'd like to read about EFAs, a good place to start is the article titled "Omega-6 Fatty Acids" on the University of Maryland Medical Center's Web site (http://umm .edu/health/medical/altmed/supplement/omega6-fatty-acids). Another good reference is the Web site of Dr. Thomas Greene, a Texas chiropractor who provides a good primer on vitamins, minerals, and EFAs, along with other nutritional information (http://dcnutrition.com/home.cfm).

If you can find a copy of Rachael Moeller Gorman's article "Captain of the Happier Meal," which appeared in the May–June 2010 online issue of *Eating Well* (http://www.eatingwell.com), I highly recommend reading it. Joe Hibbeln, MD, is a captain in the U.S. Public Health Service and acting chief of the section on nutritional neurosciences. He is a specialist in mental illness and is most interested in the connection between low levels of omega-3 fatty acids along with high levels of omega-6 fatty acids and mental health—bipolar conditions, schizophrenia, depression, and so on. In 1995, Dr. Hibbeln and a colleague published a paper in the *American Journal of Clinical Nutrition* (volume 62) that presented their theory: mental illness may be a result of omega-3 deficiency. According to the doctor, the American diet is too far out of balance; we eat ten to twenty-five times more omega-6s than omega-3s because of the prevalence of soybean, safflower, and corn oils. That imbalance, he says, may be the cause of many of the mental health problems that plague our nation. His next mission? To change the entire American military diet to include more omega-3 fatty acids and fewer omega-6s. He believes this change will reduce posttraumatic stress disorder and depression among veterans.

OTHER MAJOR NUTRITIONAL VILLAINS

Since the late 1980s, after realizing what a strong impact foods and nonfoods have on the brains and behavior of my students, I have continued to experiment, research, and read about nutrition and the brain. And for over three decades, two culprits continue to crop up time and again, whether I am reading magazine articles or major scientific studies: artificial sweeteners and high-fructose corn syrup.

Aspartame

Aspartame and I came into conflict personally after I started dating a cowboy who was hooked on diet soda. (Aspartame is the main ingredient in artificial sweeteners like NutraSweet, Equal Measure, and Equal.) A nonsoda drinker until that point, I started drinking the occasional diet soda. Before long, I found myself craving them, just as my friend did. At the time, I was living in southern New Mexico, where hot is an understatement much of the time and crunchy-ice sodas, as my friend referred to them, tasted especially good. Before long, I graduated from 12-ounce drinks to the typical 41-ounce bucket of chemicals, preservatives, flavorings, and artificial sweeteners that comprise most commercial sodas today. And within a few months, I started noticing some physical changes—brittle fingernails, hair falling out and landing on my bathroom counters, a little spare tire around my middle, and chubbier than normal thighs. I didn't connect those changes to the diet sodas until I started having serious bladder issues. My doctor suggested that

I stop the sodas. I did. But giving up diet sodas turned out to be difficult—even more difficult than quitting smoking, which I had done several years earlier. Eventually I did quit, and within a few days my health started to improve. That's when I realized there was something shady in that soda, and my research led me to the culprit: aspartame.

Once again I was amazed at the amount of research and data that had been ignored or buried along the rocky road to governmental approval of food substances and additives. In 2010, aspartame could be found in over 5,000 American foods and drinks, in spite of the mountains of paperwork and testimony from doctors and scientists who had warned the government about the dangers of artificial sweeteners in general and aspartame in particular.

- Dozens of books written by medical doctors and scientists warn against consuming aspartame, citing the same basic fact: aspartame is composed of aspartic acid (40 percent), phenylalanine (50 percent), and methanol or wood alcohol (10 percent).

- There is general consensus that artificial sweeteners interfere with the body's delicate and critical insulin balance. One of the best of the many books I have read is the well-documented and comprehensive *Ultrametabolism* (Atria Books, 2008), by Dr. Mark Hyman, who writes about artificial sweeteners: "One of the side effects we know these sweeteners have is stimulation of hunger through the cephalic, or brain-phase, insulin-response.... Artificial sweeteners do not act as sugar does and do not balance your insulin. As a result, you end up with excess insulin in your body, so you end up eating more food to take care of this problem. This whole pattern disrupts your appetite control system in serious ways. What's worse, it can lead to insulin resistance" (pp. 98–99).

- Studies funded by the food industry invariably show no danger posed by aspartame and other artificial sweeteners, but the vast majority of independently funded studies show just the opposite. Dr. Hyman's reference: "Of 166 studies on the safety of aspartame, 74 had at least partial industry funding; 92 were independently funded. While 100 percent of the industry-funded studies conclude aspartame is safe, 92 percent of independently funded research identified aspartame as a potential cause of adverse effects" (p. 99).

- The U.S. Food and Drug Administration's (FDA's) own reports show that over 10,000 consumers complained of adverse reactions to aspartame (including seizures and death). In 1995, FDA epidemiology branch chief Thomas Wilcox confirmed that aspartame was responsible for over 75 percent of all consumer complaints filed between 1981 and 1995 (*Food Chemical News*, June 12, 1995, p. 27).

- The U.S. Department of Health and Human Services released a list of ninety-two symptoms, including headaches, dizziness, seizures, nausea, weight gain, heart palpitations, depression, fatigue, irritability, vision problems, joint pain, and memory loss, in its 1994 list of Adverse Reactions Associated with Aspartame Consumption.

- In 2007, twelve U.S. environmental health experts asked the FDA to review potential health risks of aspartame because of recent studies linking cancer to aspartame. You can read a copy of the letter at http://cspinet.org/new/pdf/aspartame_letter_to_fda.pdf.

- The clincher for me was reading the Congressional testimony of doctors and scientists who petitioned the U.S. government to disapprove aspartame because of previously documented side effects. Those health experts were successful in blocking aspartame's approval as a food additive until Arthur Hull Hayes was appointed FDA commissioner by then-president Ronald Reagan. Shortly after aspartame was approved, Hayes left the FDA to work for NutraSweet's public relations firm, Burson and Marsteller, and subsequently refused all interviews.

High-Fructose Corn Syrup

You know something is up when food manufacturers spend millions of dollars on advertising campaigns and television commercials touting the safety of their products. The basic gist of the commercials is that person A warns person B not to eat HFCS. Person B says, "Why not?" and person A has no answer. Gloating, person B then asks, "Because it's perfectly safe in reasonable amounts?" or some such question. A more factual comment from person B might be, "Because it won't kill you or make you sick immediately?"

HFCS is another one of those food additives (I hesitate to label it as food) that is at the center of years of controversy. Again, we have government approval versus throngs of medical experts and consumers claiming that it may not be deadly in small doses but that it should not be consumed regularly because it interferes with metabolism and can be linked to diabetes.

After suffering from a terrible reaction after drinking iced tea with lots of HFCS in it, I conducted my own unofficial research. First, I asked everybody I knew about HFCS. Folks at the health food store and the gym laughed and said, "You didn't know?" Internet searches revealed all kinds of warnings, many claiming that HFCS was responsible for everything from ADD to diabetes and fatty liver. And I read the same explanations over and over, in article after article, book after book. Following is my understanding, stated in laywoman's terms, of course.

When we eat food, our bodies create insulin to carry the sugars (sucrose and glucose) in that food to our cells so it can be used. And our brains secrete a chemical called leptin that tells us when we're full, so we stop eating. Regular table sugar, sucrose, is a combination of glucose and fructose. Our bodies use glucose for energy and metabolism; it's one of the key building blocks of all carbohydrates, and if the carbs are of the complex variety then the glucose is slowly absorbed by the body as it should be. Fructose is most often found in fruit, and it's best eaten in the whole fiber-containing fruit package rather than as juice because it is absorbed more slowly that way and contains more nutrients and fiber. Slower is better when it comes to sugar absorption.

Fructose doesn't stimulate our bodies to create insulin, and it doesn't trigger our brains to release leptin. When fructose is turned into high-fructose corn syrup, it's absorbed much more quickly than other sugars, and it ignores the insulin that our bodies create when we eat food. Unlike glucose, which needs insulin to be absorbed by cells, HFCS bypasses the insulin and goes directly into our cells, and that's where the damage begins. Inside our cells HFCS turns into carbon, which is then made into cholesterol and triglycerides. It makes our cholesterol levels shoot up and can interfere with liver function, In fact, according to Hyman, it is "probably the biggest reason for the increase in cholesterol levels we have seen in our society over the last twenty years" (p. 98).

Here's an interesting tidbit from my reading: when researchers want to create diabetes in laboratory rats for experimental purposes, they feed them HFCS. It does the trick every time. HFCS is 100 percent effective at creating diabetic rats. Princeton University researchers confirmed that rats with access to HFCS gained more weight than rats given sugar, even when both groups of rats ate the same overall number of calories (*ScienceDaily*, March 22, 2010, http://www.sciencedaily.com/releases/2010/03/100322121115.htm).

In the interest of fairness, you can read the Corn Refiners Association statement claiming that the Princeton researchers are off their rockers at http://www.corn.org/princeton-hfcs-study-errors.html. Given that the corn refiners have a huge financial stake in such studies, and the fatness of the rats, I tend to side with the Princeton guys. Decide for yourself.

Now, when you see those television commercials and person B asks why we shouldn't eat HFCS, you can impress your friends and family by answering the question: because research indicates that HFCS leads to increased appetite, obesity, high blood pressure, and diabetes.

Bovine Growth Hormone

Common sense seems to be the key here. The point of bovine growth hormone (BGH) is to make baby cows grow and adult cows grow fatter. Aside from the fact that humans are not cows, hormones are delicate things. We humans have our own hormones, which regulate our intricate systems. Introducing bovine growth hormones may or may not be responsible for the early development of breasts and menstrual cycles of preadolescent girls. However, since there is absolutely no nutritional requirement for humans to consume bovine growth hormones and there is so much controversy over the long-term effects of human consumption of BGH, it doesn't make sense to me to eat food that contain them if we have a choice.

WE NEED TO USE OUR NOODLES

I have read about so many scientific studies in which nutritional changes and supplements resulted in drastic reductions in violent and aggressive behavior as well as dramatic decreases in ADHD symptoms and allergies. I am thoroughly convinced that if we spent more time and money on nutrition instead of powerful prescription medicines that can have serious side effects, we would have much healthier children who would be better able to learn and behave in our schools. The only real question that remains is whether we value our children's health and mental well-being more than we value the goodwill of the insurance companies, pharmaceutical manufacturers, and test makers who reap billions of dollars in profits from the desperate parents and teachers of children who are unable to sit down, concentrate, and learn.

My thinking is that adults have the right to abuse their bodies any way they see fit but that children deserve a chance to grow up as healthy and strong as possible: not just so they can support us when we are in our old age but also because it's the right thing to do. Current research proves that human brains require more than 20 years to fully develop. During that time, everything children eat and drink affects their brain development—and their future children. But I think it's a huge mistake to worry and fret about every morsel we eat because stress is a real killer. Again, I harken back to the same idea: let's use some common sense. We can pay attention to what our bodies are telling us. If what we eat makes us sick, then we are silly to keep eating those foods. With the skyrocketing cost of health care, it makes good financial sense to be proactive about our health and the health of our children.

We can't count on doctors and health care experts to spoon-feed us every bite of information. We can learn the basics of how our metabolism works and the best natural sources of vitamins and minerals. We can take responsibility for our own health and retrain our taste buds. America tends to lead the way, and the rest of the world follows. We don't have to follow the unethical food companies and advertisers who are leading us toward obesity, diabetes, and learning disorders. There are ethical food and drink manufacturers in this country and legions of health advocates who read the research and distill the statistics and scientific studies and make that information palatable for us. We can chart our own course toward making healthier choices and raising happier, healthier, smarter children. As teachers—gatekeepers of information and influential role models for our nation's children—we should take our place at the head of the parade.

WHAT DO YOU THINK?

1. What is your experience with the effects of nutrition on student behavior and learning?

2. How can we help children when their parents and grandparents practice poor nutrition?

3. Visit your local grocery stores—how many healthy snack products and drinks can you find (without corn syrup, artificial sweeteners, or artificial colors)? Consider making a list for your students or making this a class project so that they can take a list home to use for family shopping.

4. How can we incorporate exercise into our schools in addition to physical education courses?

Teacher Talk

When I give a keynote presentation or conduct a workshop, teachers often call me aside to discuss their particular classroom problems. They hesitate to discuss these situations with teachers or administrators at their own schools because they don't want to jeopardize their jobs or betray their students' confidence. Because so many teachers face variations of the same problems, I thought it might be helpful to share some of their questions and concerns, along with my answers. I hope these letters will highlight the universality of our experience as teachers and spark discussions, because I believe that a problem is halfway solved once we shine the light of discovery on it. Even a seemingly impossible situation feels less hopeless and overwhelming when we have sympathetic souls to help us share the burden. And sometimes it can help just to know that we are not the lone ranger when it comes to facing classroom challenges. (For more questions and answers, or to ask me your own question, please visit my Web site, http://louannejohnson.com.)

QUESTIONS AND ANSWERS

Q: *Even after teaching for 8 years I still seem to spend more than half my class time refereeing arguments and fights among students and redirecting their attention to their work. I am so tired of fighting the same battles every day. What can I do?*

First, I would announce to your class that you will not tolerate verbal abuse in your classroom. Tell the students that they are in charge of their own behavior but that you are in charge of your classroom. Anybody who wants to stay in the room must follow the rule of treating everybody in the room with respect—including themselves.

Name calling, insults, and rampant disrespect were the reasons that I devised my only classroom rule: treat everybody in this room with respect—no put-downs of other people based on their race, religion, ethnic background, skin color, native language, gender, sexual preference, intelligence, body shape, or body size. (Students are entitled to their opinions and prejudices, but they are not permitted to express those opinions publicly in the form of insults or attacks on other people. You can read more about my discipline approach in Chapter Six.)

In spite of my rule mandating respectful behavior, sometimes one particular group of students seems to include a high percentage of instigators, hotheads, or bullies. When I encounter this situation, I frequently remind them of my rule and post it in very large letters in the classroom. I also suspend my instruction temporarily for a lesson in psychology. I explain to the students that psychology can help them understand how other people play you or psych you out (or whatever term they will understand).

First, we discuss why people tease each other: some people are trying to make themselves feel better by making other people feel small. Some people are afraid they are stupid themselves, so they try to get smart students in trouble. Some people are bored, and they want to create problems just to make life interesting. Some people are unable to do the work in class but don't want people to laugh at them, so they try to distract the teacher and the other students.

Some people just get a kick out of controlling others' behavior, and this is the motive that kids find most interesting. When kids understand that by becoming angry or responding to verbal insults, they are doing exactly what the other person wants them to do and that they are being manipulated, some kids will stop playing the game. Some students find this a difficult concept to grasp. You may have to restate it in various ways and perhaps stage an example in your room.

Helping your students understand themselves and each other isn't enough. You need to help them learn how to withstand the peer pressure and verbal assault. Teach them what to say and role-play some situations so that they can practice. I teach them power statements; just calling them power statements makes them sound attractive. Word your power statements to suit your students' age level. Some of my favorites include the following:

- You can say what you want, but it isn't important to me.
- I know you want me to get mad, but I control my own mind.
- You are not the boss of me. I don't want to fight with anybody.
- You have your opinions, and I have mine. We just don't agree.
- Doing mean things doesn't make you strong.
- We are all human beings. I think we should try to get along.
- You can think whatever you want. I think for myself.

Some children really don't understand why they tease other people; we need to teach these children other ways to get attention from their peers. They usually don't have any real friends because they don't know how to be a friend. We talk about this, too, in class. I ask students to write in their journals what they think is important in a friendship, what they look for in a friend, how to make friends, and so on. Then we have a class discussion, and we write our thoughts about friendship on the board. Many students have reported that after our discussion on friendship, they feel more confident about being able to make friends.

Another thing you might consider is watching video clips of how other teachers begin their school terms by outlining rules for behavior. There is a clip featuring British teacher Andy Bell where he asks his students to fill out a worksheet he has designed, in which they list things they want the people in their classroom to do. He discusses students' suggestions, which leads to creating rules for the room. When done this way, students are much more apt to agree with and abide by rules than they are when rules or imposed or when they are tasked with creating a list of rules without first being asked to describe the classroom environment they prefer. You can find Bell's videos on the Internet if you search for his name and "Establishing the Ground Rules."

Q: *How do you make your students realize the importance of education? I teach middle school in a suburb, and I have so many students who just don't seem to care.*

I learned the hard way that I can't *make* students do anything, but I also learned that my own enthusiasm can be an irresistible magnet for students. If I truly believe something is important, my students tend to at least give me a good listen. I don't discuss the value of education until students know me well enough to believe that I am on their side and that I want them to succeed in their lives (according to their own definitions of success).

One popular strategy is to ask students to create a hypothetical budget to get a general idea of how much it costs to live. Then they view charts showing how much money the average person with a high school diploma makes versus the person with no diploma. This sounds like a good plan, but it doesn't seem to be effective with students who have already decided that they are destined for failure. They don't really believe they have the power to change their future.

Because their peers or relatives have advised many unenthusiastic students to drop out and just take the GED, I keep one of those bulky books containing actual GED tests on my desk so that students can see that the tests aren't easy and that GED classes involve as much work as high school, if not more. Students are invariably surprised to see how much information they will be expected to know as adults, and most change their minds about dropping out.

I don't try to convince students that they will use everything they learn, because they won't. I explain Bloom's Taxonomy of cognitive domains (see Chapter Five) to describe the different levels of thinking and why each is important to master. We then look at ways that we use synthesis or evaluation, for example, in different classes. I repeatedly remind my students that I want to help them be successful people in life and in school. I tell them: "The more education you have, the better you learn to think, the more worlds are open to you, the better decisions you can make, and the more options you have in your life. Even if you don't like your job, if you have an education you can earn a good living at something while you put yourself through school or training to do something else. Without an education, most people work to survive from day to day, and their options shrink with each passing year."

But the bottom line is this: I can't make students care about their education. However, if I can convince them to care about themselves and understand that they have the power to change their lives for the better, then they begin to care about their education. So my focus is on convincing them that I care about them—by telling them over and over and over until they finally get the message.

Q: *I am completing my teacher training. Being the kind of in-the-middle student that you describe in your workshops, I'd like to know how you evaluate and recognize those types of students in your classroom without losing them through the cracks since they are not a part of the two extremes. Is there anything you would suggest to a future teacher on how not to lose those quiet kids in the middle?*

I make copies of my roll sheets and keep them at home so I can include student names on my worksheets and tests, making sure that I get everybody's name at least once. Kids really respond to seeing their own names in print, even if it is just on a vocabulary quiz. I make a tickler file with student birthdays, and on their special day I give them a "magic pencil" that earns only As. Students who have weekend or summer vacation birthdays get their pencils on Friday afternoon or on the last day of school.

To prevent students from being lost in space, I place my desks in a U-shape pattern so that nobody is more than three kids away from me, and I walk around the room constantly and talk to each student. I pat them on the back or shake their hands if they are doing a good job. I encourage them to keep working and ask for their opinions on the assignments.

I use journals to give extra attention to the kids who are shy or quiet. If I find a book at a library sale that I think they might like, I buy it for them.

I ask my silent students to help me collect papers, distribute tests, and so on. If they don't want to, I don't pressure them. I ask them to deliver messages or get things from the office for me. I may assign one to be the official door-answerer during class.

These things may work for you, or perhaps they will inspire you to develop your own strategies for remembering the middle kids. Just being aware that they tend to be ignored will make you less likely to forget about them. If you have an old school photo of yourself, why not tape it someplace near your desk where you will see it and remember how you felt as a child? When your students notice the photo (and they will), you will have the opportunity to begin conversations that may lead to wonderful places.

Q: *How do you get students to see themselves beyond being at risk and then to excel?*

First, I tell my students that I don't accept labels and I don't think they should, either. For example, I don't use the term *at risk* because it doesn't accurately describe students who are tempted to give up or who have already quit caring about school. All children are at risk in today's society. One boy told me that when he heard himself described as at risk, he felt as though the people were saying he was a hopeless loser. I prefer the term *disenchanted* because it more accurately describes students have given up on school or themselves—or both. Perhaps they are tired of failing or fighting with teachers who don't understand their learning styles. Perhaps they feel like outcasts among their peers, or they are angry about their difficult personal lives. Perhaps they decided at some point that working hard in school didn't pay off. Regardless of the reason that students have given up on school, I firmly believe that kids who claim they don't care do, in fact, care very much. But they have learned to project the opposite image to protect themselves from further pain and embarrassment.

The key to helping disenchanted students is to separate the child from the learner, to see each child as a human being and not merely as a student. I search until I find some natural strength or skill—and everybody has at least one. I praise students for their patience, wit, compassion, fashion sense, artistic ability, musical talent—whatever makes them special. I tell them how I see them. By truly seeing a different image of a child and communicating that image, often I am able to change a child's perception of self; she can no longer go on thinking of herself as a failure or a loser or whatever vision she previously had.

Once I have established some rapport, I find out what interests or hobbies a student has, and I point out that writing a song, lifting a 100-pound barbell, learning to drive, or knowing how to take care of a turtle are all skills that this student has successfully mastered. Then I encourage him to take on academic challenges with the promise that I will be his helper. I start with something small but difficult (learning five college-level vocabulary words or five difficult spelling words) so that accomplishing the goal will result in a true feeling of success. Each success builds more confidence.

One more important thing I discuss with my students is the nonimportance of grades. Grades are important only in a certain context. We all know people who earn As but are not very likable or successful in any other area. In fact, some people who earn As are F people: they have terrible personalities. And we all know people who earn Ds and Fs but who are popular, charming, talented, and successful in other areas; they are A people who earn Fs. In my opinion it is far better to be an A person who can work to improve his or her grades than an F person who earns academic honors. Grades can always be improved; given the choice, I would opt for a lovely person with lower grades over a super achiever with an obnoxious personality. Many students claim that teachers treat students who earn high grades better than they treat students with average or low grades. If we do, then we have ourselves to blame when students focus on grades so much that they are willing to lie or cheat to earn them.

Q: *In one of your books, you mentioned that you eliminated tests. How did you grade students without testing?*

Oh, how I wish I could eliminate tests! At least the overabundance of standardized ones. But, as it turns out, people actually like tests, within reason. Once, when students complained about all the testing, I announced that we aren't going to have any more tests or grades. Students cheered. Then, after a few days of no grades, they started asking for some feedback on how they were doing. I'd say, "Oh, never mind that. Let's just learn things." They insisted on some measurement of their work. They wanted a grade or some indication of how well they were doing. It is human nature to want to know we are making progress. I also think it's human nature to become nervous and perform poorly when there is too much pressure. So the trick is to create assessments that truly test learning and progress but that don't place undue pressure on students or make one or two test scores so important that they overshadow all the learning and achievement students make that are not directly testable. One of my most popular lessons—and one where students learn the most—is when they work in small groups to create their own quizzes about what they have learned. They exchange quizzes and then critique each other's quiz format and content. This activity has the added benefit of grading itself!

Q: *I went through teacher training and earned straight As. My professors said my lesson plans were great, and I thought I was prepared to teach. But when I got into the classroom, I couldn't cope with all the paperwork in addition to lessons, and I didn't know how to manage the classes. I was so overwhelmed that I ended up taking everything home at night and working until midnight. Even though I taught elementary school, I was afraid to look the students in the eye. I was afraid that they would laugh at me or belittle me. After a short while, I gave up teaching because it became clear to me that it wasn't what I was meant to do. Do you think I was just naive, or do you think my experience was common among people who believe they want to be teachers?*

I think you have highlighted some of the most important failures in some teacher-training systems. Many colleges and universities have revamped their programs recently to include a heavy focus on classroom management and discipline, so perhaps fewer teachers will face the dilemma you faced. But I don't think your situation is unusual at all. I think the statistics show that most teachers who quit teaching do so during the first 5 years for exactly the reasons you mentioned. They can create great lesson plans and learn all the latest theories, but they aren't prepared to face real students who challenge their authority and refuse even to look at those beautiful lesson plans. And, sadly, they often fail to get the support they need from administrators.

Teaching involves far more than being educated and wanting to teach children. It involves a great deal of psychology, leadership, and time management—and the ability to motivate people who aren't inclined to be motivated. Those skills can be learned, but they require practical experience and real-world application. I think student teaching should last at least a full year and should be completed during the second year of teacher training instead of the last so that teacher candidates can get a better idea of whether they really want to teach and have time to work on the classroom management or discipline skills that need the most improvement. I hope it will help to know that every teacher struggles. It's a steep learning curve for the first few years, but if you hang in there, eventually you will reach a plateau and you'll be able to catch your breath and get ready for the next ascent. In the meantime, there are a number of good Internet sites for teachers where there are active chat rooms. You'll find lots of good advice on the Web sites—and some questionable advice as well. Be selective.

Q: *I am an ESL teacher here in a high school. Usually I have good rapport with my students and, apart from my first year of teaching, I haven't had any problems with classroom management or discipline over the last 3 years. I have a very lively class of 14-year-old students (twenty-seven students total), and it is their first year of English. I find it hard to establish a good rapport with them because they are constantly fidgeting and turning around. However, the most annoying habit they have is that normally one of them (although never the same one) repeats something I say. At first I ignored it, but it's starting to become an annoying habit. If it was only one person I would talk to this person in private, but I am not really sure what to do about this problem. My mentor suggested that I should adopt a more communicative, student-centered approach when teaching them. However, as they still lack basic grammatical structures, I don't know which kind of activities I could do with them. Do you have any suggestions?*

Since you normally don't have problems establishing rapport with students or managing your classroom, then it would seem that your current problem is particular to this class of students. Mocking somebody else is common behavior among children who are trying to push the buttons of another child. They are seeking attention and trying to force a reaction from the person they are mocking. Why would students do this in school? Several possible reasons come to mind. They may be flirting with you and trying to get you to see them as people instead of students. They may be trying to force you to be more human and less teacher. Or perhaps they are trying to distract and make you argue with them—because if you are focused on disciplining them you won't be focused on making them do work they find difficult. Perhaps the difficulty of the work is the reason. Students who are used to doing well in school will sometimes act out when they are faced with a truly challenging lesson. They may feel vulnerable or lack faith in their ability to successfully learn this new language.

One of the most successful strategies I have used when working with reluctant learners is to surprise them by putting them in charge. I assign them the task of designing lessons and activities to achieve an assigned objective. I tell them what I want them to learn and ask them how they believe they could learn it. Sometimes their lessons are wonderful and effective. Sometimes they are big flops. Either way, they learn something valuable—and so do you.

I would also recommend trying to connect with your students on a more personal level. I don't mean to suggest that you become their best friend or share details of your personal life. But if you could mention some hobbies or interests of your own and find out what interests they have, you could incorporate those things into your lessons and lectures. Here's a simple example: when you create a grammar lesson, insert the names of your students into the sentences you ask them to read. Make sure you include each student's name one time so nobody feels left out. They will be delighted to see their names, and the enthusiasm will skyrocket for that lesson.

I do think it's important, however, to maintain your authority. Don't let students get the feeling that they are dictating or controlling your behavior. I've had classes where students believe they can force me to stop giving homework if they all refuse to do it. Ha! I start giving extra credit, abundant praise, and special privileges to the few students who do their homework. Soon, the rest give up and do the work. This proves the theory that positive reinforcement is more effective than punishment.

Q: *I am currently finishing my student teaching in a fourth-grade classroom. I share your sentiments in creating a classroom of self-respecting learners. I explained to my students that my only rule is that they respect themselves and others, and then we did several activities to define respect and practice it in the classroom. I got off to a great start, but then the environment I had wanted so badly to create turned out to be a flop. I realized that, although my beginning was wonderful, my follow-through was horrendous. The students knew what I expected of them, but I never truly made them responsible for their behavior. I believe it is possible to create a classroom in which the focus is not on controlling student behavior but rather on teaching them to control their own behavior. Because of this philosophy, I met opposition from every direction: the other teachers at school, who often resorted to yelling to manage students; administration, who did not support the teachers in giving purposeful consequences; my educational supervisor, who believes that an authoritarian approach is much more effective; and the students, who became confused about my approach after I became discouraged and tried to pull in the reins only to find they rebelled against my more authoritarian approach (understandably so; this was a mistake). Is a respectful classroom of students who are responsible for their own behavior a possibility at the elementary level? Or do I need to redefine my philosophy? Outside sources are making me question whether I am too idealistic and therefore need to teach with a more authoritarian approach.*

I hope it will make you feel better to hear that I have had a similar experience—and I know dozens of other teachers who have, as well. Creating the environment where students are self-directed learners is easy if you are very clear about your expectations for student behavior and adamant about requiring them to reflect on their own behavior and change it immediately when they stray from the right path. For many of us, though, accepting the necessity of being the boss can be a difficult one. Our personalities and natural inclinations just don't bend in that direction. We aren't comfortable in the role of strict authoritarian, but we have to learn how to exert our authority because students need rules and guidelines and boundaries. Without them, they flounder. The younger the students, the more strict guidance they need because they are developing future habits. If we allow them to be lazy learners and irresponsible students, they will either continue to be lazy and irresponsible or will have to work hard to overcome their bad habits in the future.

As we all know, it's much harder to break a bad habit than to establish a good habit in the first place. Therefore, I have learned through experience that I must begin by forcing myself to be strict at the start of every grading period or term (not just at the beginning of the school year). Once students are on track, I can relax a bit and allow them to make mistakes so they will have the opportunity to learn from them. But if they haven't practiced being responsible, self-directed learners, then they won't have that default to fall back on. They need to experience what it feels like to cooperate, demonstrate initiative, and take full responsibility for their own behavior and success in my classroom. That way, when they do get off-track they know what they need to do to get back on the road to success.

As for those people who disagree with you, they are not necessarily wrong. Most likely, they have experienced or witnessed situations similar to yours, and they know how difficult it can be for even a good teacher to create and maintain a learner-directed classroom where the majority of responsibility for student behavior lies with students. It is much quicker and easier for adults to take responsibility for student behavior and success than it is to teach them how to take charge of themselves. Those critical veterans know that even the best students will push the boundaries from time to time, just to check the teacher's response, and the worst students will push and push and push every day. But if you are up for the challenge, I believe it is worth the effort. When you create a classroom where you can step aside from time to time and let your students lead the way, they tend to go much further than anybody (anybody except you, that is) would expect. And when we take the chance occasionally to act as an observer and guide rather than always insisting on being the leader of the pack, we learn valuable lessons from our students that make us far better teachers in the end.

Q: *I'm a third-year eighth-grade English teacher at a middle school, and people keep telling me to give up on particular students—that I can't save them all. I know this, but I can't give up on Joey. He came to my class 2 years ago, a tall, skinny kid with spiky hair and an easy smile. He was a fairly good kid in class; the girls loved him, but he wasn't a player. Often he would miss my class so that he could stay home to babysit while his parents worked. When Joey left middle school, I felt confident that he would continue his education, at the very least getting his GED. Fast-forward to last week. I hadn't seen this kid in 2 years, and he sauntered into my room during open house. I hugged him and then inquired about school. He dropped his head in shame and then told me a story about how he stole a car and had a gun. I suspect he is in a gang. When I told him he had talent and could do anything he wanted with his life, he looked at the girl he was with and said, "I told you someone thought I had talent." I cried for this kid, and then I enrolled him in a special program. I just found out that he is back in jail, and I don't know what to do. I absolutely refuse to give up on this kid. He has talent—I mean true talent. Please give me some advice (other than you are sorry, but we can't save them all).*

I would never tell you that you can't save them all because I believe we can save all young people—if they are still alive. I have had so many students like your Joey, and they broke my heart again and again. But going to jail isn't the end of the world. He will keep thinking about your opinion of him. Clearly, you connected. He just has to work out his own perception of himself. This is my theory: kids have a script in their heads for how the movie of their life will play out. Then they meet us, and we see a different script. We try to change the script by telling these kids that they have talent and choices in life, but they don't understand because they have always felt powerless and they really believe their script is their destiny. We can't change the script by trying to rewrite it; however, we can help them change their perceptions of themselves as people by telling them how we see them: we see them as intelligent, talented, capable, and so on. This doesn't change their script, but it changes their perception immediately and keeps it changing the more they have contact with us. Even when those students are far away, those new thoughts keep crowding out the old ones until they decide that they can indeed change their scripts. This can take years. I have had many students who believed they would end up in jail (and most of them did), but I encouraged them to use their time in jail to study and learn and think. Many of them got GEDs and good jobs afterward.

Sometimes we can intervene early enough to change a student's perception enough for him to change his script before he goes to jail. If not, we can continue to try to change the perception by calling and writing letters. If you can get an address, write to this kid every week. See if you can go visit at least once. Whether or not he answers, whether or not you see him, whether or not he ever comes to see you again, your belief in him may be the lifeline that keeps him going. I spoke to a psychiatrist about this once, and he assured me that finding one adult who offers unconditional love and acceptance is enough for many kids. That acceptance will be the lifeline they cling to until they are able to stand on their own feet.

I would like to say something about the people who tell you to stop worrying: they are not heartless people; they simply can't afford to make the kind of emotional investment you are willing to make. Just as we all have to decide how much of our income we can afford to donate to charity, we have to decide how much emotional energy we can afford to expend trying to save students. Some of us can afford to give more, and some of us can tolerate the loss when our investment shows no return. Just be careful that you don't bankrupt your supply. Find some way to recharge periodically.

Q: *I sometimes hear teachers complain about overinvolved parents, but I can't even get parents to give me a phone number. I live in a suburb, not inner-city New York. I sent notes home with my students asking for contact information, but only a few parents bothered to respond. Some students have even reported that their parents laughed and threw the notes away. How can I convince these parents to care about their children's education?*

You are not the lone ranger. So many teachers face apathetic parents, and it breaks their hearts because they can see how much the children want their parents to care about their success in school. After spending weeks and months tracking down elusive parents, I have come to the conclusion that they have a handful of common reasons for ignoring teachers' requests for information:

1. They are afraid you are going to accuse them of something. They may have been informed by some school official that their drinking, smoking,

drug use, or other behavior has contributed to their child's learning disability.

2. Their own school days were not happy ones. Classmates, teachers, or administrators bullied, humiliated, or mistreated them. They still hate school.

3. They are ashamed of their own lack of education and afraid you will judge them for having unfashionable clothing or for using poor grammar.

4. English is not their native language, and they don't feel confident about talking to a teacher.

5. They are poverty-stricken, exhausted, depressed, abused, and simply unable to cope.

6. They really are selfish, apathetic people who shouldn't be parents.

You should be able to get the phone numbers from the guidance office because parents have to provide contact information when they enroll their children. Or ask the attendance office for the numbers they call to report student absences. Sometimes the phone numbers that parents provide turn out to be invalid. If so, I ask the child to give me the name and number of anybody older who might be willing to talk to me: a sister, brother, neighbor, aunt, cousin, grandparent. Then I send a note inviting that person to call or visit my classroom. Some families never do make contact, and in those cases I try to find a coach or counselor or somebody to mentor the child. Sometimes bus drivers will develop a good rapport with kids. One bus driver told me that she always asked to see students' report cards and that some kids said she was the only person who ever looked at them. You might also consider holding a parent meeting in their neighborhood at a community center, library, or church. Many parents feel more comfortable on their own turf. When they realize that your goal is not to blame them but to help their children, many of them will change their attitudes and work with you.

Don't give up. Just the fact that you make such an effort to contact parents sends an important message to your students, and they are listening.

Q: *When is it that you decide that it's not the students who are having a problem learning but you who is having a problem teaching an idea? I enjoy teaching most of the time. Sometimes, however, I wonder if I am doing as good a job as I think I am.*

For me, honest and direct questions work best. If students don't seem to be learning something, I stop and look at them quietly. Then I ask: Are you guys really trying here, or is there something wrong with the way I am trying to teach you this information? Or is this maybe just too hard for you? I explain my objective and what I want them to know and be able to do. Then, I ask for their feedback. Are they trying or not? If they are trying and not learning, then I adjust my lessons or try something completely different. If they weren't trying, usually they will make the effort to show that they can learn if they want to.

After my first few years of teaching, I switched my perspective about lessons. Instead of assuming that students weren't trying or weren't learning or didn't care or some such thing, my first question at the end of every day is: How can I fix my teaching to help my students? By taking that approach, I have solved a lot of problems. If I have students who are consistently but unapologetically late for class, for example, then I ask: What have I done to make those students believe their tardiness is acceptable?

As for my instruction, if more than 25 percent of the students miss a question on a test, do a poor job on an assignment, or tune out during class discussions, then I know I need to question my lesson design or presentation. I try to remember that there are more visual and kinesthetic learners than auditory learners in any given group, so I need to use different approaches to any new material. Often I ask students who get it if they can help me figure out a way to help those who don't; this helps everybody, including me, because we all learn new ways to communicate information. For example, if I want students to learn how to analyze a literary short story, I may put them in small groups and ask them to create an assignment, or a series of assignments, designed to let them learn and practice their analytical skills. Together, we have designed some interesting projects—and some real disasters. But we learn as much or more from the disasters because we sit down and analyze where they went wrong.

One way I work to avoid communication problems in the first place is by modeling the assignments. I try to complete every assignment I give to my classes with them, if possible. When I do the assignment with them, they like to watch and see how I approach a problem, which is a good way to teach them problem-solving skills. If I do an assignment as homework, I can see whether the work is too hard or easy or too short or long. And I use a lot of feedback forms, asking whether the lessons are too hard, too easy, or just right. Some students get smart, but most students tell the truth. I listen to them.

Q: *I am a high school English teacher. I love my job, but I am exhausted after only 3 years. I wonder how I will manage to make it to retirement. Teaching is so hard. How do you avoid burning out?*

That's a tough question—and one I struggle with even now, after 25 years of teaching. I didn't listen when I started teaching high school, and veteran teachers warned me that I needed to hold back, keep some energy reserved, let some things slide. I kept charging ahead, determined to save every child I met. Of course, they were right. After 5 years of teaching non–English-speaking and at-risk teens, I abruptly ran out of gas. I woke up one day and couldn't get out of bed. So I took a break and went back to graduate school for a year. I think the reason I am still here and still enjoying my work is that I have given myself breaks from time to time.

If I were queen of education, I would decree that after 5 years in the classroom every teacher would be required to take a one-semester break from teaching. They could design curriculum, provide professional development training, mentor new teachers, coordinate student activities and clubs—some work that does not involve daily lesson plans, testing, and grading. Even teachers who don't want a break (I wouldn't have wanted one) would be required to get out of the classroom. Some teachers might decide not to return, which would be for the best. Most would be eager to return, which would be even better.

Since I'm not yet wearing the queen's crown, I gave myself permission to stop teaching for a year or two when I needed a break or to teach part-time. I switched from teaching public high school to teaching ESL classes at a community college. Then, after a few more years of teaching high school, I taught graduate students in a teacher-training program. I went back to school myself and took classes in creative writing. I taught high school dropouts in a diploma program.

Today, I have finally found a method that works for me. I teach high school full time in rural New Mexico. I enjoy teaching better when I live in a small town where parents are more directly involved in school activities, even if they sometimes seem to care more about sports than academics. Yes, I have a talent for motivating hard-core inner-city kids—but I was born and raised in the country, and I just don't enjoy city living. In addition to choosing a town of the right size, in a sunny climate where my health is much better than it was back in Pennsylvania (where I seemed to have the flu all winter long), I also learned to be selfish. I learned that if I don't take care of myself I can't take care of my students.

Now I don't stay at work until 10 p.m. even if I have papers to grade, lessons to plan, and projects to design. I set a time to go home, and I go. I leave everything where it is—and where it will be when I return the next day. I make sure I get at least 20 minutes of exercise every day. I used to wear myself out at the gym before I realized that overexercising didn't help. On warm days, I ride my bicycle to and from school. On cold or rainy days, I ride my exercycle and watch a funny or inspiring video. And every night, I do at least 10 minutes of meditation and yoga. Sometimes I do more, but I always do the minimum.

I try to practice gratefulness. Each night, before I go to sleep and every morning when I wake up, I look in the mirror and list several things for which I am grateful. It's so easy to find things to complain about with today's crazy educational bureaucracy. At first, it may seem difficult to find things to be grateful for, but with a little practice it becomes easy. It really does work.

Be good to yourself. You deserve it. Teaching is darn difficult and exhausting work, but it is definitely worth the effort. You are touching lives in a way that few people ever do. If you decide to switch careers, however, don't beat yourself up. Congratulate and thank yourself for the time you spent helping young people. You don't have to teach forever to earn your teacher wings. You have earned them already.

Now the Good News

Teachers are inundated with negative news: test scores are down, testing requirements are up, lunch duty has doubled, prep time has been halved, American students are falling behind those in other countries, state standards have changed once again, politicians believe they know more about teaching than licensed teachers do, and the list goes on. Many teachers become so overwhelmed by all the negativity created by the educational bureaucracies that they lose sight of the positive side of teaching. We can turn our focus to the bright side, though: just as we can change our default setting so we notice the good things students do instead of the bad things, we can change our perspective so we focus more on the research, innovations and people continue to prove every day that teaching does count. The love and care you put into your daily work does matter.

POSITIVE THINKING FOR TEACHERS

If you don't have colleagues or mentors to provide the professional and emotional support so necessary to maintaining a positive attitude amid the insanity of our educational bureaucracy, here are just a few Web sites that offer inspiration and hope. As you browse the links, you will find more sources of good news that you can read to counteract the bad news the American media love to publicize.

Following the URL of each Web site, I list just a few of the many articles I found during a recent visit to the site:

http://www.goodnewsnetwork.org/tag/education

- Strangers in New York City who donated almost $200,000 in a matter of minutes to send poor children on a field trip to Harvard
- A sixth-grade teacher in Bakersfield, California, who started a free clothing bank for students and inspired the entire town to participate
- An invitation to take a free online course in positive psychology

http://positivenews.org.uk/tag/education-2/

- A program about putting Scottish teachers behind bars so that they can better support the thousands of pupils whose parents are imprisoned
- Chilean president Michelle Bachelet's proposal to provide free tertiary education to 1.2 million students
- An interview with Eulery founder Ben Byford, whose goal is to connect socially minded entrepreneurs with academic organizations

http://globalgoodnews.com/education-news.html

- A Texas program designed to produce business-savvy prison inmates
- Ability of transcendental meditation to reduce hyperactivity
- Adults in Israel who are working to create stress-free schools

http://humaneeducation.org

- This inspiring and uplifting site, established by Zoe Weil, offers news and feature articles, video clips, conferences, training, and resources for teachers who are dedicated to the concept of humane education.

One last happy note: In his October 2013 EdWeek article titled "Some Good News About Public Schools," author Brian Cleary reminds us that four of five Americans who won Nobel prizes in 2012 were educated at public schools: David J. Wineland, physics; Robert K. Lefkowitz, chemistry; Brian Kobilka, chemistry; and Alvin Roth, economics. He also lists several celebrities who graduated from public high schools, including musicians Wynton Marsalis and Carlos Santana, writer Maya Angelou, and movie director Steven Spielberg. And I would like to add to the list the thousands of successful teachers across our country who graduated from public high schools and whose only prize is the knowledge that they have touched and improved the lives of countless children—a prize worth more than any trophy or plaque in the world.

TWENTY YEARS FROM NOW

Twenty years from now you may not remember your students, but they will remember you. They may not remember the lessons you taught them, and they may have forgotten your face, but they will remember quite clearly the way you made them feel about themselves. They'll remember your criticisms and your compliments—often word for word.

First, let's look at the negative side of those student memories.

I once complimented a bank teller on her beautiful handwriting. She blushed. Thinking she might have misunderstood, I repeated my comment.

The teller looked down at her hands and said, "My second-grade teacher used to hit my knuckles with a ruler because my handwriting was so bad. I loved my teacher and I wanted her to like me, so I sat at my kitchen table every day for months and wrote my letters over and over."

"Well, she must have been pleased to see how beautifully your handwriting turned out," I said.

"I never did meet her standards," the teller said, "but I kept practicing, even after I left her classroom. When I was in fourth grade, I went back and showed her how nicely I could write."

"Certainly, she praised you for working so hard," I said.

The teller sighed and shuffled through the deposit slips on the counter.

"She didn't remember me." After a moment she forced a smile. "But that was a long time ago, wasn't it?"

Hundreds of other people have written to tell me about their teachers. Clearly, time doesn't seem to diminish people's recollections of their experiences with teachers as it does with other memories. Although age may allow people to put their childhood experiences in perspective, it doesn't necessarily dull the memory—or the joy or pain, as the following excerpts from readers' letters demonstrate.

> One instance really sticks out in my mind. My eighth-grade teacher asked us to write our opinion on a certain subject. I do not remember the subject or how I responded; however, I do remember the teacher practically snickering, the red F for failure, and the comment, "This is not the correct answer," written at the top of the first page. When I questioned the grade, reiterating the fact that she wanted my opinion, she just laughed and said she felt I was wrong . . . . I'm 42 years old now, and I just learned in the past 3 years that my opinion is valuable and I am worth something.
>
> **Diane, St. Albans, West Virginia**

> I remember my first-grade teacher, a woman I can still envision after all these many years, who taught me to read, a habit that has brightened my life for over 50 years since then. I remember a very demanding teacher from whom I took a class in Old English when I worked on my first undergraduate degree—how troublesome he was, how wise he was, and what a great gift he gave me in demanding excellence. We have remained friends over the ensuing years. Many teachers stand out like bright stars in my sky.
>
> **Arthur, Suffield, Connecticut**

> My mother and father were divorced when I was about 9 or 10, and my mother had only an eighth-grade education. We worked very hard to survive, and I can still remember vividly the stiffness of the shirts I wore made from feed sacks. It was through the help and

encouragement of coaches and teachers with the love, compassion, and commitment such as yours that I continued my education. I received an athletic scholarship to college and enlisted as an airman basic in the U.S. Air Force in the middle of my junior year. I then entered the flying training program and graduated with wings and a commission on the same day. I spent 20 years as a fighter pilot and 4 years in the Pentagon, rising to the rank of colonel. I completed my bachelor's degree under the bootstrap program and my master's degree at night school. I also completed the War College national security management program. I am now vice president and general manager of an aviation company. I am not telling you these things to brag but to let you know that successful lives and careers often begin by warm and loving teachers.

Bud, Springdale, Arkansas

THE FLIP SIDE

Now, let's take the positive perspective. For every negative letter I have received about a teacher, I received a hundred positive ones, which confirms what we all know: there are many more good teachers than bad. Some years ago, while visiting New York City, I had the good luck and pleasure of meeting Bill Parkhurst, a broadcast journalist and author. The conversation turned to teachers at one point, and Bill shared something truly remarkable. As a research project for a true crime novel he was writing, he had spent a year working closely with a private detective so he could write more accurately and realistically about the fictional detective in his novel.

"You'll be interested and surprised, I think, to know the most common reason that people hire private detectives," Bill told me. "It isn't matrimonial surveillance, as many people think. I interviewed over 150 detectives, and every time I walked into an agency one of the first things I'd hear would be somebody asking for help in locating a former teacher. People want to find their teachers and thank them."

Bill was right. I was delighted to learn that so many people go to so much trouble to track down their teachers. And I suspect that for every person who hires a detective, there must be hundreds of others who are considering the idea—which means that teachers in this country are doing their jobs, educating and inspiring children, despite all the bad press about the failures of our schools.

Of course, there is no way to tell what your students will remember about you, but perhaps you will see something of yourself in these excerpts from three of the many letters I've received in response to *My Posse Don't Do Homework* and "The Girls in the Back of the Class." The first one is from a man who took his teacher for granted.

Dear Miss LouAnne,

I really don't know where to start. Last night I read *Reader's Digest*, and I found your story, "The Girls in the Back of the Class." I usually can't read anything longer than a paragraph, but I used my whole lunch hour reading and thinking about that story. I know you don't know me. As you can tell, my English is not that great. I even hate to write. But I felt the need to write to you. Don't ask me why. Maybe it's because you made me cry. I never cry. Only when somebody in my family dies.

After I read that story I went outside. It was a cold and dark night. I work on a loading dock from 9:00 p.m. until 7:00 a.m. I walked and walked where no one could see me, and I cried. I cried hard. I had a teacher just like you in high school who did everything she could to help me. She must have said to me, "You can do it," a hundred times a week. She got me to believe in myself so good that I thought I could do anything.

The main reason I wanted to write to you is because I really didn't know how my teacher felt about me. Reading your story gave me some insight—ooh, big word. I know that y'all are two totally different people, but I bet you she felt the same way about her students as you did. As I read, I saw myself in the story a lot of times. I was selfish. I cared about only my feelings. Now I know that she really cared, and I wish I had just one more chance to tell her thanks.

See. There you go again, making me want to cry. But really I wish that I could hug her real tight and tell her thanks for everything. She played a very important role in forming the foundation of my life.

Rick, Abilene, Texas

The second letter is from a young woman who wrote from Germany, where she was attending medical school. Her letter is about a teacher she met when she came to the United States as an exchange student during high school.

Dear LouAnne,

When I came to the United States as an exchange student, I was put into English-as-a-second-language classes. That day I decided not to like the teacher. This teacher was just as stubborn about keeping me in the ESL program as I was about trying to get out. I finally gave up, not knowing that this would save my life.

I was sure she would hate me for making all this trouble. I expected her to reject me, but instead she kept asking me how I was doing and how things went. For a long time I was suspicious of her behavior toward me, since back then I could not imagine that somebody was truly interested in me and my life. I still remember the day when she offered me to talk to her. She was sitting at her desk, and when I was leaving the classroom she called to me. She said that she would always be there if I wanted to talk. I had never heard that before. At that point I had a choice. I could take advantage of her offer or reject it. I figured I had nothing to lose, since I would leave the States anyway once the school year was over, so I took the risk and started to open up bit by bit.

In an environment that was filled with respect, understanding, and love, I was able to tell her things I had denied for a long time. By the end of the school year, the teacher I had once decided not to like became the most important person in my life, and she still is today. She was the first person who told me she loved me and cared about me. She always believed in me and my abilities. Though she was on the other side of the world, she helped me get through one of the hardest times in my life. Shortly after I returned to Germany from the United States, I was diagnosed with cancer. I had an ovarian tumor. I had surgery, followed by chemotherapy, which was hell. What kept me going through this treatment was the knowledge that somewhere out there was somebody who loved me and respected me for the kind of person I am. At times when I was about to give up, she was there in my mind and reminded me of my strength that I have inside of me. When there is somebody who loves you and cares about you, you can handle almost everything in life.

Liesl, Dusseldorf, Germany

And the last letters come from a young man in India who has written twice to tell me about his wonderful teachers—a college professor and a high school teacher. This is the first letter he wrote, when he was still in high school.

Dear Madam,

I am a 16-year-old boy. My name is Jaskirat, but you can call me Anu, as I am called at home. The day I read your article I am desperately wanting to contact you. The reasons are many, but the main one is that I had a teacher very much like you. I adored her very much, but after teaching us for a few months she went to Canada. I was really shocked, but I could do nothing. I lost her, maybe forever, but her sweet memories shall remain in my heart for all the remaining days of my life. As I went through your article I could see her in you. I began to think what is the magic in the people like her that they make such long-lasting impressions on the minds in such short periods of contact. The day the results of our tenth standard exam were reported, I stood there with tears in my eyes and hoped that she could know that I, an average student for others, had topped in the whole class with 91 percent marks in her subject (general science).

I am writing this letter to you because I wanted to tell her how I felt about her and express my gratitude, but I could not. So I want to tell it to you because I find you just like my good-natured, sweet, loving young madam. I want to be your friend, maybe because my feelings require an outlet, which I am not able to express to very many people. I hope you will accept my friendship. I promise that I will not bother you much. With love and affection, yours faithfully.

Anu, Modeltown, India

Several years later, I received another letter from Anu. He wrote to tell me about another teacher, a college professor who took him under his wing and helped him during his difficult freshman year. "Thanks to that professor and other caring teachers, I graduated with high marks," Anu wrote. "I thought you would like to know this."

Anu's letters are proof that teaching with compassion and love is worth the emotional risk. Someday the students you are teaching now will want to thank you for helping them, although you may never know. And it won't be your A students who wish they had thanked you; most of them will have thanked you already. The ones who will wish they could thank you will be those difficult students—the ones who sometimes make you want to give up teaching. The irony is that those obnoxious, difficult students are the very ones who need you to love them the most. In some cases, you may be the only adult who does love them.

On behalf of those students who won't be able to find you or will be too embarrassed to admit how slow they were to appreciate you, I would like to thank you for being a teacher. Thank you.

Thank you. Thank you. And thank you again.

THE POSSE UPDATE

People often ask what happened to the students who were depicted in my book *My Posse Don't Do Homework* and later portrayed in the 1995 movie adaptation, *Dangerous Minds*, starring Michelle Pfeiffer. I'm delighted to report that many of those students still stay in touch, sending me occasional progress reports about their educations, their jobs, and their families. Many of them are parents, and many of them are delighted to report that they now make more money than I do—they don't know how much I make, exactly, but electronics engineers, software developers, and video game designers tend to make a bit more money than teachers do. I am happy for them, and I like to tell them how happy I am because if I ever become a destitute bag lady I will have so many doors on which I can go knocking for handouts!

Seriously, I am immensely proud of those students. They overcame tremendous challenges—including poverty, physical abuse, and neglect, along with learning disabilities and language barriers—just to finish high school. Established in the early 1990s and funded by a government grant, our school-within-a-school computer academy enrolled fifty at-risk high school sophomores who became a cohort and studied with a team of four teachers for the 3 years until they graduated. When the first fifty became juniors, a new group of sophomores enrolled until we reached our capacity of 250 at-risk students. Eight students in the first class of graduates from our program earned full college scholarships. Sixteen graduates took home scholarships the following year. The program continues to thrive—but now, instead of being dubbed by students as the program for losers, it has a long waiting list of students from all backgrounds who hope to participate.

In 2004, 12 years after the first program graduates hugged me good-bye, I visited California on a quick business trip, and one of my former students arranged a mini-reunion. What a thrill to see those smiling students and their spouses and children. I was even more thrilled to learn what they were doing with their lives. In that small group there was a school secretary, a nurse, an insurance agent, two electronics engineers, a delivery truck driver, a software developer, an office manager, a realtor, a mortgage loan officer, and a professional musician. They filled me in on the occupations of the students who couldn't attend the reunion: a FedEx supervisor, a UPS truck driver, a big rig driver, a grocery chain produce manager, a dental hygienist, an ESL teacher, an art instructor, a lactation coach, a systems analyst, a navy journalist, a corporate executive, a day-care center manager, a rancher, two music producers, and two football coaches. (One of these coaches had been drafted by the San Diego Chargers and tried out for the team—he didn't make the team, but that didn't diminish our pride in his accomplishment. We all recalled our steadfast belief during high school that he was good enough to play with the pros.)

Here is a quick peek at the current lives of the four key players from the movie adaptation of the book—Raul, Gusmaro, Callie, and Emilio. (You can find photos and stories of more students at http://www.louannejohnson.com.) These students are a representative sample of the students in our program and the hundreds of thousands of struggling students in similar programs throughout this country. Their stories and their lives inspire me to continue believing in the potential of America's disenchanted students. And I hope their stories inspire other teachers to continue believing and inspire other young people to continue striving.

Raul

Raul attended college for a year before leaving to work at a family business. (And, yes, he did repay me for the jacket on the day he graduated from high school at age 21.) At last report, Raul found himself on the wrong side of the law and is temporarily a guest of the U.S. justice system, but his wit and sense of humor remain intact. I have several manila envelopes filled with letters and photos from him, and regardless of the circumstances of his life his letters always end with a smile, a hug, and a plan for the future.

Oscar (Gusmaro)

Oscar started working as a receptionist at the Stanford Linear Accelerator Center during high school, stayed on with the lab full time after graduation, and was promoted to a job in quality control. Although he steadfastly refused to attend college (he never learned to like school, even when he earned high grades), he had a knack for computers. Soon, he found himself facing the delightful dilemma of having to choose between two good job offers. A year or so later, I saw him at a book signing in Palo Alto. Oscar arrived a bit late and breathless.

"Hey, Miss J," he said, grabbing me in a hug. "Sorry I'm late. A cop pulled me over because I'm driving a shiny silver SUV, and you know I'm not supposed to be doing that in this neighborhood."

Seeing my dismay, Oscar patted my shoulder and reassured me.

"I'm cool," he said. "I know he was probably just pissed because I drive a lot better car than he does." He laughed. "And I make a lot more money than he does. I probably make more than you, too."

He then filled me in on his job. We reminisced about his first job in high school, when he resisted going for a job interview because he didn't want to talk to "White guys wearing three-piece suits." He insisted that they wouldn't like him or hire him, although they had specifically requested that our students apply for their positions. I asked him how he felt about his job now.

"Those guys are all right," he said. "They don't have no fashion sense and they tell stupid jokes, but they're okay."

About 2 years after that meeting, Oscar phoned me to discuss a problem. His new job was on the other side of the freeway and a world away from his neighborhood in East Palo Alto. He had the opportunity to buy a house near work.

"But my homies say if I leave the neighborhood I'm a backstabber," he said. "What do you think?"

"Real friends don't hold you back," I told him. "They lift you up. Just like your family does. I say go for the house. And if your EPA homies are true friends, they will come visit you, and you will visit them. If they turn out not to be real friends, then you'll have to make new friends. Your concern now should be creating the best life for your family."

Oscar bought the house and later called to let me know he was happy with his decision. We lost touch for a few years, but then I received an e-mail from him after my novel *Muchacho* was published. He deemed it a "pretty good book," which was high praise from him, and he thanked me for "turning him on" to *The Four Agreements,* which he and his daughter were reading together. Today Oscar works as a computer technician for a company in Silicon Valley and is happily married.

Shirmel (Callie)

"Sorry it took me so long to earn my business degree," Shirmel's e-mail began. I laughed out loud. As I read more of her message, the laughter turned to tears. She had married her high school sweetheart, a young man who lived on the edge and was killed when their third child was young. Shirmel raised her children alone as a working mother, and when her sons were in middle school one of them became involved in some dangerous business and was shot—fortunately not killed.

"My girlfriend called me and said, 'Have you had enough?'" She continued:

> I said yes and moved to Georgia, outside Atlanta, and started going to school. I just finished, and I wanted to let you know because you always gave me support. Now I have a good job at a big nonprofit organization. I have a lot of school loans to pay back, and I was going to get two jobs so I could pay them back faster. But my daughter is starting middle school this year, and I remembered that my mother worked at night when I was in middle school and that's when I started stepping out. So I decided I'm just going to work one job. We don't have too much money, but I know where my daughter is at night.

Recently I reconnected with Shirmel, who has grown into a beautiful and successful businesswoman and parent. Her most recent e-mail concluded with a note about realizing that after age 30 she realized she couldn't eat and drink everything she wanted to if she expected to maintain her trim figure: "This year I began participating in a couple of 5K runs. I'm no Flo Jo, but I'm happy with at least being able to place second and third in my age group. In October I will be flying to California to run in my first half-marathon."

I can see Shirmel in my mind, running like the wind, with a smile on her beautiful face.

Jose and Juan (Emilio)

And whatever happened to Emilio? In my book, Emilio's character was actually a composite of two boys—two very different boys with the same basic badass attitude. He didn't really die as he did in the movie (one of my biggest complaints about the discrepancy between my book and the film adaptation). The first Emilio, Jose, spent 4 years in the Marine Corps before settling down with his wife and two daughters in what he calls his "new, improved life."

The other inspiration for the Emilio character, Juan—the bigger and more belligerent of the two—graduated from high school while in jail after threatening a teacher who taunted him. (There were witnesses who heard the teacher's remarks, so Juan was permitted to finish his assignments and final exams in jail.)

About a month after graduation, I received a phone call from Juan, who was working as a baggage handler at San Francisco International Airport. He said the handlers worked in shifts and that some of the groups, including people from his shift, had started breaking into passengers' bags and stealing cameras, electronics, and money. He said his supervisor was getting suspicious and he was worried because he didn't want to get arrested. I suggested that he request a transfer to a different shift, one that wasn't stealing. He called me a few days later to tell me he had been transferred and things were going well. But he called again a few weeks after that.

"I got a problem," he said, to open the conversation. "My new boss is a pain in the ass. He keeps dogging me, so I might have to hit him."

"Absolutely not," I said. "You don't hit your boss at work. Period."

"Okay." Juan promised not to hit his boss. Two days later, another call. This time from a jail cell.

"Don't freak," Emilio said. "I'm not going to be here that long, but I didn't want you to hear it from somebody else." He had hit his boss after all.

"But you promised you wouldn't hit your boss," I said. Juan had very strong ethics, and once he'd given his word he usually didn't break it.

"I didn't hit him at work," Juan said. "You said I shouldn't hit him at work. So the next time he started dogging me I asked him what time did he get off work. He told me and I told him I'd see him outside the parking lot. Then I hit him."

Fortunately, the boss didn't carry a grudge, and Juan's job was waiting for him when he returned to work. I haven't had a phone call from him since. I take that as a good sign.

A PERSONAL MOVIE REVIEW

First, I'd like to say that Michelle Pfeiffer is not only a fine actress, but she's also a fine person. She read my book, and she spent 3 days in my classroom with my students, getting to know them and observing their interactions with me. She got it right. After watching the movie, one boy said, "It creeped me out, seeing her do the exact same things you do, like push your hair a certain way or give that hard look that makes you shut up and sit down."

Michelle's visit transformed our classroom—not physically but mentally. Prior to her visit, we were dubbed the dummies, and even our own students bought into that negativity. But her stardust remained after her visit, and it gave our room a new stature. Suddenly everybody wanted to be part of "that cool program." For that, and for her compassion and generosity, I am eternally grateful.

But my Hollywood experience made me seriously reflect on the idea of authors selling the rights to their books to movie production companies. Mine was a frustrating and expensive lesson. I stupidly signed for a percentage of the net profit before I learned that there is no such thing as net profit in Hollywood. The agent who negotiated the contract told me I should have known better. For a long while, the money (or lack of it) was my focus. I blamed the agent and the producers for taking advantage of my naiveté. Then I finally accepted reality. Commercial movie producers are in the business of making money. Anybody in the business of making money tries to negotiate the best possible terms on any contract. The agent was correct: I could have called the Authors Guild or contacted other authors and asked for advice, but I didn't. I signed the contract without really understanding it. I also realized that if I had needed to be a millionaire, I never would have become a teacher in the first place.

The real issue here, I think, is whether or not to hand over your creation, your vision, to somebody who has his or her own vision for it. When an author writes a book, whether it's fiction or nonfiction, that author has a clear vision of the events and characters in the story. Every reader creates his or her own image of the story, which may or may not match the author's. Movie producers tend to create very clear visions of their own—and their visions are influenced by every previous producer's visions. Unless an author is absolutely certain that the producer's vision and the author's vision reside somewhere in the same solar system, the author shouldn't sell the rights to her work. Period. If it's purely a matter of money, then the author should sign the contract, cash the check, and never look back. If artistic integrity or clarity of vision is the key factor, the author should say, "Thanks, but no thanks," and put that book back on the shelf.

Despite my whining and moaning, and despite the ethnic stereotyping and emotionally manipulative moments, I believe *Dangerous Minds* is a good movie. It touched people's hearts. It inspired a lot of people to become teachers or to become the teachers they always wanted to be. It encouraged many students—students who might otherwise have dropped out—to stay in school. It produced Coolio's incredibly beautiful song, "Gangsta's Paradise." And it gave a lot of talented but unknown actors a chance to star in a movie with Michelle Pfeiffer. I have to credit the producers for that.

One day, I was whining about the inaccuracies of movie to my sister, Susan. She said, "Boohoo. You just aren't going to find people to feel sorry for you because somebody made a movie about your life and it isn't a hundred percent accurate. Only idiots think movies are true. Most people would be excited to have a movie made about them, even a terrible one." Yikes.

For years, I still kept whining —until I whined to my friend and fellow teacher, Tawana Washington. She said, "I don't care. That movie spoke to black people. We saw ourselves portrayed on screen, and we're hungry for that—whether that portrayal is accurate or not. Black kids need to see themselves reflected in our society."

Tawana's comments made me step back and see the bigger picture, instead of taking the experience so personally. She was right. *Dangerous Minds* is a good movie, in spite of its stereotypes and imperfections, because it touched people's hearts. It inspired people to follow their hearts and their dreams. And it shined a bright light, for a few moments, on a group of students who deserved their

15 minutes of fame and so much more—the unteachable students who turned out to be so talented and intelligent and who taught me how to be a true teacher.

WHAT DO YOU THINK?

1. Describe your own best and worst teachers. How will they influence the way you teach?

2. What do you want your students to remember about you 20 or 30 years from now?

3. Take a look at your class rolls. How many students have you touched with love and compassion? How many have touched you?

4. How do you respond when you see movies that are clearly unrealistic in their portrayal of "real-life" teaching?

APPENDIX

There are so many wonderful bibliographies already available for teachers, so I am limiting myself to sharing here my very favorites among the dozens of bookmarked Web sites and articles on my computer.

Accelerated.org. www.accelerated.org Educators who need proof that it's possible to create a successful school will find inspiration on this Web site. Two idealistic young teachers in inner-city Los Angeles started a charter school in 1994. Every child at the Accelerated School is treated as a gifted child—and they live up to the high expectations. The school's curriculum incorporates culture, fine arts, and physical activities such as yoga, and the combination seems to work. Attendance averages in the high nineties, test scores in reading and math continue to climb, and the school continues to expand into additional sites.

Ad Busters. www.adbusters.org This is a great Web site for teachers seeking thought-provoking articles to spur class discussions, research, and essays. The site's spoof ads for tobacco, fast food, and fashion will definitely appeal to kids who are beginning to realize how advertisers manipulate them. Beware, though—this site is sponsored by creative folks who occasionally use four-letter words.

Annenberg Foundation. www.learner.org A wonderful resource for both teachers and learners and funded by Annenberg Media, this Web site contains over 2,000 online videos about teaching and learning, organized by subject. Teachers can search by grade level or subject and many of the videos have additional resources and links. You would have to spend a fortune just to buy a small percentage of what's available here.

BBC Learning. www.bbc.co.uk/learning If you visit only one Web site today, make it this one. Make sure you have a little time to spare, because you will want to stay a while. Hosted by the British Broadcasting Corporation, this site allows visitors of all ages—preschool to adult—to go to school online. The home page provides a selection of topics ranging from religion and ethics to art and design. My favorite section is under the Education and Teaching subject listing, which brings up several choices, including "BBC Schools—Teacher Resources." Teachers have the option of choosing by age group: preschool, ages four to eleven, eleven to sixteen, or sixteen and up. Each age group offers lessons, games, and quizzes, without the annoying commercial pop-up ads that plague American educational games online.

Behavior Advisor. www.behavioradvisor.com/CatchGood.html Unfortunately, the main Web site requires registration and is heavily devoted to advertising. Fortunately, though, you can read this excellent article, "Ways to Catch Kids Being Good," without signing up. Here you will find direct links to real-life experiences of teachers who extol the rewards of focusing on what kids do right instead of what they do wrong.

"Dialing, Authenticating, Connecting: Thinking Differently and Deeply about Student Engagement." http://www.bigpicture.org/2014/03/dialing-authen ticating-connecting-thinking-differently-and-deeply-about-student-engagement/ This article, published in March 2014 by the National Association of State Boards of Education outlines the approach of teachers at Big Picture Learning schools in the pursuit of "authentic and sustained student engagement in deep learning."

Block Center. www.blockcenter.com This Web site is hosted by Dr. Mary Ann Block, author of *No More Ritalin* (Kensington Books, 1996). A licensed osteopathic physician, Block entered medical school to learn how to help her own sick child when traditional treatments failed. Her method focuses on underlying causes of attention-deficit disorder and attention-deficit/hyperactivity disorder (ADHD) such as hypoglycemia, allergies, environmental factors, and hyperthyroidism. She provides case histories, dietary guidelines, a series of programs for purchase and use at home, and a bibliography of scientific research on ADD and ADHD.

Born to Explore. www.borntoexplore.org One of the most comprehensive and competent sites for parents who struggle with the ADHD issue, it is hosted by an environmental scientist who home-schools her two children. Here she posts information about "creativity, learning styles, and giftedness to counter the idea that all those kids labeled with attention deficit disorder actually have something wrong with them." The site has nutritional and scientific information, links to an array of resources, book reviews, articles, and essays.

Busy Teacher Cafe. www.busyteacherscafe.com A Web site for K–6 teachers, it has with themes, strategies, and resources such as printables for reading, writing, math, and Spanish. Customizable calendars, behavior charts, and classroom newsletters are also available.

Edible Schoolyard. www.EdibleSchoolyard.org This eye-appealing Web site offers a superb model for any school, but especially for science teachers who want to give students an unforgettable hands-on experience. The Edible Schoolyard is a nonprofit program located on the campus of Martin Luther King Jr. Middle School in Berkeley, California. The cooking and gardening program began with a collaboration between chef Alice Waters and the school's former principal, Neil Smith. This site offers advice and guidelines to teachers who want to start their own garden projects, along with a variety of links and resources.

Educator Pages. www.educatorpages.com This site lets teachers build their own free Web sites with unlimited pages.

ESL Café. www.eslcafe.com Dave's ESL Café is a great site for English as a second language learners, but the grammar quizzes are just as useful for native English speakers. Most of the material is too advanced for elementary students (except grammar whizzes), but the site has quizzes on a number of subjects, including geography and American idioms as well as links to a wide variety of other online sites. The "Pronunciation Power" link under Stuff for Students in particular is especially helpful for those who need to hear the words spoken.

Fred Jones. www.FredJones.com First-rate teacher and author Fred Jones has published books and training videos to share his methods. You can find video clips and a series of links to his articles on Education World's website: http://www.educationworld.com/a_curr/columnists/jones/jones.shtml

Greater Good. http://greatergood.berkeley.edu/article/item/nine_things_educators_need_to_know_about_the_brain# This article by psychology Louis Cozolina explores the connection between neuroscience and the classroom. This Web site will appeal to the growing number of teachers who actively try to incorporate mindfulness into their lessons because it addresses topics such as social-emotional learning and teaching compassion and gratitude.

Just Walk on By. http://homepage.smc.edu/zehr_david/brent%20staples.htm This Web site provides the full online text of Brent Staples's brilliant essay, "Just Walk on By: A Black Man Ponders His Power to Alter Public Space," which first appeared in print in *Ms. Magazine* in 1986. Born into urban poverty, Staples earned his doctorate in psychology before becoming a respected journalist who serves on the editorial board of the *New York Times*.

PARCC. www.parcconline.org/about-parcc Teachers who find themselves wondering what the Partnership for Assessment of Readiness for College and Careers is all about will find answers on this Web site, along with information about the PARCC tests that are being adopted by some states and rejected by others.

PBS Frontline documentary "Medicating Kids" www.pbs.org/wgbh/pages/ frontline/shows/medicating Direct link to the PBS Frontline documentary "Medicating Kids: A Report on Parents, Educators, and Doctors Trying to Make Sense of a Mysterious and Controversial Medical Diagnosis—ADHD." This is the program that first publicized the connection between the organization Children and Adults with ADHD (CHADD) and the pharmaceutical corporation that funded the group's pro-Ritalin videotape. As of June 2011, the documentary can be viewed online in five chapters. There is also a follow-up posted about the four children and their families who were the subjects of the documentary.

Positive Discipline. www.positivediscipline.com The nonprofit Positive Discipline Association is based on the work of psychiatrist Alfred Adler, who believed all human beings are worthy of dignity and respect. This program promotes and encourages the development of life skills and respectful relationships in families, schools, businesses, and community systems. Although this Web site heavily promotes the association's books and speakers, it does offer a number of intelligently written and helpful articles for teachers and parents, including "18 Ways to Avoid Power Struggles" and "How Do You Motivate a Teen?" Includes some free videos that are also available on YouTube.

"Teaching Reading Is Rocket Science" American Federation of Teachers This article (Item No. 39–0372; http://www.aft.org/sites/default/files/reading_ rocketscience_2004.pdf) This article offers an in-depth look at reading instruction, advice, and suggestions for improving classroom instruction, teacher in-service, and professional literacy training. It concludes with an excellent list of references and an Appendix that guides teachers through the core curriculum standards and how they apply to reading instruction.

Sites for Teachers. www.sitesforteachers.com/index.html This Web site contains pages of links for lesson plans, Internet study, songs, clip art, social networks—all for teachers.

Teachers.net. http://teachers.net This Web site contains chat boards, lesson plans, projects, blogs, articles by Harry Wong and others, job listings, and printables for teachers of all grade levels and subjects. If you have a great lesson plan, you can submit it here.

INDEX

Page references followed by *fig* indicate an illustrated figure.

American diet: abundance of high-fructose corn syrup in the, 267; aspartame and diet soda problem of the, 269–271; attention deficit and learning issues related to poor, 266–267; bovine growth hormone (BGH) in the, 273; childhood and adult obesity due to poor, 264–266, 274; high-fructose corn syrup (HFCS) in the, 267, 271–273; imbalance of omega-3 and omega-6 fatty acids in the, 269. *See also* Nutrition

American Journal of Clinical Nutrition, 269

Amygdala, 103

Angelou, Maya, 295

Antibullying Web sites, 149

Anu (student), 300–301

Anxiety: how cognitive function decreases with, 183; over reading outloud, 180, 183

AP Eng III Student Survey (feedback form), 222, 223

Araceli (student), 257–258

Arachidonic acid (AA), 267–268

Arthur (student), 296

Aspartame, 269–271

Assignments: "The Brain Project," 41–43; considerations for disciplining through writing, 146; designed to eliminate the potential for cheating, 39–43; do some diagnostics of student strengths and weaknesses through, 124–125; Gender Gap project, 230, 232–233; IA-Independent Assignments for button pusher students, 77–78; introduce metacognition approach to completing, 130–131, 133; Learning Brain project, 230, 231; making detention worthwhile with interesting, 166–167; open-ended writing, 124–125; plagiarism, 38–43; postreading Shakespeare essay,

200–201; Project-Based Learning, 42–43, 223–233; required reading, 180, 190–191; short story project, 201–202; story on the theory of personality, 42; student folders for, 75–76. *See also* Homework; Journals

Association for Supervision and Curriculum Development, 104

Association of Texas Professional Educators, 215

Attendance monitors, 93

Attention: how many students do you need?, 121–122; poor American diet related to problems with, 266–267; *Sharing Expectations* video on getting student, 119; silent signals and nonverbal cues to pay, 120–121; strategies to gain student, 119–120; understanding that children crave, 244–245

Attitudes: check your own, 241; help students believe in success, 245–247; power of choice to adjust a student's poor, 238–241, 257–258

Audiovisual staff, 93

Auditory learners: identifying, 250–251; reaching, 289

Australian Journal of Remedial Education, 216

Authority: delegate to student some, 127–128; establishing rapport with students while maintaining your, 284; example of Craig Cameron for how to deal with students who resist, 141–143; shoes that convey, 170; students who are resistant to, 180, 193, 219, 234–258

Authors Guild, 306

B

Bachelet, Michelle, 294

Band-Aids, 67

Bathroom breaks, 25–27

Bathroom passes, 26

Be careful with students note, 48

Behavior. *See* Student behavior; Student misbehavior

Behavior cards, 160

Behavior contracts, 163–164

Beliefs: guarding against racial/ethnicity prejudice, 29–32; how they impact your teaching, 28; raise the bar and help students to develop success, 245–247, 278–279, 280–281; respect others,' 90. *See also* Values

Bell, Andy, 119–120, 121, 277–278

Biting behavior, 143

Black, Al: on classroom management, 23–24; on establishing your optimal agenda, 27–28

Blacks: author's experience with facing her prejudices against, 31–32; facing your own prejudices against, 29–31

Bloom's Taxonomy of Cognitive Domains, 130, 131*e*–132*e*, 230, 278

Book exchange activity, 190–191

Boot camp instructors, 104

Bovine growth hormone (BGH), 273

Brain: the amygdala of the, 103; how learning is affected by brain chemistry of the, 104; as open to suggestion when surprised, 102–103

Brain gym exercises, 248

Brain hemisphere dominance: additional resources on the, 104, 248; brain dominance quiz on, 248–249; McGilchrist's *The Divided Brain* (TED Talk video) on, 40–41, 248; right-brain activities, 249*e*–250*e*; understanding the learning significance of, 247–250*e*

"The Brain Project" assignment, 41–43

Brain science research: on behaviors that disable the brain's cognitive security system, 102–103; on the counterproductive impact of long-term use of external rewards, 237–238; on how brain chemistry affects attention and learning, 104; on new information

processed by daydreamers, 55; on process of learning, 41; on right- and left-brain dominance, 247–250*e*; study on 2-second video clips, 70–71; on yellow food dyes impact on disruptive behavior, 262

Brainstorming solutions, 203

Bribing: the debate over persuasion and, 236–237; long-term use as counterproductive, 237–238

Brodeur, K., 56

Brooks, David, 233

Brooks, Garth, 195

Bud (student), 296–297

"Bullet in the Brain" (Wolff), 202

Bullies: identifying class, 148; teachers as the first line of defense against, 149

Bullying: antibullying Web site resources on, 149; when staff members engage in student, 150–151. *See also* Teasing behavior

Burnout: emergency meltdown plan to pull back from, 168–174; tips on avoiding, 290–291

Button pusher students: assignments (IA-Independent Assignments) for, 77–78; description of, 77

Byford, Ben, 294

C

Call-and-response activity, 91–92

Cameron, Craig, 141–143

"Captain of the Happier Meal" (Gorman), 268

Casey, J. M., 56

Cell phone detention, 147

Central Alternative High nutritional program, 262

Cheaters: designing assignments that eliminate potential for cheating, 39–43; what to do about, 38

Childhood obesity, 264–267, 274

Choice: adjusting student attitude through the power of, 238–241, 258; Araceli' story of being given a, 257–258; to respect or not respect a teacher, 32–35; steps to take for the I HAVE TO and I CAN'T exercise on the power of, 238–240; when a student decides to be a gang member, 35–37

Choice video (RSA Animates), 236

Cialdini, Robert, 236

Classroom calendars, 68–69

Classroom environment: challenge of creating a self-directed learning, 284–286; controlling it and not your students, 23–25; establishing a private zone as part of the, 65–67, 67*fig*; how learning is impacted by the lighting, 180, 182, 205–217; sensory details of the, 53–56; train your students to create your desired, 21–23; when you need to make changes in your, 171

Classroom management: communicating your expectations for behavior, 21–23; control your classroom instead of your students, 23–25; example of Craig Cameron for effective, 141–143

Classroom policies: on bathroom breaks, 25–27; design your discipline code as part of the, 89–90; mandatory thinking time, 123–124; Miss J's Welcome Handout on, 85*e*–86*e*; no-phone, 146–148; on self-respect and respect for others, 32–35; Welcome handouts on, 84–86*e*, 125–126. *See also* Respect

Classroom preparation: checklist for, 95*e*–96*e*; deciding on open seating or seating charts, 62–64; establishing a private zone, 65–67, 67*fig*; importance and benefits of, 52; post your agenda, 68–69; the psychology of seating, 57–62*fig*; rules of order, 69–71; sensory details, 53–56; supplies and storage, 67–68

Classroom procedures: end-of-class (EOC), 122–123; establish routines and rituals, 118–123; for oral responses, 109–110*fig*; planning your, 87–88; rules versus, 143–144

Classroom rules: Andy Bell's *Establishing the Ground Rules* for, 277–278; on behavior that will not be tolerated, 143; deciding on consequences of breaking the, 145–146; give students a fun practice exam on the, 126; negative versus positive, 145; no-phone, 146–148; procedures versus, 143–144; on respecting yourself and everybody in this room, 145; rules for creating, 144–146. *See also* Discipline policies; Student behavior

Classroom sensory details: air purifiers for allergies, 54; making your classroom inviting and interesting, 54–55; painting the walls, 54; putting up motivational quotations on the walls, 55–56; sound and smell, 53–54

Classrooms: check out your own, 94; holding an honest discussion with your students about problems in the, 172–174; how learning is impacted by the lighting in, 205–217; posting your agenda in the, 68–69; preparing your, 52–71, 95*e*; red, yellow, and green zones in, 159; seating arrangements in, 57–64, 171, 279

Cleanup crews: cleanup time signals, 88–89; establishing your, 127–128

Cleary, Brian, 295

Cline, Vicki, 184

Clothing: appropriate teacher, 20–21, 92; comfortable shoes, 21, 92; shoes that convey authority, 170

Coaches: remove the perpetrator and ask for supervision by, 165; when to send for reinforcements and/or a, 164

Dress codes: check your wardrobe to follow appropriate, 92; matching your teacher persona, 20–21; shoes that convey authority, 170; wear comfortable shoes, 21, 92

Durham trial, 264–268

Dutton, Kevin, 102, 103

Dweck, Carol, 236

Dylan, Bob, 195

Dyslexic students: Durham trial findings on early nutrition history of, 268; Emily's journal entry on her memories of learning to read, 186–187; IQ test story on a, 123; who also have light sensitivity, 182. *See also* Remedial readers

E

Eating Well (online journal), 268

Education: GED, 278; help students to believe they can success in, 245–247, 278–279, 280–281; making sure students realize the importance of, 278–279; students who may need extra motivation but do care about their, 219, 220–234. *See also* Schools

EdWeek, 295

EFAs (essential fatty acids). *See* Essential fatty acids (EFAs)

"Effects of School Deign on Student Outcomes" (Tanner and associates), 209

Ego (Maslow's Hierarchy of Needs), 130e

Eicosapentaenoic acid (EPA), 265

Einstein, Albert, 55

Elementary-level project-based assignments, 226–227

Embarrassment: as cost of loss of control, 156; don't let students laugh at others' mistakes, 253; how peer interviews can cause, 117; when misbehavior is caused by fear of, 112–113; when used as a discipline strategy, 140–141

Emergency meltdown plan for yourself, 168–175

Emergency misbehavior folder, 76–77, 258

Emergency plan, 72

Emily's journal entry, 185–186

Emotions: school experience and related, 45–46; social and emotional learning (SEL) training on, 46; teach students how to take control of their own, 150, 156–157; when misbehavior is caused by fear of embarrassment, 112–113. *See also* Fear

Empathy: created between you and your students, 106–107; to students who disciplined by being humiliated, 140–141; take a difficult course to remind yourself how it feels to struggle, 241

End-of-class (EOC) procedures, 122–123

Equal, 269

Equal Measure, 269

ESL (English as a second language) teachers, 283–284, 299–300

Essential fatty acids (EFAs): additional information resources on importance of, 268–269; Durham trial findings on, 266–268; as necessary for brain function and health, 264–265; ratio of omega-6 to omega-3 EFAs as key to good health, 265–266

Establishing the Ground Rules video (Andy Bell), 277–278

Ethics: don't make promises unless you can keep them, 255; Ethics Exercise, 255–257; grading policy that reflects your, 37–38; how your teaching agenda is shaped by your, 28; respecting your students,' 34; teaching values without imposing your own, 255. *See also* Justice (sense of)

Ethics Exercise, 255–257

Ethnic stereotypes, 29–32

Eulery, 294

European Council of International Schools conference (Germany, 2003), 264

Everybody-starts-with-an-A technique, 106

Excellent teachers, 7, 9

Expert-level project-based assignment, 227–228

Extroverted students, 117

Eye-hand coordination, 248

Eye problems, 180–182

F

Failure: as cost of loss of control, 156; reading aversion due to fear of, 180, 188–189; as something that no one wants, 138

Fairness, 143–144

Families. *See* Parents

FarmersFridge.com, 263

Fats: the American diet and problem of, 264–267; EFAs (essential fatty acids), 264–265; ratio of omega-6 to omega-3 EFAs as solution to problem of, 265–266

Faulty logic, 252–253

Fear: of being told that their opinion is wrong, 180, 192–193; as the enemy of learning, 136; reading aversion due to fear of failure, 180, 188–189; when misbehavior is caused by fear of embarrassment, 112–113. *See also* Emotions

Feedback: AP Eng III Student Survey form for, 222, 223; for effective reading instruction, 204; making curriculum changes in response to student, 223; request students to provide you with frequent, 221–223; Self-Critique Form, 229; on using transparent colored overlays for light sensitivity, 210–212,

213–215; when behavior improve provide positive, 149, 154–155

Feingold, Benjamin Franklin, 262

Feingold diet, 262

First day/week of school: be prepared for "test the teacher," 110–113; choose an engaging opener on the, 100–102; create a daily do-now activity, 113–116; don't forget to smile on the, 98; establish class routines and rituals, 118–123; establishing the "everybody-starts-with-an-A" policy, 106; grab your students by their brains, 102–104; introduce students to each other, 116–118; introduce your students to metacognition, 130–133; learn the names of your students, 108–109; Miss J's welcome speech on the, 105–106; provide clear instructions on the, 102; show your gratitude to, 133; what is support to happen on the, 97–98; where you should be by the end of the, 133–134. *See also* Preparation; Schools

Flexible seating arrangement, 58, 59*fig*

Flipnosis: The Art of Split-Second Persuasion (Dutton), 102

Fluorescent lighting: with a colored overlay to correct the color spectrum, 206; full-spectrum with electronic ballasts, 182, 206; humming problem with overhead, 206; light sensitivity to, 206; regular, 206; scotopic sensitivity syndrome and, 182, 209–217

Folders: crates for organizing student, 75–76; daily lesson, 72; emergency misbehavior, 76–77, 258; fun lessons, 73–74; IA-Independent Assignments for button pusher students, 77–78; makeup work, 74; sub (or substitute), 72–73; when to hand out student, 125

Food Chemical News, 271

Formula vs. mother's milk, 267–268

The Four Agreements (Ruiz), 304

Friendship journal assignment, 277

Full-spectrum fluorescent lighting, 182, 206

Fun lessons folder, 73–74

G

Gang members, 35–37

"Gangsta's Paradise" (Coolio), 307

GED, 278

"The Gender Gap at School" (Brooks), 233

Gender Gap project, 230, 232–233

Gentle Horse-Breaking and Training video (Cameron), 143

Get-acquainted activity, 116–118

"The Girls in the Back of the Class" (Johnson), 298

"Give Me Five" (Bell's *Sharing Expectations* video), 121

Glucose, 272

Golden Rule, 167–168

Gonzales, Alex, 209–211, 215

Good teachers, 7, 9–10

Gorman, Rachael Moeller, 268

Government testing regulations, 6

Grade book system, 78–79

Grade policy: on cheaters, 38–43; deciding on your, 37–38; everybody-starts-with-an-A, 106; student learning versus your, 38

Grades: discussing with students the nonimportance of, 281; keep a paper grade book, 78–79; punitive discipline through lowing student, 139; student learning versus, 38; studies linking lighting with higher, 208–209. *See also* Tests/quizzes

Granet, David, 181

Gratitude: be sure to show students your, 133; student memories expressing their, 297–301

Green classroom zone, 159

Greene, Thomas, 268

Group 1 students. *See* Motivation strategies (Group 1 students)

Group 2 students. *See* Motivation strategies (Group 2 students)

Group work: break it down individual tasks and practice, 226; Level I student abilities to do, 224, 225; Level II student abilities to do, 224, 225; Level III student abilities to do, 224, 225–226; Level IV student abilities to do, 225, 226; Project-Based Learning goal of getting good at, 224–226

"Guantanamera" (Hispanic folk song), 195

H

Haiku story, 159–160

Hand cleaner, 67

Hand-raising class procedure, 109–110*fig*

Handouts: Miss J's Welcome Handout, 85*e*–86*e*; Third-Grade Welcome, 86*e*–87*e*; "Welcome to My Class," 84–85; when to pass out, 82

Harvard- University of California study (2007), 70

Hathaway, W. E., 207

Hayes, Arthur Hull, 271

Health: Alberta Education research findings on light and, 207; EFAs (essential fatty acids) impact on, 264–269; effect of light on, 206; impact of stress on, 274; mental, 269. *See also* Nutrition

Healthy vending machines, 263

Hemingway, Ernest, 152

Hibbeln, Joe, 268–269

High-fructose corn syrup (HFCS), 267, 271–273

"Hills Like White Elephants" (Hemingway), 152–153

Hispanics: author's experience with facing her prejudices against, 31–32; facing your own prejudices against, 29–31

grade, 254; writing on what they think is important in friendship, 277. *See also* Assignments; Writing assignments

Julio (student), 242

"Just Walk on By" (Staples), 31

Justice (sense of), 255. *See also* Ethics

K

Kinesthetic learners: behavior cards for, 160; identifying, 250–251; reaching, 289

Kobilka, Brian, 295

L

Learning: AP essay assignment on brain science on, 40–43; brain hemisphere dominance impact on, 40–41, 104, 247–250*e*; covering curriculum issue of, 43–45; fear as the enemy of, 136; how classroom lighting impacts, 180, 182, 205–217; how nutrition impacts, 261–274; how stress affects, 104; poor American diet related to problems with, 266–267; Project-Based Learning used for, 40–43, 223–233; social and emotional learning (SEL), 46; Vygotsky's theory on motivation and, 220. *See also* Metacognition; Motivation

Learning Brain project, 230, 231

Learning disabilities: dyslexia, 123, 182, 186–187, 268; light sensitivity mistaken for, 180, 182, 210–217; vision problems mistaken for, 181, 182. *See also* ADD (attention-deficit disorder); ADHD (attention-deficit/hyperactivity disorder)

Learning preferences: auditory, 250–251, 289; kinesthetic, 160, 250–251, 289; visual, 160, 198, 199*fig*, 250–251, 289

Learning to read memories: online discussion by future teachers on their, 194–195; student journals on, 185–186

Left-brain dominance, 247–249

Lekowitz, Robert K., 295

Lesson planning: activities included in your, 82; consideration of standards in, 81–83; include stakeholders in, 83–84; master lesson plan draft, 79–83; online Project-Based Learning, 223–224; recharging yourself by creating a week's worth of lessons, 171; school templates used for, 81; for timing of handouts, 82; www.teachers.net resources on, 171. *See also* Curriculum; Planning

Lessons: daily lesson folders, 72; fun lessons folder, 73–74; raise the bar by building on the curriculum with challenging, 246–247; recharging yourself by creating a week's worth of, 171; "sub folder" for substitute teachers, 72–73. *See also* Activities

Liesl (student), 299–300

"Light at the Brain" link (www.dyslexia services.com), 217

Light sensitivity: colored transparent overlays used in case of, 210–212, 213–215; feedback on using transparent colored overlays for, 213–215; passing the word on, 215–216; reading aversion due to, 180, 182; research findings on, 216–217; signs of, 213. *See also* Scotopic sensitivity syndrome (SSS)

Lighting: examining how it impacts learning, 205; fluorescent, 182, 206; full-spectrum incandescent, 206; natural daylight via windows or skylights, 206; regular incandescent, 206

Lighting research: Alberta Education study (1992), 207; "Illuminating the Effects of Dynamic Lighting on Student Learning" (2012), 207; linking a room with a view with higher grades, 208–209; Mahone Group research

poor, 180, 191; suggestions for improving, 191–192

Reading instruction: for eager readers, 201–202; how to give effective feedback during, 204; memories of learning to read and, 185–186, 194–195; reading upside down, 203; *Read Right! Coaching Your Child to Excellence in Reading* (Tadlock) for ideas on, 203–204; short story project, 201–202; teaching Shakespeare for everyone, 72–73, 188, 197–201; use music to introduce poetry, 195–197

Reading outloud: eager readers and, 201; student fear of, 180, 183

Reading phobia, 45. *See also* Reading aversion

Reading skills: how students hide their poor, 178–179; importance of teaching, 177–178

Reading speed: assuring student that they don't need a fast, 184; fear over having slow, 180, 183–184

Reading upside down, 203

Read Right! Coaching Your Child to Excellence in Reading (Tadlock), 203–204

Reagan, Ronald, 271

Red classroom zone, 159

Remedial readers: light sensitivity and, 180, 182, 209–217; *My Posse Don't Do Homework* (Johnson) on introducing Shakespeare to, 236–237; reasons and solutions for not liking reading by, 180, 180–193; understanding why they developed aversion to reading, 178–180. *See also* Dyslexic students

Removing troublemakers, 165–166

Required reading assignments: solutions for lack off interest in, 190–191; students who have zero interest in, 180, 190

Resignation. *See* Teacher resignation

Respect: by allowing students to back down gracefully, 153; classroom rule on, 145; discipline that uses the Golden Rule and, 167–168; how military discipline principles can teach students to, 136; making students responsible for being respectful and showing, 284–286; Miss J's Welcome Handout on, 85*e*; recall your own childhood teacher and if they gave, 36–37; respecting yourself, 32–35, 145; self-respect by students, 174; toward your classroom custodian, 93; as an unbreakable classroom rule, 90. *See also* Classroom policies

Responsibility: learn to relinquish your own responsibility for student behavior, 257–258; of students for their own behavior, 149, 151–153; of students for their respective behavior, 284–286. *See also* Power of choice

Rewards: the debate over persuasion and giving, 236–237; long-term use as counterproductive, 237–238

Rick (student), 298

Right-brain dominance: description of the, 247–248; designing activities that encourage, 248; Right-Brain Word Puzzles, 250*e*; Wacky Wordics, 249*e*

Roadmap to Healthy Foods in School (documentary), 262

Robinson, Smokey, 195

Roll sheets: assigning a student helper to take attendance, 127; making spare copies of your, 74–75; used for parent public relations, 75

Romeo and Juliet lesson plan, 72–73

Roosevelt, Eleanor, 55

Roth, Alvin, 295

RSA Animates, 236

RSA Shorts–The ABCs of Persuasion video, 236

the movie version and write essay), 200–201; introducing the vocabulary and creating a glossary, 198; *My Posse Don't Do Homework* (Johnson) on remedial readers and, 236–237; the opening curtain (explaining basic setup of the play), 199–200; *Romeo and Juliet* lesson plan, 72–73; Rules for Reading Shakespeare, 198–199

Shakespeare plays: *The Merchant of Venice,* 188; *Othello,* 188; *Romeo and Juliet,* 72–73; students who end up enjoying the, 188; *The Taming of the Shrew,* 188, 198, 199*fig,* 200, 236

Sharing Expectations video, 119

Shark feed: emergency disaster plan in case of a, 169–175; story on young teacher caught in a, 168–169

Shaw, G. B., 56

Shepard, Diane Herrera, 210–211

Shirley, Alyce, 56

Shirmel (Callie) [*My Posse Don't Do Homework* student], 304–305

Shoes: that convey authority, 170; wear comfortable, 21, 92

Short story project, 201–202

Shy/in the middle students, 117, 279–280

Silent signals: to get students to pay attention, 120–121; response to misbehavior with, 159

Silent thinking time, 110*fig*

Skin color prejudice: author facing her own, 31–32; facing your own, 29–30; "Night Walker" (Staples) on experiencing, 30–31

Slow reading groups, 180, 185–186

Small-group activities seating, 58

Smartphones, looking up vocabulary words on, 131

Smell (classroom), 53–54

Smiling: and don't keep your distance from students, 99–100; on the first day

of school, 98; have students leave your classroom, 109

"Smokers" (Wolff), 202

Smooth transitions, 88–89

Social and emotional learning (SEL), 46

Social interaction needs, 129*e*

"Some Good News About Public Schools" (Cleary), 295

Sousa, David, 104, 248

Southwestern New Mexico State Fair, 141

Speaking right up policy, 110*fig*

Speech recognition software, 178

Spelling tests experiment, 221

Spielberg, Steven, 295

Spurlock, Morgan, 262

St. Francis College (NY), 194

Staff: don't let them disrespect your students, 150–151; find a friend among the, 92–93; meet the administration and support, 93; when to send for reinforcements and/or other, 164

Stakeholders (lesson planning), 83–84

Standards: Common Core State Standards, 40, 82–83; grading policy that reflects your, 37–38; lesson planning consideration of, 81; Partnership for Assessment of Readiness for College and Careers (PARCC), 82; your optional agenda regarding, 27–28

Staples, Brent, 30

Street gangs, 35–37

Stress: emergency meltdown plan for teachers in case of too much, 168–175; how it affects learning, 104; impact on health by, 274; take a mental health break from, 169

Stress relief techniques, 156–157

Student behavior: avoid posted rules of order on, 69–71; clearly state your expectations for future, 149, 154; communicating your expectations for, 21–23; control your classroom instead of your students, 23–25; focus

306–307; private detectives asked to locate former teachers of, 297; racial or ethnicity prejudice by and against, 29–32; school as an emotional experience for, 45–46; showing your gratitude to, 133; shy/in the middle or introverted and extroverted, 117, 279–280; understanding how impressionable they are, 46–48; when they are members of a gang, 35–37; when they don't share their teacher's enthusiasm, 219; when to remove from class the, 165–166; who care about education but may need external motivation, 219, 220–234; who resent authority and being told what to do, 180, 193, 219, 234–258. *See also* Dyslexic students; Power of choice; Teacher-student relationships

"A Study into the Effects of Light on Children of Elementary School Age: A Case of Daylight Robbery" (Hathaway), 207

Substitute teachers: benefits of having one or two regular, 73; providing a "sub folder" with lessons for the, 72–73; strategies for preventing student behavior problems with, 73

Super teaching, 7, 8–9

Supersize (documentary), 262

Supplies and storage, 67–68

Support staff, 93

Suspensions, 139

T

Tadlock, Dee, 203

Taking breaks, 94

"Taking the Fifth Amendment," 118

"Tambourine Man" (Dylan), 195

The Taming of the Shrew (Shakespeare), 188, 198, 199*fig*, 200, 236

Tanner, C. Kenneth, 208–209

Teach Every Child About Food TED Talk (Jamie Oliver), 262

Teacher candidates: examining why they sometimes crash and burn as teachers, 17–18; getting feedback on transparent colored reading overlays from, 213–215; take a full year of student teaching, 11–12; take the opportunity to take elective courses, 12. *See also* Teaching and Learning Theory (online course)

Teacher homework: choose your persona, 18–20; dress the part, 20–21; examining what it takes to be the best teacher possible, 17–18; train your students, 21–23

Teacher material, 5–7

Teacher persona: choosing your, 18–20; dress the part, 20–21

Teacher resignation: emergency meltdown plan in case things escalate to, 168–174; overcoming failures in teacher-training systems to avoid need to, 282; when you have no choice but, 174

Teacher-student relationships: be prepared for "test the teacher," 110–113; catch kids being good and write them notes about it, 244–245; choose an engaging opener on the first day, 100–102; connect through private journals, 253–255; creating empathy between you and your students as part of the, 106–107; delegate some authority, 127–128; don't forget to smile o the first day of school, 98; don't keep your distance from students, 99–100; establishing rapport with students, 283–284; how your teaching philosophy impacts your, 14; no more teacher versus student approach to the, 104–109; positive communication with parents and impact on, 233–234; raise

Teacher-student relationships *(continued)*
the bar by helping students believe in
success, 245–247, 278–279, 280–281;
rewire your connection to improve
your, 162–163; show your gratitude
to students, 133; understanding how
impressionable students are, 46–48.
See also Student-student relationships;
Students

Teacher talk questions/answers: on
apathetic parents, 287–288; on
avoiding burnout, 290–291; on
changing a kid's self-perception about
themselves, 242–244, 286–287; ESL
teacher problem with establishing
student rapport, 283–284; how do you
grade students without testing, 281;
how to make sure students realize the
importance of education, 278–279;
on how to not lose those quiet kids
in the middle, 279–280; how to stop
fighting the same behavior battles
every day, 276–278; making students
responsible for being respectful,
284–286; on overcoming failures in
the teacher-training systems, 282; on
self-assessing and improving your
teaching skills, 288–289

Teacher-training programs: overcoming
failures in, 282; recommendation of
full year of student teaching as part of
your, 11–12; taking the opportunity to
take elective courses as part of your,
12; what to look for in, 11

Teachers: benefits of having a basic
understanding of psychology, 235;
characteristics of super, excellent,
or good, 7–10; checking your own
attitude through self-reflection, 241;
desire to see students be successful by
excellent, 138; don't make promises
unless you can keep them, 255; emergency meltdown plan for, 168–174;

ESL (English as a second language),
283–284, 299–300; find a friend
among the staff or other, 92–93; as the
first line of defense against bullies,
149; how you'll be remembered by
students twenty years from now,
295–301; Johnson's Dear Teacher
letter to, 1–3; journal assignment on
discipline given to, 137–138; learn to
relinquish responsibility or student
behavior, 257–258; modeling the
behavior you expect from students,
149, 150–151; need to actually like
children, 6–7; need to collaborate
to design humane school policies,
26; the optional agenda or, 27–28;
positive communication between
parent and, 233–234; positive thinking
for, 294–295; private detectives asked
to locate former, 297; proof that the
emotional risk is worth it, 301; recall
your own childhood, 36–37; student
name test for, 108; substitute, 72–73;
when their enthusiasm isn't shared by
students, 219

Teaching: the challenges and possible
rewards of, 7; characteristics of super,
excellent, or good, 7–10; checking your
own attitude and self-refection on,
241; the extra knowledge and exper-
tise required for, 10–12; just covering
curriculum as not being, 43–45; multiple opportunities for different types
of, 12–13; a personal movie review
about a movie celebrating, 306–307;
self-assessing and improving your
abilities for, 288–289; student memories of their teachers and influence of
their, 295–301; sub folder for substitute, 72–73; when you realize that you
don't want to continue, 170; when you
want to resign but have to continue,

170–171; as worth the emotional risk, 301; your optional agenda for, 27–28

Teaching and Learning Theory (online course): feedback on transparent colored reading overlays from students of, 213–215; learning to read memories of students in the, 194–195; students used as guinea pigs to test various theories or research, 220–221. *See also* Santa Fe Community College; Teacher candidates

Teaching challenges: facing your own prejudices, 29–31; interpersonal communications skills, 7; Project-Based Learning, 42–43; your academic knowledge, 7; your leadership ability, 7

Teaching philosophy: developing your own, 13–15; how it impacts your teacher-student relationship, 14; understanding that it will evolve, 15

Teaching With the Brain in Mind (Jensen), 104

"Tears of a Clown" (Robinson), 195

Teasing behavior: don't allow it from either students or adults, 150–151; don't let students laugh at others' mistakes, 253; giving students a psychology lesson on, 276–278. *See also* Bullying

TED Talk videos: *Teach Every Child About Food* (Jamie Oliver), 263; *The Divided Brain* (Iain McGilchrist), 40–41, 248

"Test the teacher," 110–113

Tests/quizzes: being prepared for the "test the teacher" by students, 110–113; brain dominance quiz, 248–249; DIBELS reading test, 184; experimenting with spelling, 221; GED, 278; giving a fun practice exam on class rules, 126; how to grade students without, 281; reading aversion due to fear of failing, 180, 188–189; student name test, 108; studies linking lighting with higher scores on, 208. *See also* Grades

Theory of personality assignment story, 42

Third-Grade Welcome Handout, 86*e*–87*e*

Three checklists (classroom, paperwork, and yourself), 95*e*–96*e*

Time-outs, 161–162

Tissue box, 67

Twain, Mark, 56

20/20 vision, 181

Tyeisha (student), 128

U

U-shaped and modified U seating, 58, 59*fig*, 279

Ultrametabolism (Hyman), 270

University of California, 181

University of California–Harvard study (2007), 70

University of California–Irvine School of Medicine, 216

University of Cambridge, 102

University of Georgia, 208

University of Maryland Medical Center, 268

University of New Mexico, 217

University of Sydney, 216

University of Utah School of Medicine, 217

U.S. Department of Health and Human Services, 271

U.S. Food and Drug Administration (FDA), 270–271

U.S. Naval Education and Training Center, 217

U.S. Public Health Service, 268

V

Valerie (student), 211–212

Values: how your teaching agenda is shaped by your, 28; respecting your students,' 34; teach ethics without

Values (continued)
imposing your own, 255. *See also* Beliefs

Vending machines, 263

Vision problems: double vision (convergence insufficiency), 180–181, 212; light sensitivity, 180, 182, 209–217; reading aversion due to, 180–182

Vision theory research, 182

Visual learners: behavior cards for, 160; identifying, 250–251; reaching, 289; Shakespeare instruction using art for, 198, 199*fig*

Vygotsky's learning theory, 220

W

Ward, William, 55

Wardrobe: appropriate teacher, 20–21, 92; comfortable shoes, 21, 92; shoes that convey authority, 170

Warm-up activities: common traits of good, 114; creating a daily do-now, 113–116; suggested adaptations for older or young students, 115–116

Washington, Tawana, 307

Wastebaskets, 67–68

"We Shall Be Free" (Brooks), 195, 197

Web sites: antibullying, 149; Dr. Mac's behavior advisor, 244; Dr. Thomas Green, 268; Durham trial, 268; FarmersFridge.com, 263; Feingold, 262; LouAnne Johnson, 276; National Farm to School Network, 263–264; *New York Times,* 181; positive thinking

articles for teachers, 294–295; University of Maryland Medical Center, 268; www.teachers.net, 171. *See also* Internet

Weil, Zoe, 295

Welcome handouts: Miss J's Welcome Handout, 85*e*–86*e*; Third-Grade Welcome, 86*e*–87*e*; "Welcome to My Class," 84–85; when to hand out the, 125–126

Western Horseman (magazine), 143

Whiting, Paul, 216

A Whole New Mind: Why Right-Brainers Will Rule the Future (Pink), 248

Wilcox, Thomas, 271

William Tell Overture (as cleanup time signal), 89

Wineland, David J., 295

Wolff, Tobias, 202

Writing assignments: considerations for disciplining through a, 146; making detention worthwhile with interesting, 166–167; open-ended writing used for, 124–125; postreading Shakespeare essay, 200–201; short story project, 201–202; story on using humor to get students to write haiku, 159–160. *See also* Journals

Writing phobia, 45

Wurtman, R. J., 205

www.teachers.net resources, 171

Y

Yellow classroom zone, 159

Yellow food dyes, 262